THE SCOPE AND STRUCTURE OF UNJUST ENRICHMENT

This ambitious book grapples with the complex ongoing debates on the structure of unjust enrichment, proving to be a major contribution to the field.

Responding to the subject's critics, it presents a clearly articulated structure for this branch of private law, arguing that while unjust enrichment has the function of reversing defective enrichments (whether by performance or in another way) there is scope for normative pluralism in how the law achieves this.

Drawing heavily on comparative material from Germany, Scotland and South Africa, the book then argues for a legal framework which combines elements of the absence of basis and unjust factors approaches. It assesses how that structure can be mapped against the causes of action that make up unjust enrichment, arguing that some are performance claims – reversing a deliberate, intentional performance – and some are non-performance claims. Other claims, often included in books on unjust enrichment, such as 'necessity' should be excluded from the subject area. The book concludes with a treatment of defences.

Volume 46 in the series Hart Studies in Private Law

The Scope and Structure of Unjust Enrichment

Duncan Sheehan

•HART•
OXFORD • LONDON • NEW YORK • NEW DELHI • SYDNEY

HART PUBLISHING
Bloomsbury Publishing Plc
Kemp House, Chawley Park, Cumnor Hill, Oxford, OX2 9PH, UK
1385 Broadway, New York, NY 10018, USA
29 Earlsfort Terrace, Dublin 2, Ireland

HART PUBLISHING, the Hart/Stag logo, BLOOMSBURY and the Diana logo are trademarks of Bloomsbury Publishing Plc

First published in Great Britain 2024
First published in hardback, 2024
Paperback edition, 2025

A catalogue record for this book is available from the British Library.

A catalogue record for this book is available from the Library of Congress.

ISBN: PB: 978-1-50994-243-5
ePDF: 978-1-50994-246-6
ePub: 978-1-50994-245-9

Typeset by Compuscript Ltd, Shannon

ACKNOWLEDGEMENTS

As is true for many, it was the late Peter Birks who first got me fascinated in an enduring way by this area of law in BCL restitution seminars and as an ex-DPhil supervisee of his, I owe him a debt of gratitude. He would have disagreed with much of this book, but I am sure would have generously and painstakingly given of his time to help me make it better. Over the years, I have sometimes changed my mind, but the sense that we can, as English unjust enrichment lawyers, learn from the civilian and mixed systems like South Africa and Scotland has never gone away. Nor has the sense gone away that while classification and taxonomy are important it is possible to get carried away and be too doctrinaire about it. This book reflects those two senses.

I must take the opportunity to thank a few people who have helped me put this book together. Not all have read chapters although many have; others have merely cheerfully put up with questions about this or that, to which in many cases I probably ought to have known the answer already. So, in alphabetical order many thanks go to Elise Bant, Kit Barker, Rob Chambers, Niamh Connolly, Jacques du Plessis, Alex Green, Steve Hedley, Peter Jaffey, Sonja Meier, Rob Stevens and Graham Virgo. Ideas that would later become chapter two were presented at the SLS conference at Durham in September 2021 (although like many I was at home on zoom), ideas from chapters three and six were presented in person at the 2022 SLS conference at Kings College London and from chapters one and three at an IDEA-CETL seminar in Leeds in November 2022. I would like to thank all those who participated in the discussions and perhaps especially Jamie Dow, Martin Fischer and Eoin O'Dell. While the book is better for all your input, of course any remaining errors, infelicities and so forth are entirely down to me. Finally thank you to my wife, Sukhuma, who refers to this enterprise merely as 'book three', for her support and to the twins, Danica and Rosie, whom I have not yet scarred for life with talk of the *condictio indebiti* (but there is still time).

I have attempted to state the law as of 1 July 2023.

Duncan Sheehan
July 2023

CONTENTS

TABLE OF CASES

Australia

Canada

England and Wales (and Ireland)

Germany

New Zealand

Scotland

Singapore

South Africa

United States of America

TABLE OF LEGISLATION

United Kingdom (common law jurisdiction)

Germany (civil law jurisdiction)

1

Justifying Legal Concepts

Introduction

Legal scholarship in the area of unjust enrichment and restitution has got into a mess. There are two broad camps of scholars, although this characterisation hides considerable complexity and nuance between scholars in each camp. The first might be labelled the pro-unjust enrichment group. They often take their inspiration from Peter Birks, but their work has moved on considerably. Birks' great innovation in *An Introduction to the Law of Restitution*[1] was to provide a theoretical structure on which the material found in Goff and Jones[2] could be hung. Birks illustrated this theory using his famous grids, the first versions of which can be found in *An Introduction to the Law of Restitution* itself. Later iterations of the grids were all slightly different from the previous one; however, an important theme was that Birks formed a series of 'events' – consent, wrongs, unjust enrichment and the fourth miscellaneous 'other' category. This category of 'events' comprised a series of things that happen to which the law responded – restitution was such a response and therefore in Birks' final analysis restitution for wrongs was hived off from unjust enrichment into its own category. Restitution was multi-causal, sometimes responding to consent, sometimes to unjust enrichment and sometimes to wrongs.[3] Birks suggested that a series of questions must be answered in deciding liability in unjust enrichment.[4]

1. Is the defendant enriched?
2. Is that at the expense of the claimant?
3. Is there an unjust factor – a positive reason for restitution?
4. Is there a defence to the claim?

[1] PBH Birks, *An Introduction to the Law of Restitution*, rev edn (Oxford, Clarendon Press, 1989).

[2] At the time of the first publication of Birks' book in 1985 this was R Goff and G Jones (eds), *The Law of Restitution*, 2nd edn (London, Sweet & Maxwell, 1977); the third edition published in 1986 was current when Birks' book was revised in 1989.

[3] This switch from the view in Birks, *An Introduction to the Law of Restitution* (n 1) was first found in PBH Birks, 'Misnomer' in WR Cornish et al (eds), *Restitution: Past, Present and Future. Essays in Honour of Gareth Jones* (Oxford, Hart Publishing, 1998).

[4] Birks, *An Introduction to the Law of Restitution* (n 1) 21.

In later writing, Birks suggested that the multiplicity of unjust factors – that the payment was mistaken, made under duress etc – should be replaced by one: that there was no basis for the payment.[5]

In either model, the category of unjust enrichment is then taken by its proponents in the first camp, the 'pro-unjust enrichment camp', to be a normative category with unifying normative features that justify and help shape the way the law is. Further, the underlying or unspoken assumption is often that enrichment is always dealt with in the same way, and that 'at the expense of' should be dealt with in the same way even if the unjust factor is different. That view – that the approach to enrichment (say) is unified – is part and parcel of the view that it is a unified normative category. Indeed, Lionel Smith has argued that Birks probably always thought that there was only one cause of action in unjust enrichment because the defences were all the same, and the elements of the action in terms of 'enrichment', 'at the expense of' were again the same for all the different 'unjust factors'.[6] Despite the fact that case law regularly invokes the existence of unjust enrichment as an area, the 'pro' view is now under increasing strain and attack by the second group of scholars – the 'sceptical camp'. As with any group of scholars there are differences between them, but a common line of attack is simply to deny that the cases the pro-unjust enrichment camp draw together under the banner of unjust enrichment can be grouped together. The idea is that they are simply too different to be gathered together in this way. Jaffey has therefore argued that there is no unifying principle of unjust enrichment; if anything, it is a mixture of property, tort and contract justifications. Restitution in mistaken payments cases, for instance, is granted by reference to a property principle.[7] This in turn entails treating services cases separately as imputed contracts. Hedley argues for an expansion of contract law and, like Jaffey, suggests that no unifying unjust enrichment principle exists. Even some formerly pro-unjust enrichment theorists have moved into this camp. Stevens, rather than arguing for the overthrow of the whole area, reconfigures unjust enrichment to performance claims, understood in the same way as in civil law systems such as German law. Stevens argues first, however, that the law of unjust enrichment as commonly understood comprises a collection of claims with nothing much to tie them together and that they have nothing much to do with enrichment in the commonly understood sense of the word.[8]

The pro-unjust enrichment camp has a standard-ish response to these criticisms. Members of the camp often 'dig in' and refine their theories even further. Hedley has therefore traced the way in which unjust enrichment theory has become ever

[5] PBH Birks, *Unjust Enrichment*, 2nd edn (Oxford, OUP, 2005) ch 6.

[6] LD Smith, 'Restitution: A New Start?' in P Devonshire and R Havelock (eds), *The Impact of Equity and Restitution in Commerce* (Oxford, Hart Publishing, 2019) 93; this despite PBH Birks, 'The Independence of Restitutionary Causes of Action' (1990) 16 *University of Queensland Law Journal* 1.

[7] P Jaffey, *Private Law and Property Claims* (Oxford, Hart Publishing, 2007) ch 6.

[8] R Stevens, *The Laws of Restitution* (Oxford, OUP, 2023) 3; R Stevens, 'The Unjust Enrichment Disaster' (2018) 134 *LQR* 574.

more complex and refined with ever greater theoretical rigour.[9] This has proven to be a dead end. The pro-unjust enrichment camp run into ever greater problems with their insistence on ever greater theoretical rigour and the application of general concepts. Lionel Smith has pointed this out through several examples. The easiest one to illustrate the problem is rising heat. The rising heat problem derives from an example given in the case of *Edinburgh Tramways v Courtenay*.[10] The owner of a downstairs flat puts on his heating. Heat rises and this means that the owner of the upstairs flat has a lower heating bill than he would have had otherwise. Is the upstairs owner unjustly enriched? No. But the pro-unjust enrichment camp can have surprising difficulty dealing with it. Some authors, such as Ball, have talked of abandonment.[11] Birks called it a grudging gift.[12] Neither suggestion is particularly plausible, but excluding the rising heat scenario is not something that should cause difficulty. The difficulty begins with the very starting point of the upstairs owner's economic gain rather than the interests of the downstairs owner. It is a theme of this book, therefore, that unjust enrichment scholarship has, at least sometimes, started in the wrong place. We need to concentrate on identifying whether there is a substantive reason for reversing the alleged enrichment.

This book aims to chart a middle way between the warring camps. It is not true that to justify a category of unjust enrichment we must prove that all cases have a very tight normative connection and that each step in the way to deciding liability is decided in the same way. Law does not work like that. Nor do we need – as the sceptics suggest – to say that because this cannot be done there is no connection between the cases and that the area of law needs scattering to the winds, except (maybe) for performance claims. Law does not work this way either. It is a way of thinking about unjust enrichment and private law foreshadowed by the work of Barker. Barker has identified four different possible roles for a concept of unjust enrichment.[13] The first is that it is a classificatory unit, grouping homogenous things. In this context it has no intrinsic normative force, any more than the category 'triangles' has intrinsic normative force. The second is that it is an extrinsic norm outside the realm of law. It prescribes what the law should do. The third possibility is that it is a legal principle with legal status and intrinsic legal normative force. It can operate to change legal rules and in that sense is dynamic but has limited dispositive power in that it is mediated via a set of lower-level concepts. Finally, it could be a dispositive cause of action. Some work in Canadian unjust

[9] S Hedley, 'Justice and Discretion in the Law of Restitution' (2019) 48 *Common Law World Review* 94.

[10] *Edinburgh Tramways v Courtenay* 1909 SC (HL) 99.

[11] E Ball, 'Incidental Benefits and Abandonment in the Law of Restitution of Unjust Enrichment' [2011] *Restitution Law Review* 49.

[12] Birks (n 4) 158.

[13] K Barker, 'Understanding the Unjust Enrichment Principle in Private Law: A Study of the Concept and its Reasons' in J Neyers et al (eds), *Understanding Unjust Enrichment* (Oxford, Hart Publishing, 2004) 84–90.

enrichment law – particularly that of McInnes – rests on this.[14] Barker has more recently restated these potential roles in slightly different terms, but the thrust remains the same.[15]

Unjust enrichment is, this book argues, best seen as an example of the third possibility. It is a legal category, a legal concept, a set of normative principles. But this begs the question of what such a legal normative category might be. This chapter aims to start the argument by seeing how law does work. How do we categorise in private law and what difference does it make? In previous work I have relied on a Dworkinian theoretical framework, and I do so again here, accepting that Dworkin's views are intensely controversial.[16] I will also add Wittgensteinian ideas of family resemblance, as Barker did,[17] but also ideas from Weber to make my point. The general thrust of all these theorists is such that they complement each other and allow us to better illustrate important aspects of legal concepts and taxonomy. Essentially, this chapter will argue for a looser idea of how concepts and categories work and interact in a dynamic and developmental manner and that analogical reasoning driven by significant family resemblances is at the core of how this operates. Three related questions arise.

1. How do we get from the intension of a cause of action to its extension? What process allows us to say that this set of facts is covered by that set of idealised conditions?
2. How can we account for conceptual change? How do we account for the category-concept of unjust enrichment changing and developing under the influence of lower-level concepts?
3. What process allows us to gather concepts horizontally in a wider conceptual category?

The chapter begins in its first section by asking what a concept is, and what a cause of action is. In the second section we look to how to categorise them before returning to the three questions above. It is impossibly purist to demand that each category of law have one unique controlling principle informing each cause of action. Instead, there are multiple cross-cutting principles from different areas of law all interacting and influencing the formulation of causes of action.[18] At bottom this is why Dworkin puts little emphasis, at least not in *Law's Empire*, on areas of

[14] See, eg, M McInnes, *The Canadian Law of Unjust Enrichment and Restitution*, 2nd edn (Ottawa, Lexis, 2022) 110–12, drawing on *Pettkus v Becker* [1980] SCR 834; *Garland v Consumer Gas* 2004 SCC 25, [2004] 1 SCR 629; *Kerr v Baranow* 2011 SCC 10, [2011] 1 SCR 269.

[15] K Barker, 'Unjust Enrichment in Australia: What Is(n't) It? Implications for Legal Reasoning and Practice' (2020) 43 *Melbourne University Law Review* 903.

[16] For a hyper-critical examination of Dworkin's jurisprudence, see B Leiter, 'The End of Empire: Dworkin and Jurisprudence in the 21st Century' University of Texas School of Law Public Law and Legal Theory Working Paper No 70, available at: ssrn.com/abstract=598265.

[17] Barker, 'Understanding the Unjust Enrichment Principle in Private Law' (n 13) 93–95.

[18] In the contract context see P Saprai, *Contract Law Without Foundations: Towards a Republican Theory of Contract* (Oxford, OUP, 2019) ch 3; if contract cannot be explained by one universal principle, it seems plausible to say the same of unjust enrichment.

law, referring only to the importance of local priority. We do, however, categorise or 'compartmentalise' areas of law and 'no competent interpretation' can ignore this.[19] We identify ways, based on Dworkin, in which law and legal reasoning have a republican character and how a developmental view of concepts grounds them in past practice. We conclude that an area of law, such as unjust enrichment, is **functional**. A critical point to emphasise is that how we categorise depends on the purpose for which we do so. We might put this differently: what question are we asking when we classify? The law is also **normatively pluralistic**; we draw on substantive principles from across the law and group them together according to their normatively significant family resemblances.

This methodology is at odds with that strand of private law theory proceeding from a more formalistic standpoint. Private law is not the apolitical or pre-political realm the Kantian/Hegelian camp of legal philosophical thought would have it; private law relies on public choices and collective values.[20] Independence from others, treated as foundational by such scholars, is not therefore absolute. It is important and must be considered, but it is not a be-all and end-all.[21] This is vital, for example, in our defence of 'mistake' claims in chapter three.

I. Concepts and Causes of Action

In explaining what a concept is we must distinguish between its *intension* – the set of conditions that a thing must satisfy to fall under the concept – and its *extension* – the sets of facts that satisfy those conditions. Two concepts may share one, but not another. Frege gave the example of the names for the planet Venus. 'Morning Star' and 'Evening Star' clearly do not mean the same thing, but in conceptual terms designate the same thing.[22] They have the same extension, but not the same intension. Specifying a concept, therefore, requires engaging both with its intension and its extension, because it is not possible to say whether a concept expresses a given predicate or referent merely from extensional information as two concepts may have the same extension but different intension.[23] In law this would be unusual, and we might say that a cause of action that only covered an area fully covered by another cause of action was redundant, but it remains true to say that we must both understand the differing interlocking sub-principles that make up our subject's intension, and their extension. As a legal example, we might take the concept of

[19] R Dworkin, *Law's Empire* (Cambridge, MA, Harvard University Press, 1986) 252.
[20] H Dagan and A Dorfman, 'Just Relationships' (2016) 116 *Columbia Law Review* 1395, 1397–98.
[21] ibid 1426; K Barker, 'Theorising Unjust Enrichment Law: Being Realist(ic)' (2006) 26 *OJLS* 609, 611.
[22] G Frege, 'On Sense and Reference' in P Geach and M Black (eds), *Translations from the Philosophical Writings of Gottlob Frege* (Oxford, Blackwell, 1952) 57.
[23] A Gupta and N Belnap, 'A Note on Extension, Intension and Truth' (1987) 84 *Journal of Philosophy* 168, 168.

estoppel. Estoppel, we might say (crudely), comprises three sub-concepts: representation, reliance and detriment. If I **rely** to my **detriment** on the truth of your **representation**, there is an estoppel. That is its intension. Its extension comprises all those facts in the real world where we say the requirements of estoppel are met. The same can be said of causes of action. A mistaken payments claim, we might say (crudely), comprises three sub-elements: payment, mistake and causation. If I **pay** by **mistake** and I would not have paid **but-for** my mistake, there is a claim. That is its intension, and its extension is again the set of real-world facts to which it applies (although there is a qualification to which we come later).

At this point we must note that confusion arises from the fact that we use 'cause of action' in different ways. One sense (the first sense as I call it) is that where we say that A has a cause of action against B it is just a conclusion to the effect that if A sues B, A will succeed. Another sense (the second sense) of the 'cause of action' is that it is a statement of the general conditions both necessary and sufficient for the claimant to succeed. Judicial definitions frequently concentrate on yet another sense (the third sense). One classic judicial definition of cause of action is found in *Letang v Cooper*.[24] Diplock LJ said:

> A cause of action is simply a factual situation the existence of which entitles one person to obtain from the court a remedy against another person. Historically, the means by which the remedy was obtained varied with the nature of the factual situation and causes of action were divided into categories according to the 'form of action' by which the remedy was obtained in the particular kind of factual situation which constituted the cause of action. But that is legal history, not current law.[25]

This focus on facts is found in other jurisdictions. In *Danyluk v Ainsworth Technologies Inc*[26] it is said that 'A cause of action has traditionally been defined as comprising every fact which it would be necessary for the plaintiff to prove, if disputed, in order to support his or her right to the judgment of the court'. *Cooke v Gill*[27] prefaces this. Brett J commented that, 'Cause of action' has been held from the earliest time to mean every fact which is material to be proved to entitle the plaintiff to succeed, – every fact which the defendant would have a right to traverse'.[28] That quotation and references to rights to traverse harks back to the rather different world of the form of action.

While this concentration on facts has appeal and historical pedigree it does not work for our purposes in this book. There must be a normative element as well. We can show this by, for example, pointing out that in order to prove a cause of action in negligence we must set out a legal duty of care, which is not merely a legal requirement for the tort, but also itself a product of normative legal reasoning. In

[24] *Letang v Cooper* [1965] 1 QB 232.
[25] ibid 242–43.
[26] *Danyluk v Ainsworth Technologies Inc* 2001 SCC 44, [2001] 2 SCR 460, [54].
[27] *Cooke v Gill* (1872) LR 8 CP 107.
[28] ibid 116.

order to justify a remedy, there must be a normative as well as a factual element to the action. To concentrate purely on facts is to describe an extension of the cause of action. It is to describe a (hypothetical or actual) set of facts on which the claimant can base a successful action. The facts whereby I do unduly influence you comprise (an example of) the factual extension of the action.[29] We also need to identify the intensional aspect, the internal conceptual relations between normative criteria comprising the action. This is recognised in some contexts. In the context of *res judicata* it has been commented that a claim evidences a new cause of action (and therefore not one barred by *res judicata*) if the change in facts pleaded is material under a rule of substantive law different from that under which the matter was first pleaded.[30] Rules of substantive law are different when (a) the facts on which liability is predicated are different (ie, the extension is different) or (b) if the different legal rules protect different interests or have different consequences (other than simply in quantum) (ie, the intension is different). The third sense of cause of action is therefore inadequate and the first sense conclusory. The elements of a cause of action are not extensional. They do not merely refer to facts, although they do refer to facts. Those facts are part of their extension; they also have a normative, conceptual intension. As well as a description of the conditions for liability, a cause of action is also a unique interrelationship between its conceptual elements (its intension) which designates or references a set of real-world things that fall under the concept or satisfy the conditions for the action's availability.[31]

We will therefore use cause of action in the second sense. There is another aspect to this. Lionel Smith is concerned that the account of any given cause of action be sufficiently general. His example is the ludicrousness of trying to differentiate between being hit with a haddock and a hammer so that haddock-battery is a different cause of action from hammer-battery. It is not. The distinction between the objects is not normatively material – at least not in this context. He is also concerned it not be too general. We do not talk of a cause of action in 'tort'[32] for example, but divide up nuisance, battery and defamation etc.

To divide up the causes of action of unjust enrichment we need to identify the normative bases on which they lie, and Lionel Smith has come to talk of each cause of action evincing a claim norm that provides a justification for liability.[33] A cause of action for him is the set of matters individually necessary and collectively sufficient for relief to lie. This conclusion emerges in part from a discussion in his

[29] There may be a little more to it than this in that, taking an example from negligence, my particular duty of care not to harm you in any given circumstance (which is normative) is also an extension of the general idea of duty of care (which is also normative).

[30] E Schopflocher, 'What is a Single Cause of Action for the Purposes of the Doctrine of Res Judicata?' (1942) 21 *Oregon Law Review* 413.

[31] TT Arvind and D Sheehan, 'Private Law Taxonomy: Reframing the Debate' (2015) 35 *Legal Studies* 480, 490.

[32] LD Smith, 'Defences and the Disunity of Unjust Enrichment' in F Wilmot-Smith et al (eds), *Defences in Unjust Enrichment* (Oxford, Hart Publishing, 2018) 42–43.

[33] ibid 39.

work about the individuation of laws.[34] The classification and individuation of laws presupposes according to Raz an answer to the question – 'What is to count as a complete law?'[35] That in turn means that it is sensible to ask what counts as a complete cause of action. These too need to be individuated in the same way. Individuation of laws seems an unnecessary digression, however. Dworkin pays the question no heed at all.[36] Lawyers use rules and principles to report legal information – they may, if they are writing a text, need a strategy of exposition – but it is wrong to treat these reports as canonical.[37] That cannot though mean that there is no such thing as a cause of action separate from another cause of action. Dworkin will be happy to say that a given normative reason for a claim will extend to some facts, but not be made out by others. It is the courts' task to explain what the normative basis is and what its extension is in terms of the facts it covers. Like all legal statements, it will be an argument and one with which others will disagree either because they seek to argue the principle(s) can be improved normatively and ethically, or that it does not 'fit' the cases well enough, or just that these facts are not covered by it. Dworkin would agree that the reason there is pressure not to make causes of action 'too big' is that we would not be able to make distinctions that we wish to make. We describe or interpret the law differently in different contexts and 'too big' a cause of action would be insufficiently nuanced to capture this.

Having established this, a final point becomes vital. This is that the description of a cause of action is idealised. No matter how detailed your cause of action's description there will be some difference between it and the facts to which it is applied. We can make this more explicit through a recognition that a cause of action is an ideal type in Weberian terms. Ideal types are purely mental constructs that model certain aspects of social reality, but which do not exist in pure form.[38] An ideal-type's relationship to empirical reality is problematic in every case.[39] Weber pointed out that every object treated as an instance of an ideal type will deviate from the ideal. Weber argued, however, that ideal types were useful, because they made it possible for researchers to 'analyse historically unique configurations … by means of genetic concepts'.[40] Perfect competition, for instance, is an ideal type; it explicitly posits conditions that have never existed and will never exist.[41] This applies equally to legal concepts such as 'unjust enrichment'. The perfect example of 'unjust enrichment' does not exist. Just as every actual example of a market is different from every other example and from perfect competition or any other idealised

[34] ibid 37.
[35] J Raz, 'Legal Principles and the Limits of Law' (1972) 81 *Yale Law Journal* 823, 825.
[36] R Dworkin, 'Social Rules and Legal Theory' (1972) 81 *Yale Law Journal* 855, 885.
[37] ibid 885–87.
[38] M Weber, *The Methodology of the Social Sciences* (New York, Free Press, 1969) 90.
[39] ibid 103.
[40] ibid 93.
[41] D Shivakumar, 'The Pure Theory as Ideal Type: Defending Kelsen on the Basis of Weberian Methodology' (1996) 105 *Yale Law Journal* 1383, 1399.

micro-economic model, every actual example of unjust enrichment differs from every other, with the result that a completely specified category would be infinitely complex, just as a completely specified category of market would be insanely complex. Every actual example will possess a mix of the elements rival (legal or economic) theories have emphasised. In selecting one of these as the primary point around which to organise a theory, we do no more than assert that characteristic has some greater significance for our purposes than another in determining how to deal with a particular factual problem that has arisen. As I have said before, what we select is a normative question which depends on what we are doing and why. For what purpose are we classifying? What question are we asking?[42]

One question for this book – in chapters four to eight – is therefore one of exposition of the principles behind the causes of action and defences said to be included in unjust enrichment. It is to describe – at the right level of generality – the preconditions of liability and to justify what we select as significant. Another, also explored in those chapters, is to identify the significant family resemblances that justify classifying our causes of action together. This chapter explains why the identification of such resemblances is necessary and sufficient to justify such groupings.

II. Categorising Causes of Action and Legal Concepts

Accepting therefore that legal concepts are Weberian ideal-types, we need to identify how they operate within legal reasoning. Dworkin's theory of legal interpretation is well known, and I will not reprise it in detail. The first subsection elucidates how legal concepts are interpretive concepts and how local priority in Dworkinian terms allows for categories like unjust enrichment while still respecting the global coherence required by law as integrity. The second subsection shows that legal concepts are dynamic and developmental in contrast to the more static view adopted by some unjust enrichment theorists. The third subsection shows how they are defined, categorised and classified by reference to Wittgensteinian family resemblances and how this is compatible with overlapping concepts. The fourth subsection returns to our three questions outlined in the main introduction to the chapter.

A. Local Priority and Interpretive Concepts

Dworkin begins by examining the idea of interpretive concepts – these are concepts that cannot be understood except through a process of interpretation. They can be contrasted with criterial concepts, such as 'triangle' which involve

[42] Arvind and Sheehan (n 31) 483.

the convergence of linguistic criteria or an external 'thing' with which they correspond.[43] Interpretive ideas are not like that. There is no external thing, waiting to be found. In *Law's Empire*, Dworkin posits three distinct stages: the pre-interpretive, interpretive and post-interpretive.[44] In the first stage we identify the practices to be interpreted; in the second we put the best light on them; and in the third we adjust our sense of what the practice really requires, although Dworkin abandons this three-stage process in *Justice for Hedgehogs* for the recognition that interpretation is interpretive 'all the way down'.[45] *Justice for Hedgehogs* also involves an acceptance that – again contrary to his earlier views – law and morality are not separate evaluative practices; there is one unified field of enquiry. Doctrinal legal and moral concepts are then both examples of interpretive concepts, the result of an interpretive argument.[46] This sits well with the claim above that causes of action, and indeed all legal concepts, are Weberian ideal-types, which are constructed by selecting (by a process of interpretive argument) significant normative features, significant for what we are trying to achieve and why.

There is a social aspect to this. Dworkin argues that the moral authority of the law depends on our being part of a community of integrity. Obligations between members of such groups are regarded as special; they flow from an obligation of equal concern for others.[47] Interpretation then is an interaction between the participants in the practice and the practice itself.[48] It involves a community of integrity in which concepts are shared – not necessarily because we agree on them – but because of the way in which we share in the practice of interpreting them[49] in the morally best light. The claims a participant makes about a concept are therefore about what it is and what it represents, not just what the participant means. To debate a social practice, however, parties must share a vocabulary and recognise the sense in one another's claims. They must, according to Dworkin, share, 'what Wittgenstein called a form of life'.[50] This social aspect of interpretation and integrity takes concrete form in several ways. An interpretation must be communicated and influenced by what the judge knows of other's opinions, what he has internalised from his community and so on. Dworkin explains that a number of forces temper the differences between judges – the effect of legal education, process of selecting lawyers, the general legal intellectual landscape and the common language that reflects it.[51] The point about common language is vital because, as Dworkin notes later, the act of having a thought and choosing words

[43] R Dworkin, *Justice for Hedgehogs* (Cambridge, MA, Harvard University Press, 2011) 124.
[44] Dworkin, *Law's Empire* (n 19) 65–66.
[45] Dworkin, *Justice for Hedgehogs* (n 43) 131.
[46] ibid 402.
[47] Dworkin, *Law's Empire* (n 19) 204.
[48] D Cornell, 'Institutionalization of Meaning, Recollective Imagination and the Potential for Transformative Legal Interpretation' (1988) 136 *University of Pennsylvania Law Review* 1135, 1151–54.
[49] Dworkin, *Justice for Hedgehogs* (n 43) 158.
[50] Dworkin, *Law's Empire* (n 19) 63.
[51] ibid 88.

to express it are not different.[52] We cannot have a concept more fine-grained than the words we use to express it.[53]

This social aspect has wider connotations for legal reasoning and taxonomy. As is well known, Dworkin expresses his theory of interpretation with reference to a super-human judge, Hercules. Hercules, in answering a given question, will ask whether his interpretation could form part of a coherent theory justifying the entire law.[54] He looks backwards at the cases to check his interpretation 'fits' the law, but also looks forward at the best moral justification of the given practice. This practice of Hercules of looking across the whole law poses a problem for our thesis. How can it be reconciled with the idea of local priority, where a judge allocates a question to a given, discrete area of law – like unjust enrichment? Local priority is about more than making the law digestible; Saprai argues it renders the law and legal reasoning republican in character.[55] For earthly judges, global coherence is likely impossible to achieve and trying to achieve it could make the law less predictable. The assignment of a question to a particular area of law should, however, match popular opinion, promote predictability and guard against large-scale uprooting of areas of law.[56] This seems at first glance to go against law as integrity. If the compartments make sense, however, it promotes the ability of everyone – not just judges – to interpret the law and encourages 'the protestant attitude integrity favours'.[57] That said, what most people think is not necessarily justifiable. Dworkin responds to this as well, discussing the distinction between nuisance and negligence;[58] Hercules might need to reject a proposed test for liability as 'silly'. This signals a shift from popular morality to critical morality and a recognition that, however popular the 'silly' test there may be much more (objectively) just ways of carving up the law. Dworkin says little more about this, but the tension between local and global priority creates a tension – a Hegelian dialectic if you will – between the two. Saprai does not invoke Hegel, but maintains that only by requiring judges to interpret existing or conventional legal categories in light of contingent public or popular views can we invite ordinary people into legal reasoning and inculcate the required protestant ethic.[59] Law as integrity which, on its face, requires global coherence may to preserve itself require respect to legal categories that are not completely or perfectly justified on the basis of integrity, so long as they are accepted by the community,[60] as unjust enrichment seems to

[52] ibid 315.
[53] C Peacocke, *A Study of Concepts* (Cambridge, MA, MIT Press, 1992) 5.
[54] Dworkin, *Law's Empire* (n 19) 242–49.
[55] Saprai (n 18) 53–62.
[56] Dworkin, *Law's Empire* (n 19) 252.
[57] ibid.
[58] ibid 254.
[59] Saprai (n 18) 52–54.
[60] T Brooks, 'Between Natural Law and Legal Positivism: Dworkin and Hegel on Legal Theory' (2007) 23 *Georgia State University Law Review* 513, 553; see also T Khaitan and S Steel, 'Areas of Law: Three Questions in Special Jurisprudence' (2023) 43 *OJLS* 76, 83–84.

be. To stress, the reason for this is that for Dworkin, legal obligations are associative obligations. Members of a community must see themselves as owing duties of equal concern and respect to others in the community, allowing a public culture of discussion of matters of principle and rights. Without that citizens cannot partake in the collective effort of determining the law, which is essential for the legitimacy of the system as a whole.

The importance of this for our purposes is that we must develop a unity to, or theory of, unjust enrichment.[61] Such a theory of unjust enrichment, which accepts the republican and Dworkinian character of legal reasoning, is **contingent** on the moral values its community actually accepts. Unjust enrichment is, as stated earlier, **functional**. It serves a purpose: the reversal of defective enrichments, whether by performance or in some other way. As a human artefact it is always possible to ask what an area of law is for. An account of the area's function in this sense is an account of the normative reasons for having the area of law. This explains our exclusion of restitution for wrongs. If we gather cases together based on family resemblances in the rationale for liability or the core function of the area, the normative justification of relief consequential on a breach of duty and in the absence of one are significantly dissimilar. This is so even though unjust enrichment is **normatively pluralistic** in accepting ancillary purposes from other areas of law.[62]

B. Legal Concepts as Dynamic Concepts

For Dworkin, interpretation becomes a dynamic practice; the law works itself pure over time.[63] Recognising the dynamism of legal concepts allows us to see parallels with a Weberian ideal-type. Weberian ideal-types too are always a work-in-progress[64] and Weber's philosophy of the social sciences is permeated with hermeneutic principles, including their development over time and the dialogue between the interpreter (judge) and the interpreted.[65]

This can be drawn out as a parallel with a developmental taxonomy of law. A key aspect of such taxonomies is precisely that they see law as being in a constant process of change. The rules that categories contain must be able to change, but in addition the categories themselves must be able to expand, contract and develop. Realist taxonomies generally reflect this as realists see law responding to social

[61] Saprai (n 18) 55–57.

[62] ibid 62–68 on these features in Saprai's theory; and Barker, 'Theorising Unjust Enrichment Law' (n 21) 612 on normative pluralism.

[63] Dworkin, *Law's Empire* (n 19) 402.

[64] H Aronovitch, 'Interpreting Weberian Ideal Types' (2012) 42 *Philosophy of the Social Sciences* 356, 361.

[65] A Kedar, 'Ideal Types as Hermeneutic Concepts' (2007) 1 *Journal of the Philosophy of History* 318, 323–24.

change. As the normative bases of different areas respond to social change so must the relationship between them.[66] Indeed, realists argue that although the open-texture of rules, principles and doctrines invites a broad range of interpretations, the fact of interpretation's being embedded in social practice constrains judges' options in the development of the law. Dworkin holds that law is a seamless web and law should seek to resolve any inconsistencies within itself; as such it is both forward-looking to the best moral justification for the rules or doctrines and backward-looking at the fit with prior case law.[67] For Dworkin, therefore, normative evaluation is how the law develops – through the incremental improvement on the prior paradigm and the ironing out of inconsistencies. Prior decisions constrain what future judges decide but do not, in hard cases, settle what they decide and, as we have seen, social factors, including conventional understandings, help shape the republican character of legal reasoning. Legal realism and Dworkinian jurisprudence therefore have many similarities and Dworkin owes an oft-unacknowledged debt to realists, although this should not detract from their differences. In particular, realists reject the type of global coherence that Dworkin seeks as an ideal,[68] as well as the possibility of a right answer to a legal question. Despite these differences, we can see that, for Dworkin and realists, conceptual development entails incremental changes to the intensional content of our legal concepts which in turn change their relations with other neighbouring concepts.

This idea of a developmental taxonomy is also important for our thesis in this book. As we proceed to develop a normative unity to unjust enrichment, or a selection of normative connections legitimising the concept, we need to recognise an iterative and developmental process. Although the process requires us to think deeply about the best normative and justificatory rationales for the law and to be prepared to develop and change the rules within the category of unjust enrichment, the methodology is rooted in past practice. It therefore avoids the more egregious examples of prescriptive overreach by some unjust enrichment theorists such as Birks' claim that the whole of the law of knowing receipt should in effect be junked as disapplying unjust enrichment.[69] We must instead engage in analogical reasoning by way of family resemblance. What then is a family resemblance?

C. Wittgensteinian Family Resemblances

We have already seen that Dworkin draws on Wittgenstein. Wittgenstein suggests that language phenomena have no one thing in common but lots of degrees of

[66] Arvind and Sheehan (n 31) 485.

[67] ibid 486.

[68] H Dagan, 'The Real Legacy of American Legal Realism' (2018) 38 *OJLS* 127, 138–39; See also SW Smith, 'Right Answers and Realism: Ronald Dworkin's Theory of Integrity as a Successor to Realism' (2013) 64 *Northern Ireland Legal Quarterly* 504; Arvind and Sheehan (n 31) 493.

[69] Birks, *Unjust Enrichment* (n 5) 157.

affinity,[70] and this turns out to be true of legal phenomena also. Wittgenstein's example is of games.[71] He claims that there is no absolute precise definition of a game, but we all basically agree on what is and what is not a game and we do so based on family resemblances.[72] Games in short look like other things we think of as games. They are dissimilar in many respects, but similar in others. This means that the concept of game is one with blurred edges which begs the question whether there is a concept at all. But there is, and we all agree there is. Wittgenstein equally agrees there is. He argues that my idea or concept of a game is completely expressed in the explanations I can give of what one is,[73] despite the fact I cannot draw a sharp line. His point here is that there is nothing beyond what we can speak of. 'When philosophers use a word … and try to grasp the essence of a thing, one must always ask oneself, is the word ever actually used in this way?'[74] There is no second-order of philosophy. If a philosopher talks of philosophy, there is no meta-philosophy.[75]

We cannot escape our language, therefore. We cannot step outside our language, and we cannot step outside our legal system or the shared vocabulary that enables us to debate it either. Here, however, we make a different point. Games look like other things we think of as games. They are dissimilar in many respects, but similar in others. Barker has already raised the relevance of the idea of the family resemblance in law in the context of unjust enrichment. Barker contrasts family resemblance to essentialism. His critical insight is that an overly essentialist approach restricts our understanding of what unjust enrichment is.[76] Instead we group things because of the way they have similarities, despite the dissimilarities. This will be a simple question of the strength of an analogy over a disanalogy. In some cases, it will be obvious and in others – the hard cases – less so. The objection, however, is one of open texture. It is that we must group everything together, because you will always be able to find some family resemblance or analogy.[77] Wittgensteinians do not always seem to have much of an answer to this. They may see analogy as ineffable, an uncodified imaginative moment with no formal rules.[78] It is plainly though inadequate in law to ignore how judgments of similarity might be made.[79] The standard way to do this is that we concentrate on the purpose for which we are classifying.[80] Barker himself raises the question of the purpose of the area. Proper practice and

[70] L Wittgenstein, *Philosophical Investigations*, GE Anscombe et al (trans) (London, Wiley, 2009) § 65.
[71] ibid § 67.
[72] ibid § 68.
[73] ibid § 75.
[74] ibid § 116.
[75] ibid § 120.
[76] Barker, 'Understanding the Unjust Enrichment Principle in Private Law' (n 13) 93.
[77] JE Bellaimy, 'Family Resemblance and the Problem of Under-Determination of Extension' (1990) 13 *Philosophical Investigations* 31.
[78] S Brewer, 'Exemplary Reasoning: Semantics, Pragmatics and the Rational Force of Legal Argument by Analogy' (1996) 109 *Harvard Law Review* 923, 952–53.
[79] ibid 954.
[80] M Simon, 'When is a Resemblance a Family Resemblance' (1969) 78 *Mind* 408, 412.

analysis, he suggested, depend at root on a clear vision of the law's foundational aims.[81] Given the importance of the point earlier that we select the characteristics we select on the basis of their relevance to why we are engaged in selecting characteristics at all – ie, the purpose of our enquiry – this must be right. Part of the anchoring that prevents our analogies and family resemblances from spreading everywhere is a concentration on the function of the area.

Analogical reasoning also forces us not only to include things that are significantly similar but exclude things that are significantly dissimilar[82] as a means of countering the open-texture objection. Such a propositionalist account of analogy holds that analogical argument reduces in the legal context to principles or other justificatory propositions.[83] Dworkin proffers such an account of legal reasoning, and this may explain his lack of discussion of analogy per se.[84] In other words, we see if the justificatory proposition underlying the concept or cause of action has sufficient explanatory power to cover our circumstances. But we also need a sense of when competing propositions might better cover our case – even if those competing propositions are just the negation of our first (eg, no cause of action covers the case because the action is not illegal). We need the full set of interlocking categories. Andersen describes how contrast sets are formed by division of a superordinate idea, a higher and more comprehensive set, and therefore how we can construct hierarchies of concepts. Different concept sets meet in the middle with their being unable to be extended to include another example because it is already contained in a different concept set. It is important, therefore, that we mean contrasts capable of mutually limiting one another's extensions.[85] A complete taxonomy is therefore needed to stop concepts extending indefinitely in other directions of the conceptual space. Minimally in law this entails a contrast between 'estoppel' and 'not estoppel', or 'actionable' and 'not actionable'. Contradictories stop each other,[86] as will contraries like 'void' versus 'voidable' and 'valid'. This means that at the edges intermediate cases will need to be in one category or the other. This creates sharp-edged categories, which may be at odds with a Wittgensteinian view of concepts, but two points can be made.

First, a cause of action is either made out or it is not. X is either an example of legal concept Y or it is not. That, and Dworkin's right answer thesis, trivially requires some sort of hard edge to the category, derived by a process of argument and interpretation. Secondly, and much more importantly, we may find that from one point of view X is part of set Y, but from another it is part of set Z. This may mean that more research is needed to decide where X really lies, or that the judge

[81] Barker, 'Understanding the Unjust Enrichment Principle in Private Law' (n 13) 80.

[82] H Andersen, 'Kuhn's Account of Family Resemblance: A Solution to the Problem of Wide-Open Texture' (2000) 52 *Erkenntnis* 313.

[83] Brewer (n 78) 958–62.

[84] ibid 960; J Raz, *The Authority of Law* (Oxford, OUP, 1979) 205.

[85] Andersen (n 82) 322.

[86] ibid 318.

has not yet reached the answer, or it could – and this is the third point – simply indicate overlapping taxonomies.[87] Take the question whether my rights against my bank with regard to my overdrawn bank account are governed by contract law (yes) or banking law (also yes), or whether battery is a crime (yes) or a tort (also yes). This idea of overlapping taxonomies should not surprise. We have already seen in this chapter that the selection of a characteristic to pull out to construct our Weberian ideal-type cause of action depends on what we are trying to do and why; we will not always be trying to do the same thing even on the same facts. This is why it is not problematic that a cause of action as an ideal type is inherently interpretive and evaluative.[88] They are Dworkinian interpretive concepts. That constant evaluation, as we have already seen, is necessarily developmental and dynamic. It is not static at all; everything is not in place all at once.[89] A Weberian ideal-type is a work-in-progress. The taxonomy is constantly changing over time.

Barker discusses the idea that legal taxonomies should not overlap.[90] While the avoidance of overlap can legitimately be one aim of a taxonomic system it cannot, however, be the only aim. It needs to be balanced against the need to analyse ideas in a way that brings the normative connection between them to light. The defence of change of position seems in principle available to at least some wrongdoers who have accrued a gain, despite its often being said that only unjust enrichment defendants can avail themselves of the defence. That argument that only (and all) unjust enrichment defendants can avail themselves of the defence is based on the idea underlying the Birksian view of taxonomy that every concept within a system must be independent of every other concept within that system.[91] One concept may be a subset (or sub-concept) of another, but two concepts cannot overlap and this lay at the heart of the grids that Birks so often drew in his taxonomic work.[92] As we are beginning to see, this is not how law works. Concepts can draw on principles from elsewhere in the law and can overlap in their extension or share sub-concepts. For our purposes, the point is that in developing a law of unjust enrichment we can draw on principles from elsewhere in the law and develop the law by recognising a relevant and significant family resemblance. In doing this, we must keep a close eye on the purpose for which we are categorising and identifying a cause of action or another rule as one of unjust enrichment.

D. Our Three Questions

We can now return to our three questions and apply the idea of family resemblances to answer them. The first was how do we get from the intension of a cause of action

[87] ibid 316–18.
[88] Arvind and Sheehan (n 31) 492–93.
[89] Andersen (n 82) 330–31.
[90] Barker, 'Understanding the Unjust Enrichment Principle in Private Law' (n 13) 107, fn 113.
[91] Arvind and Sheehan (n 31) 492.
[92] See, eg, Birks, *An Introduction to the Law of Restitution* (n 1) 40; Birks, *Unjust Enrichment* (n 5) 24.

to its extension? The second question was how do we understand the changing nature of concepts and taxonomies over time? The third was what process allows us to gather these ideal-type concepts together in a wider conceptual category?

i. From Intension to Extension

If it is right to say that there are no empirical applications of any ideal type,[93] or more accurately that there are no cases that satisfy the conditions of an ideal type, we would appear to have a problem. No cause of action – understood as an ideal type – could ever be satisfied. This is plainly untrue. We declare the conditions of liability of different causes of action satisfied every day. Papineau, however, criticises the view that an ideal type can help in describing reality. For him, the point is not merely that an ideal type covers no actual case at all, but also that it is impossible to say what real cases approximate to the ideal type.[94] There is – he argues – no criterion of how similar a fact scenario needs to be to the ideal type to be covered. If no rules are laid down to decide this, the idea is vacuous. Anything can count. If rules are laid down, he suggests, it is hard to see what role ideal types play at all. They are no longer ideal. This objection seems to miss the point. Weber saw concepts – ideal types – as tools to understand the world.[95] The point therefore is to compare reality with the ideal type.[96] If the differences between the ideal type and the empirical case are too large, we must either change the ideal type or account for the difference. In the legal context, this simply means that if we want liability, but the ideal type is 'too far' away we must consider reform to the law.[97] The payoff for this methodology of 'confronting our ideal with reality' is not merely that we have a general grip on the situation, but that we can analyse the specifics of the facts.[98]

None of this tells us precisely how we 'confront the ideal with reality'. The answer lies in the idea of family resemblance. As we saw in the previous sections, family resemblance reasoning has been criticised as having the same problem – what counts as an insufficient or sufficient resemblance? We also saw that a way around this exists. It is to look not merely at the similarities between the ideal type and reality, but also the dissimilarities and the purpose or function of the area. An ideal type, as we have seen, is selective. It responds to the infinite diversity of real-world cases by picking out aspects significant from a particular point of view. By explicitly positioning itself away from empirical reality the ideal type avoids doing

[93] D Papineau, 'Ideal Types and Empirical Theories' (1976) 27 *British Journal of the Philosophy of Science* 137, 137.

[94] ibid 141.

[95] M Weber, *Economy and Society: An Outline of Interpretive Sociology* (1924) 19–24.

[96] R Swedberg, 'How to use Max Weber's Ideal Type in Sociological Analysis' (2018) 18 *Journal of Classical Sociology* 181, 188.

[97] The lesson of course is that there is a closer fit between ideal types and typical cases than usually allowed; Aronovitch (n 64) 361.

[98] Swedberg (n 96) 188–89.

violence to the diversity of real-world cases.[99] The distance we find between ideal types and empirical reality reinforces the need to reject essentialism, which picks out, not significant features, but common features. Picking out common attributes implies fixed attributes.[100] There is no mechanism for developing the category; as soon as we argue that it should be expanded to include a case that exhibits some, but not all, the common attributes the objection is raised that 'by definition' x is not y. An ideal type is not, however, designed to fix the meaning of social or legal phenomena.[101] There is a deep contrast therefore between essentialism – grouping things together by common characteristics (everything with characteristic x is a y) – and selectivity or an ideal-typical manner of grouping where we look for significant characteristics,[102] not all of which need to be shared in all cases. The latter allows the ideal type to change and develop; the former does not. The myriad variations of the relation between an ideal type and an example of it in the real world must therefore be of the 'family resemblance' type we find in Wittgenstein.[103] In deciding if these facts satisfy this ideal-type cause of action, we must see if there is a sufficient resemblance between the two.

Kedar elucidates how this works by drawing a contrast between the horizontal and the vertical. We return to the horizontal in the next subsection. The vertical enquiry engages the way in which the ideal type allows us a better understanding of empirical cases.[104] From a Wittgensteinian perspective, the question is whether the ideal type illuminates our understanding of the specificities of our individual case. Kedar describes the process in ways similar to analogical or propositionalist legal arguments of the sort a Dworkinian judge might use. We turn to an 'amorphous mass' of empirical material and sort through it, using the ideal-type's suggestions, identifying where and how the ideal-type's theme(s) (the governing principles, function or ideas) manifest themselves empirically; critically Kedar argues that the aim is not just to identify similarities, but to identify how the empirical cases diverge from the concept and why.[105] This allows us to see if the significant features picked out by our ideal-type cause of action are present on the facts, or alternatively whether any of the significant features we see in our empirical reality match any possible idealised cause of action. Compare how analogy works; we see the same process – just described differently. The judge abduces a proposition (that the concept covers our case), tests it against a set of explanatory or justificatory ideas lying behind the concept and comes to a conclusion confirming or disconfirming the original proposition that the actual facts before

[99] Kedar (n 65) 332–33.

[100] ibid 337; this quite plainly is true of concepts like 'triangle' which do have fixed attributes, but 'triangle' is a criterial concept with no normative content, and so while every triangle drawn on a piece of paper could be said to be the 'ideal' triangle, 'triangle' is fixed in a way that 'undue influence' is not.

[101] ibid 333.

[102] ibid 336.

[103] ibid 338.

[104] ibid 341.

[105] ibid 341–42.

us are covered (or not) by the concept or cause of action.[106] This process might also require the judge to abduce[107] and confirm a proposition that the case is relevantly (dis)similar to another concept/ideal type.[108]

ii. Developmental Taxonomies

This segues neatly into our second question. How do we understand conceptual change? In principle for a theorist with a propositionalist understanding of analogy the iterative process of abduction and (dis)confirmation seen above not only produces a conclusion as to whether our concept applies to given facts, but also a shifting understanding of the concept itself, one impossible if we look for features common to all instances of a concept, as this fixes the concept[109] and precludes development. In confirming (or disconfirming) an abduced rule that the concept applies, the reasoner looks 'up' to the rationales he takes as guiding true judgments and simultaneously 'down' at his chosen past cases before applying the concept.[110] This reflects Dworkin's theory's forwards and backwards looking nature and the iterative nature of theoretical ascent (and descent).[111] Our idea of the ideal type in question is refined and amended, and so the construction of a Weberian ideal-type is a 'work-in-progress'.[112] Every new case brings in new facts which slowly change our assumptions.[113] Cases which we would not have included under the concept in the past are brought in and others, previously included, are thrown out. Causes of action, as ideal types, have an argumentative function. Scholars and judges must find the best arguments they can to convince others and transform concepts.[114] We may find that the normative justification for (say) undue influence extends to a new case not previously included in the concept, or that it does not extend so far but that we are uncomfortable and believe a remedy can be – and should be – found. We must, as part of the iterative nature of theoretical ascent and descent, decide whether to adapt the concept or not.

iii. Categorisation

The third of our questions was how to group causes of action together. A moment of care is required here. In section I a distinction was drawn between the normative intension of a concept – the abstract set of conditions for its application – and

[106] Brewer (n 78) 962–63.
[107] ibid 945–49 for an explanation of abduction.
[108] ibid 1015–16.
[109] Kedar (n 65) 337.
[110] Brewer (n 78) 1022–23.
[111] Arvind and Sheehan (n 31) 486.
[112] Aronovitch (n 64) 361.
[113] M Sadowski, 'Language is not Life: The Chain Enterprise, Interpretive Communities and the Dworkin/Fish Debate' (2001) 33 *Connecticut Law Review* 1099, 1123.
[114] Kedar (n 65) 340–41.

its factual extension, the set of facts on which the concept operates or where the cause of action is satisfied. However, an extension can also be normative. Once we have decided that payments under undue influence are an example of unjust enrichment, we can say that the concept of undue influence is an example of unjust enrichment. The intension of undue influence is part of unjust enrichment's normative extension. However, in identifying causes of action to group together under the unjust enrichment banner, we are not merely talking about getting from the intension of a clearly accepted higher level concept to part of its (normative) extension. We are trying to generate a doctrinal and normative theme to unjust enrichment, lending it extra legitimacy and then delineating its precise scope and boundary.

This is essential,[115] and engages Kedar's horizontal aspect of ideal types,[116] the notion that ideal types can help pinpoint and identify connections between cases, phenomena and concepts. This is both how we construct larger categories of causes of action and concepts and how we develop our taxonomy over time. It is precisely, however, what unjust enrichment critics say is impossible – or at least impossible of unjust enrichment in that they claim no such significant connections exist. To decide if they are right, we must come back to the same problem as before. How much difference can a category tolerate? It must tolerate difference otherwise we fall into the essentialist fallacy of assuming that either x must have characteristic y or it cannot be an example of z (and it is an example of z) or, which turns out to be merely the flipside of the first proposition, that x cannot be an example of z because it has not got characteristic y. The methodology is the same. It is a family resemblance question. In gathering the lower-tier causes of action together to form the higher-tier category we must form a hypothesis as to what the significant features are of our higher-level concept z and then look at the case law to see how it instantiates those factors; how does the case law resemble our proposed new category concept, and critically also how does it diverge from it and why?

This sits well with the role of unjust enrichment as a legal principle.[117] A higher-level concept of this nature has normative force and legal status. It can operate as a reason for changing legal rules and lower-level causes of action; the principle is dynamic. We saw in our discussion of developmental taxonomies and conceptual change that we might find either that the normative justification for undue influence suggests a new case be included and a remedy given or not. We might then seek to adapt the principle of undue influence. While it is difficult (possibly impossible) to come up with a pithy statement of an unjust enrichment principle, such a higher-level concept might assist in this process and in doing so lend the law a forward force and momentum for change. This allows us to clarify indeterminacies in lower-level causes of action.[118] It allows for iteration between

[115] Barker, 'Understanding the Unjust Enrichment Principle in Private Law' (n 13) 81.
[116] Kedar (n 65) 341.
[117] Barker, 'Understanding the Unjust Enrichment Principle in Private Law' (n 13) 86–87.
[118] ibid 95.

theoretical ascent and descent. The higher-level unjust enrichment concept finds itself mediated to the rule disposing of the individual case by a set of intermediate principles and considerations which elucidate the significant family resemblances in play and interlock like strands of a rope – an analogy Barker takes in turn from Wittgenstein[119] – so that not all of them need support any given case of unjust enrichment.[120]

We must say a little bit more about this now. One objection to this developmental approach and role for unjust enrichment as a legal principle, despite the judicial endorsements it has received,[121] might be the relative emptiness of the idea of similarity. To lay down strict criteria in advance would be to miss the point that legal concepts are interpretive – not criterial – concepts. However, something must be said to head off the objection that I can populate my categories with anything I please.[122] This is not so. Any account must pick out morally significant values or features underlying the justification, function or purpose of the cause of action and gather actions together on the footing that they reflect those values. At the same time, there will be scope for ongoing critical analysis of those underlying values,[123] and reciprocal engagement with values drawn from elsewhere in the law,[124] and finally an evaluation of the morally and normatively significant dissimilarities with cases allocated to other legal categories. Morally significant principles are contingent. There is a conventionalist tone to Dworkin's remarks on local priority and his emphasis on public opinion.[125] This contingency is also historical and implies that the right answer in one jurisdiction is not necessarily the right answer in another.

We see how this works in more concrete form in chapter three. For now, we can say that what matters is the significance of the reason for restitution and return to the analogy of the rope. Some causes of action which I will include in unjust enrichment involve the defendant having done something to affect the claimant's intentional performance, but not all. Some causes of action I will include in unjust enrichment will attract change of position as a defence, but not all. Indeed, some causes of action I will not include in unjust enrichment will attract the defence. Unjust enrichment, as suggested earlier, is **functional**.[126] It serves to reverse

[119] Wittgenstein (n 70) §32.

[120] Barker, 'Understanding the Unjust Enrichment Principle in Private Law' (n 13) 96.

[121] In Australia see, eg, *Pavey & Matthews Pty Ltd v Paul* (1987) 162 CLR 221, 256–57 (Deane J); *Bofinger v Kingsway Group Ltd* (2009) 239 CLR 269; *Mann v Paterson Constructions (Pty) Ltd* [2019] HCA 32, (2019) 267 CLR 560, [213] (Nettle J et al); in England see *Lipkin Gorman v Karpnale Ltd* [1991] 2 AC 548 (HL); *Investment Trust Companies v HMRC* [2017] UKSC 29, [2018] 2 AC 275, [39]–[40] (Lord Reed).

[122] Webb objects to much work in the unjust enrichment field on the ground that why some things were more alike than others was never explained (although it was asserted). C Webb, *Reasons and Restitution* (Oxford, OUP, 2016) 43; see also, Arvind and Sheehan (n 31) 492–93.

[123] H Dagan, 'Legal Realism and the Taxonomy of Private Law' in C Rickett and R Grantham (eds), *Structure and Justification in Private Law: Essays for Peter Birks* (Oxford, Hart Publishing, 2008) 161.

[124] ibid 164–65.

[125] Saprai (n 18) 52–53.

[126] This list roughly tracks the way Saprai (n 18) 72 sets out the features of his contract theory.

defective enrichments be they by performance or some other way. The connections with moral principle are **historically contingent**. They are shaped by ideas of conventional morality and past political practices. Unjust enrichment is **normatively pluralistic** in that it can draw on principles from across the law, mould them in a context-specific manner, and consider incidental purposes in doing so.[127] It can do this because its function is **under-determinative**. It says nothing, for example, about what counts as a defective enrichment. Rather, the courts should take general and abstract principles and mould them based on past political practice etc. This provides the space for normative pluralism, but also for the recognition of contingency between legal systems.

III. Conclusion

This chapter has sketched out a methodology for approaching legal taxonomy and one rather at odds with the methodology – possibly ideology – which lies behind the approach of many unjust enrichment theorists. It is a much looser approach, reliant on family resemblances, analogies and moral and normative arguments illuminating the concept at hand. It is an approach that accepts the Dworkinian insistence on a right answer to questions of law, but also insists that the criteria for knowing whether a cause of action is satisfied or should cover this situation are not fixed absolutely in advance. An argument based on the underlying principles, which can be cross-cutting and drawn from other areas of law, must be made and the concept developed as judges attempt to work the law pure; causes of action and legal concepts are therefore always works-in-progress.

My description of unjust enrichment as serving to reverse defective enrichments be they by performance or some other way has civilian echoes. The next chapter, therefore, sketches out a structure for the common law of unjust enrichment, which is based on that of the civil law and, especially, the mixed jurisdictions of Scotland and South Africa. The mixed jurisdictions have a case-based system, as does English law, and they gather several rather different claims together under the unjust enrichment heading, as does English law, and so make a useful comparison.

[127] See, for ways this normative pluralism can work in practice, M Chen-Wishart and R Gregson, 'Impaired Intent Unjust Factors' in E Bant et al (eds), *Research Handbook on Unjust Enrichment and Restitution* (Cheltenham, Edward Elgar, 2020).

2

The Structure of Unjust Enrichment in Comparative Perspective

Introduction

Unjust enrichment draws on principles from at least two other areas of law. These are contract law and property law;[1] if we include restitution for wrongs in our subject area it will draw on tort and equitable principles from breach of fiduciary duty and confidence as well. This book does not include restitution for wrongs. The reason, as we saw in chapter one, is that although we can draw out similarities between restitution for wrongs and the non-wrongs claims and they may be important for some purposes – for example, understanding quantification of relief – there is a fundamental normative difference between a claim justified by the defendant's breach of a duty and where there is no prior duty to breach. The question this book asks is: when is private gain actionable in the absence of a breach of duty? That justification, and the function of the area, is different if a breach of duty is proven.

The important point is that, as Barker, argues, we can rationally group causes of action together that are not exactly alike, or share some essential unique characteristic, but because they share family resemblances.[2] These substantive similarities in the reasons for reversing the performance or other enrichment map to interests of the claimant, and by starting with the question of what those interests might be, is that we can explain differences in the approach to enrichment and attribution. Not every similarity will apply to every cause of action. Responding to corrective justice may be one thread that runs through the law, but it struggles, Barker says, to fit everything that is claimed for the area.[3] At the same time, the question that we are asking – when and why is enrichment reversed in the absence of a wrong? – justifies categorising the claims together.[4] Lionel Smith has talked of 'big unjust enrichment' and 'small

[1] D Sheehan, 'The Property Principle and the Structure of Unjust Enrichment' [2011] *Restitution Law Review* 138, 155.

[2] K Barker, 'Understanding the Unjust Enrichment Principle in Private Law: A Study of the Concept and its Reasons' in J Neyers et al (eds), *Understanding Unjust Enrichment* (Oxford, Hart Publishing, 2004) 93–95.

[3] ibid 105–06.

[4] ibid 85.

unjust enrichment'.[5] We would expect there to be multiple causes of action, multiple sets of necessary and sufficient conditions for liability. As we see later in this book that is exactly what we find and the book maps out individual causes of action and defences in chapters four to eight.

The classic central core of unjust enrichment is largely agreed to be cases of vitiated intention. That may be the wrong expression, since I may really intend the transfer – as when you put a gun to my head – but there is a flaw in the claimant's decision-making. Mistake, duress, undue influence and failure of consideration (or failure of basis) are, however, on any view central. Burrows' classic textbook, *The Law of Restitution*, sets out in the contents pages several other unjust factors. These are 'Exploitation of Weakness',[6] 'Human Incapacity',[7] 'Ignorance',[8] 'Legal Compulsion',[9] 'Necessity',[10] 'Illegality'[11] and 'Public Authority Ultra Vires Extraction and Payment'.[12] He provides a similar list in his judicial capacity in the Privy Council decision of *Samsoondar v Capital Insurance Ltd*.[13] Still other authors have proposed different unjust factors, such as the 'Policy against Accumulation'.[14] Birks in *An Introduction to the Law of Restitution* cut the unjust factors slightly differently, calling 'Necessity' 'Moral Compulsion' and referring to 'Inequality'. The major additional unjust factor on that view was that of 'Free Acceptance'. Bant and Edelman in their textbook divide the unjust factors into groups. They split ignorance and powerlessness under a new heading and chapter 'No Intention to Benefit'.[15] Illegality, incapacity, the policy against accumulation, policy concerning reversal of judgments[16] and free acceptance all come under the heading of 'Policy-Based Reasons for Restitution'.[17] This then seems to largely cover the different possible unjust factors. However, this does not exhaust the category of cases that have been included in unjust enrichment. Another – quite different – scenario is that of a proprietary claim contingent on tracing.[18] We look at this in more detail in chapter seven.

This chapter aims to outline a structure of unjust enrichment, based on the civilian system, as including what I will call performance (or *condictio*) claims, but also a range of non-performance claims including cases which would in the

[5] LD Smith, 'Restitution: A New Start?' in P Devonshire and R Havelock (eds), *The Impact of Restitution and Equity in Commerce* (Oxford, Hart Publishing, 2018) 93–94.

[6] AS Burrows, *The Law of Restitution*, 3rd edn (Oxford, OUP, 2011) ch 12.

[7] ibid ch 13.

[8] ibid ch 16.

[9] ibid ch 17.

[10] ibid ch 18.

[11] ibid ch 19.

[12] ibid ch 20.

[13] *Samsoondar v Capital Insurance Ltd* [2020] UKPC 33, [2021] 2 All ER 1105.

[14] S Degeling, *Restitutionary Rights to Share in Damages* (Cambridge, CUP, 2003).

[15] E Bant and J Edelman, *Unjust Enrichment*, 2nd edn (Oxford, Hart Publishing, 2016) ch 12.

[16] B McFarlane, 'The Recovery of Money Paid under Judgments later Reversed' [2001] *Restitution Law Review* 1.

[17] Bant and Edelman (n 15) ch 13.

[18] PBH Birks, *Unjust Enrichment*, 2nd edn (Oxford, OUP, 2005) 198.

civil law be examples of the *actio de in rem verso*. This is important as the civilian system provides an alternative structure for restitution. Although the possibility of English law's adopting a civilian structure has been much discussed, there has been no systematic attempt to map the English causes of action against this structure. This can, perhaps, most easily be done against the mixed systems as in South Africa which maintain a case law-based system and in determining whether transfers, that were not owed, can be recovered also require proof of additional circumstances like mistake. South African law provides a good comparator. There is a greater wealth of material than in the smaller Scottish jurisdiction, commentators such as Visser, in his important textbook *Unjustified Enrichment*, as well as judges (at least sometimes)[19] look for inspiration to English law materials and it has its own version of the four questions analysis.[20] Those questions are:

1. Is the defendant enriched?
2. Is the plaintiff impoverished?
3. Is the defendant's enrichment at the expense of the plaintiff?
4. Is the enrichment *sine causa*?

In the first section we outline the civilian structure to their unjustified enrichment claims, including *versio*-claims, the extended action of the *negotiorum gestor* and other non-performance claims. In the second, we roughly map the English law onto these categories to set out an important hypothesis. English law causes of action in unjust enrichment follow roughly the same map as civilian systems and this illuminates the interests that they protect and the reasons for difference in treatment of different scenarios. The similarity should not be too surprising. Both systems have the same set of problems, but this does not mean, as we see in chapter five, that English law does or should adopt a German-style absence of basis system for its performance claims.

I. Civil Law Systems

It has been said that there are in essence only two ways to do restitution. The English unjust factors approach has been called a 'restitution if' approach. If there is a mistake, or duress or undue influence restitution follows. The other is the 'restitution unless' approach. If there appears no reason for the transfer, so that it is in civil law terminology *sine causa* or without legal ground, restitution

[19] eg, *B&H Engineering v First National Bank of South Africa* 1995 (2) SA 279, referring to *Barclays Bank v WJ Simms, Son & Cooke (Southern) Ltd* [1980] QB 677.

[20] See, eg, *Municipal Employees Pension Fund v Mongwaketse* [2020] ZASCA 181; *Mndi v Malgas* 2006 (2) SA 182; *St Helena Primary School v Department of Education* 2007 (4) SA 16; *Watson v Shaw* 2008 (1) SA 350.

follows unless the claimant knew it was not due.[21] This section outlines the civil law – 'restitution unless' – tradition. Yet it is not obvious that this is a useful, or even correct, characterisation of the tradition; certainly, it is not the case in non-performance claims. As in English law, the history of unjustified enrichment is a history of argument about the presence of one overarching principle or a set of rather heterogenous cases. Historically, the civil law of unjustified enrichment emerged from two different lines of tradition – the first line originated with the Roman *condictiones* and the second from an amalgam of the *actio de in rem verso* and *negotiorum gestio*.[22] As Scott has argued, the idea of absence of legal ground is therefore a thin one. There is little coherence between the claims of German law and no general concept captures 'absence of legal ground' across the piece;[23] du Plessis even argues that one view of whether an enrichment was *sine causa* is simply whether the prerequisites of a cause of action are made out.[24] The same criticism of incoherence has therefore been levelled at civilian systems and the same suggestion of scattering the elements of unjustified enrichment elsewhere has been made.[25] The criticism that the different claims cannot be grouped together may have greater force in Germany where a single legislative provision tries to cover all unjustified enrichment claims than it has in a case law system like South African, Scots or indeed English law. If, however, the methodology outlined in chapter one is sound, both the common and civil law will be defensible as grouping cases with relevant family resemblances.

We first look at performance claims, sometimes referred to in the book as *condictio*-claims, and then at the different types of non-performance claims, splitting them into imposed enrichment and enrichment by encroachment cases, a categorisation used both by Visser and du Plessis in the context of South African law, as well as intermediary claims. German law provides an excellent example of an absence of basis system and has a codified system with a clearly defined concept of 'nullity' or *sine causa* within the context of performance claims. The picture is though muddied, as we see later, by remnants of the *condictio ob rem*. Scots and South African law are not codified and so, although they too derive from the civil law tradition, they have a much less well-defined idea of what counts as a *causa* and therefore what counts as *sine causa*.

[21] M Hogg, 'Unjustified Enrichment in Scots Law Twenty Years On: Where Now? [2006] *Restitution Law Review* 1.

[22] S Meier, 'Restitution of Undue Transfers in the Civil Law and the Common Law' (2017) 27 *New Zealand Universities Law Review* 528, 528–30; B Dickson, 'The Law of Restitution in the Federal Republic of Germany: A Comparison with English Law' (1987) 30 *ICLQ* 751, 769.

[23] H Scott, 'Rationalising the South African Law of Enrichment' [2014] *Edinburgh Law Review* 433, 449.

[24] J du Plessis, *The South African Law of Unjustified Enrichment* (Durban, Juta, 2012) 148–52; J du Plessis, 'Labels and Meaning: Unjust Factors and Failure of Purpose as Reasons for Reversing Enrichment by Transfer' [2014] *Edinburgh Law Review* 416, 431–32.

[25] N Jansen, 'Farewell to Unjustified Enrichment?' [2016] *Edinburgh Law Review* 123; for a common law response see S Hedley, 'Farewell to Unjustified Enrichment? A Common Law Response' [2016] *Edinburgh Law Review* 326.

In German law, the traditional unified view of § 812 was replaced in the second half of the twentieth century, following work by Walter Wilburg and Ernst von Caemmerer, by the division between the *Leistungskondiktion* and the *Nichtleistungskondiktion*: the performance and the non-performance claim. The directness requirement – that the enrichment be directly at the expense of the claimant – was replaced by the intent and purpose of the transfer and by the different actions of the non-performance claim.[26] It is divided into several actions and despite attempts both to diversify the classification and to further unify it, this remains the accepted typology. These are first, the *Eingriffskondiktion* – dealing with cases of gains made through infringing others' rights, a categorisation also found in South Africa although the non-codal nature of the law in that jurisdiction lends itself to greater argument as to whether the actions lie in unjust enrichment or delict. Second, there is the *Verwendungskondiktion* – dealing with expenditure on another's property, and here again South African and Scots law deal with the scenario outside the context of the performance claims; in the case of South Africa, this is through the extended action of the *negotiorum gestor*. Third, there is the *Rückgriffskondiktion* – dealing with payment of another's debt. Intermediary cases where the *actio de in rem verso* had been used have been largely expunged from the modern law in German, Scots and South African law, although there are some areas where the action remains.

A. Performance Claims

There are two main points to cover in this subsection. The first provides an answer to the question: what is a performance claim and how do we identify the basis for a claimant's performance? The second leads on from this: how do we identify performance in complex three-party cases? In German law, the crux of the *Leistungskondiktion* or performance claim is a claim for the return of a performance proffered to the defendant on the grounds of the failure of the basis for the transfer; this is typically that there was no obligation to make the payment and therefore no legal ground for it. The standard German way of finding a legal ground is to look to the intention or purpose of the claimant. This is the subjective method of identifying the putative basis of a transfer. The claimant must act with a purpose directed towards the defendant (which fails) for there to be a claim. That purpose might be to discharge a debt – *causa solvendi*, or to induce counter-performance – *causa ob rem*, or to make a gift – *causa donandi*. In practice to substantiate the claim the German claimant must explain how and why he wants restitution. Sanders describes this pleading practice as coming close to an unjust factors approach,[27] although this may be misleading

[26] T Krebs, *Restitution at the Crossroads* (London, Cavendish, 2001) 208–10.

[27] A Sanders, 'Absence of Basis: A German Perspective' in S Elliott et al (eds), *Restitution of Overpaid Tax* (Oxford, Hart Publishing, 2013) 233.

as the German claimant is attempting to prove – not mistake – but failure of a purpose to discharge a debt. The other method in German law of identifying the basis for the transfer is the objective method, although the differences between the approaches are small. The objective method involves multiplying sets of fact in which a ground is present and concluding if none are present, there is no basis.[28] There is some evidence that Scots law might follow this route,[29] and the general tenor of the Canadian cases suggest that it might be moving to an objective method.[30] However, the subjective method is dominant in German law and has important advantages over the objective approach. The first is its automated nature. If party A intends to discharge a debt and it does not exist, restitution follows. That is caveated in German law by the fact that if A knew the payment was not due, restitution does not follow. It is then deemed a gift (although this characterisation is not uncontroversial). The second advantage is that 'at the expense of' is baked in. If my purpose was to pay you and discharge a debt owed to you, there is putative performance and automatically your enrichment is at my expense.

The mixed jurisdictions, just mentioned, such as Scotland and South Africa do not have the general unitary action of German law but are also said to rest on absence of legal basis,[31] although questions of the subjective/objective methods of identifying that basis may be best avoided.[32] They are multi-actional systems with a set of distinct *condictio* claims,[33] envisaged as based on failed performance or transfer. There are moves in South Africa, after the decision of *McCarthy Retail (Pty) Ltd v Shortdistance Carriers Ltd*,[34] to recognise a general unjust enrichment action and an increasing tendency to deploy South Africa's own four questions analysis (maybe unwittingly) as such a general action and to ignore requirements such as that the mistake be excusable.[35] There are dangers to the recognition of a general action. The most obvious might be a tendency to its imperial growth. Recognising the dangers, the South African court said first, few cases would succeed which would not have done so under one or other of the traditional actions and second, less energy would be spent on arguing as

[28] H Scott, 'Restitution of Extra-Contractual Transfers: Limits on the Absence of Legal Ground Analysis' [2006] *Restitution Law Review* 93, 100.

[29] Sir George Mackenzie, *Institutions of the Law of Scotland*, book 3, ch 1 (Mackenzie I 3.1); R Evans-Jones, 'Some Reflections on the Nature of the *Condictio Indebiti* in a Mixed Legal System' (1994) 111 *South African Law Journal* 759.

[30] But see, D Sheehan, 'Unjust Factors, Absence of Juristic Reason and the Development of Canadian Unjust(ified) Enrichment Law' (2016) 49 *University of British Columbia Law Review* 619.

[31] *Shilliday v Smith* 1998 SLT 976, 978.

[32] du Plessis, 'Labels and Meaning' (n 24) 432.

[33] Hogg (n 21) 8.

[34] *McCarthy Retail (Pty) Ltd v Shortdistance Carriers Ltd* 2001 (3) SA 482.

[35] J du Plessis, 'Basic Features and Problems of the South African Law of Unjustified Enrichment' (2022) 86 *Rabels Zeitschrift für Ausländisches und Internationales Privatrecht* 531, 539–49; see also, G Glover, 'Reflections on the *Sine Causa Requirement* and the *Condictiones* in South African Law' (2009) 20 *Stellenbosch Law Review* 468.

to which of those *condictiones* was appropriate;[36] that said, it seems clear that the traditional *condictiones* will remain a feature of South African law for some time to come. Each *condictio*-claim refers to a distinct purpose that the claimant had. The purposes with which a person might pay are thought to be mutually exclusive and so are the *condictiones*.[37] The *condictio indebiti*, for example, refers to a failed *causa solvendi*. The claimant pays with the intention to discharge a non-existent debt and so can recover. The *condictio causa data causa non secuta* applies when, outside the contractual context, the claimant makes a transfer to induce a non-forthcoming counter-performance (*causa ob rem*). Consequently, the *condictio causa data* should not apply where a contract is terminated for breach or is frustrated. We find the logic followed to the letter in German law where restitution following termination of a contract for breach is a liability in contract and not unjustified enrichment.[38] This is because when the performance was proffered by the claimant there was a valid basis for it; termination does not retrospectively invalidate the contract and so the provisions for restitution after termination are found in the contract section of the Civil Code. The flipside is that the *condictio ob rem* in German law only has a role to play in extra-contractual cases where the parties never intended to create mutual obligations.[39] The second sentence of § 812(1) provides:

> This duty (of restitution) also exists if the legal grounds later lapse **or if the result intended to be achieved by those efforts in accordance with the contents of the legal transaction does not occur.**

Krebs gives three main examples of the *condictio ob rem* which derive from the highlighted segment: a case from 1924[40] where to induce an estranged wife to move back in (as § 1353 BGB suggested she should) a farmer gave her all his lands and then livestock. When she failed to move in, he sought them all back. Second, there are cases of transfers made in anticipation of a contract being formed when it fails to materialise and last, cases very similar to the Quistclose trust in English law. The *condictio ob rem* in German law is very limited and does not fit well with the abstract reasoning inherent in other examples of the *Leistungskondiktion*, because it involves a positive reason for restitution, the non-fulfilment of an agreed or understood (but non-contractual) condition. Section 817 provides for restitution if the purpose of a performance was illegal or immoral. This is the *condictio ob*

[36] (2001 (3) SA 482, 488–89, a point alluded to in *Financial Services Board v De Wet NO* 2002 (3) SA 525, 622–23 as to whether the action there was properly the *condictio ob turpem vel iniustam causam*, *condictio indebiti* or *condictio sine causa specialis*.

[37] R Evans-Jones and P Hellwege, 'Some Observations on the Taxonomy of Unjustified Enrichment in Scots Law' [1998] *Edinburgh Law Review* 180, 209–11.

[38] §§ 346 ff BGB; R Zimmermann, 'Restitution after Termination for Breach of Contract: German Law after the Reform of 2002' in AS Burrows and A Rodger (eds), *Mapping the Law* (Oxford, OUP, 2006).

[39] Krebs, *Restitution at the Crossroads* (n 26) 144–45.

[40] ibid 146; RGH 118, 358.

turpem vel iniustam causam and in German law is largely swallowed, where the obligation is void, by the *Leistungskondiktion*.[41] We also find positive reasons for restitution – (excusable) mistake,[42] duress[43] and incapacity or ultra vires[44] rearing their heads as additional requirements in the South African *condictio indebiti* and the extent to which unjust factors matter is a live debate in South Africa. The question has also been raised of the reception of unjust factors as understood in English law into Scots law,[45] but the idea did not have an enthusiastic welcome.

B. Non-Performance Claims for Improvements

One example is the subcontractor case,[46] where A contracts with B that B will do work on C's land or property (sometimes without C's knowledge), A fails to pay for the work and B sues C in unjust enrichment. A performance is a conscious intentional action in favour of another person to carry out a purpose.[47] Here the action is not intentionally benefiting the defendant (C). B's legal relationship is with A – not C. There is a leapfrogging problem inherent in this therefore in that an action would allow B to avoid the risk of his contracting party's non-payment, and put it on C. That is firmly disallowed in Germany, South Africa[48] and England.[49]

There are cases, however, in which the improver can recover from the owner of the land or chattel in South Africa[50] and in Germany, where in some cases the owner/possessor model in §§ 994–96 BGB applies or otherwise the *Verwendungskondiktion*. In Scotland, these cases are dealt with via mistake. In *Newton v Newton*,[51] the pursuer believed he owned the property, which he

[41] Sanders (n 27) 219–20.

[42] *Morgan Guaranty Trust Corporation of New York v Lothian RC* 1995 SLT 299; *Willis Faber Enthoven v Receiver of Revenue* 1992 (4) SA 202 (A); *Affirmative Portfolios CC v Transnet Ltd* 2009 (1) SA 196; *Yarona Healthcare Network (Pty) Ltd v Medshield* 2018 (1) SA 513. H Scott, 'The Requirement of Excusable Mistake in the Context of the Condictio Indebiti: Scottish and South African Law Compared' (2007) 123 *South African Law Journal* 827.

[43] *Union Government v Gowar* [1915] AD 426.

[44] *Amalgamated Society of Woodworkers of South Africa v Die* 1963 Ambagsaalvereniging 1967 (2) SA 586; H Scott, *Unjust Enrichment in South African Law* (Oxford, Hart Publishing, 2013) ch 5.

[45] See PBH Birks, 'Six Questions in Search of a Subject' [1985] *Juridical Review* 227; PBH Birks, 'Restitution: A View of Scots Law' [1985] *Current Legal Problems* 57; WJ Stewart, *The Law of Restitution in Scotland* (Edinburgh, W Green & Sons, 1992).

[46] D Visser, *Unjustified Enrichment* (Durban, Juta, 2008) 203–12.

[47] On performance, see F Botha, 'The Legal Nature of Performance Reconsidered' (2020) 137 *South African Law Journal* 248.

[48] *Buzzard Electrical (Pty) Ltd v 158 Jan Smuts Avenue Investments (Pty) Ltd* 1996 (4) SA 19.

[49] *McDonald Dickens v Macklin & Costello* [2011] EWCA Civ 930; *Uren v First National Home Finance* [2005] EWHC 2529 (Ch).

[50] *McCarthy Retail v Short Distance Carriers CC* [2001] 3 All SA 236 (A); *ABSA Bank v CB Stander* 1998 (1) SA 939 (C); D Visser and S Miller, 'Between Principle and Policy: Indirect Enrichment in Subcontractor and Garage Repair Cases' (2000) 117 *South African Law Journal* 594; Visser, *Unjustified Enrichment* (n 46) 213–16.

[51] *Newton v Newton* 1925 SC(HL) 925, discussed in *Shilliday v Smith* 1998 SLT 976, 980.

improved. The mistake was explicitly relied upon. A mistake that you own the property negatives the possibility of a purposive transfer, which is why it cannot be a performance claim, and this would be a case of the *Verwendungskondiktion* in Germany, reflecting that while there are some improvement cases that can be fitted into a *condictio indebiti*, many – like *Newton* – cannot be.[52] In South Africa, *Klug & Klug v Penkin* involves almost the same facts.[53] An agent repaired four houses having been instructed by the relevant authority that they were unsafe and needed repair. However, one did not belong to his principal and was repaired by mistake. Mistake was not relied on explicitly, but as in Scotland this was not deemed a performance claim; the agent succeeded in the extended action of the *negotiorum gestor* available where he has bona fide improved the defendant's property in the belief that he was carrying out his own affairs. The extended action is an action in unjustified enrichment in a way that the 'normal' action in *negotiorum gestio* is not. *Negotiorum gestio* – where I in a reasonable manner manage your affairs without your knowledge but with the intention of benefiting you and recovering my expenditure – creates its own legal ground.[54] Du Plessis has suggested that mistake does not work in these 'extended' cases of *negotiorum gestio*.[55] To regard mistake as the critical factor is to suggest a structural link with undue payments where there is none. His basic objection is that to focus on mistake will lead to distinctions cutting across established categories of claim given that civil law has had a set of unjustified enrichment rules (outside *negotiorum gestio*) for unauthorised improvements for centuries, including for those who know perfectly well that they were not authorised to act. These latter rules for mala fide improvers have been accepted into South African law,[56] but not Scots law. These cases also lie on the edge or boundary line with property laws and alongside the extended action in *negotiorum gestio* we also find that the bona fide possessor/occupier rules developed in property law apply. In Scotland it would probably have been better to view *Newton* as a bona fide possessor claim. A claim based on bona fide possession is also a feature of South African law, where a case of a bona fide possessor or occupier can take action to improve the property or prevents its deterioration. This might be because a possessor of a car, to whom property has not (yet) been transferred, procures repairs from a garage and absconds. The garage owner might sue the car owner in the extended action,[57] or under the bona fide occupier rules.[58]

[52] J Wolffe, 'Enrichment by Improvement in Scots Law' in R Zimmermann and D Visser (eds), *Unjustified Enrichment: Key Issues in Comparative Perspective* (Cambridge, CUP, 2001) 402–07.

[53] *Klug & Klug v Penkin* 1932 CPD 401.

[54] Visser, *Unjustified Enrichment* (n 46) 565.

[55] J du Plessis, 'Towards a Rational Structure of Liability for Unjustified Enrichment' (2005) 122 *South African Law Journal* 142, 163.

[56] J du Plessis, 'The Enrichment Claim of the *Mala Fide* Improver of Another's Property' in A Burrows, D Johnston and R Zimmermann (eds), *Judge and Jurist: Essays in Memory of Lord Rodger* (Oxford, OUP, 2013). *Barbour v Halliday* (1840) 2 D 1279 bars the Scots bad faith possessor from recovery.

[57] *ABSA Bank v Stander* 1998 (1) SA 939.

[58] *McCarthy Retail v Shortdistance Carriers CC* 2001 (3) SA 482.

The overlap in South Africa is a historical accident. Roman law had no developed general action for unjust enrichment and so developed an embryonic version in its property law rules.[59]

In German law as well, special rules for example apply to the relationship between the owner of a thing and its possessor. A mala fide possessor, who knows he is not in lawful possession, cannot demand restitution where the improvements were merely useful,[60] and is relegated to the rules on *negotiorum gestio* for necessary expenditure. A bona fide possessor can claim necessary expenditure, excluding normal maintenance costs or useful expenditure if it raises the value of the property.[61] There is a question as to what counts as necessary and German courts have struggled to find a clear line on this, although the general proposition that necessary expenditure is incontrovertibly beneficial is unquestioned.[62] If an increase in the value of the asset has been realised by the defendant through sale that is recoverable. Readily realisable (but as yet unrealised) value can also be recovered if that can be done without detriment to the defendant.[63] In general, the owner/possessor model takes priority over unjustified enrichment if its requirements are fulfilled; the *Verwendungskondiktion* therefore only applies where the owner/possessor model does not.[64]

This leads to inconsistencies and demarcation issues between the claim of the possessor and the *Verwendungskondiktion*.[65] The requirements for relief in the latter are also not completely clear. The fact that my act improved your property is insufficient to ground relief. What is sufficient is controversial, although it is obvious that some substantive reason is needed[66] and the obvious candidate is mistake. The point and purpose behind the unjustified enrichment provisions of the BGB was to reverse unintended shifts of wealth or enrichments. Cases where the improver knows the asset does not belong to him and pursues his own interests in full knowledge of the position are therefore excluded and this is either justified by analogy with § 814 BGB which denies the *Leistungskondiktion* if the claimant knew the payment was not owing or by analogy with the German equivalent of estoppel, *venire contra factum proprium*. If the aim is to guide English law, the analysis is not helped by the single reported instance of *Verwendungskondiktion*,[67]

[59] Visser, *Unjustified Enrichment* (n 46) 597; see also R Evans-Jones 'Seeking Imposed Enrichment in Improvements: Classification and General Enrichment Actions in Mixed Legal Systems – Scotland and South Africa' [2008] *Restitution Law Review* 18.

[60] § 996 BGB.

[61] §§ 994–96 BGB.

[62] DA Verse, 'Improvements and Enrichment: A Comparative Analysis' [1998] *Restitution Law Review* 85, 92; BGHZ 5, 337; RGZ, 117, 112.

[63] Verse (n 62) 94–98.

[64] T Krebs, 'Unrequested Benefits in German Law' in J Neyers et al (eds), *Understanding Unjust Enrichment* (Oxford, Hart Publishing, 2004) 253.

[65] Visser, *Unjustified Enrichment* (n 46) 598; J Beatson and E Schrage (eds), *Cases, Materials and Texts on Unjustified Enrichment* (Oxford, Hart Publishing, 2003) 441–43.

[66] Krebs, 'Unrequested Benefits in German Law' (n 64) 255–56.

[67] BGHZ 140, 275; G Dannemann, *The German Law of Unjustified Enrichment and Restitution: A Comparative Introduction* (Oxford, OUP, 2009) 114–15.

which seems to turn on a misprediction by the son that the gift would not be recalled by his parents. Mispredictions are typically said in English law not to ground relief. The claimant parents transferred a property to their son but reserved proprietary rights to the use of the stables and other buildings. The son and parents fell out and the parents claimed the property back on the grounds of the son's 'gross ingratitude' under § 530 BGB which triggered the return of the house under the unjustified enrichment rules. In the meantime, the son, working on his own property (so not owner/possessor model) and on his own behalf (so not *negotiorum gestio*), had improved the house and credit needed to be given for this under the *Verwendungskondiktion*.

C. Intermediary Cases

Where there is an intermediary involved in making an unauthorised transfer of assets from claimant to defendant it is said liability only exists within the *actio de in rem verso*.[68] The *actio de in rem verso* is explicitly concerned with third-party enrichments other than by performance.[69] Its history is quite fraught. The action derives from the Roman *actio de peculio* which referred to a master's enrichment at the defendant's expense by the actions of the former's slave or servant,[70] and expanded to cover cases where a third party is enriched at the expense of the impoverished obligee via an intermediary.[71] The immediate cause was C4.26.7.3 which was seen as a clear example of the general principle that nobody should be enriched at the expense of another. The traditional core became the contract between A and B by which C is enriched.[72] Initially parallels were drawn with *negotiorum gestio*, but ever more far-reaching parallels were drawn and as more attention was placed on the defendant's enrichment, less and less was placed on the need for a middleman until the action became the general enrichment action in French and Louisiana law.[73] In the French/Louisiana tradition it is an equitable and subsidiary remedy. One of the primary requirements therefore is that no other action be available.[74] In Roman-Dutch law by contrast courts subsumed the *versio*-claim within a wider general enrichment action – the *condictio sine causa*[75] – and

[68] A Honore, 'Third Party Enrichment' [1960] *Acta Juridica* 236, 246–251; JR Whitty 'Indirect Enrichment in Scots Law' [1994] *Juridical Review* 200, 207; *Commercial Bank of Scotland v Biggar* 1958 SLT (Notes) 46.

[69] R Zimmermann, *The Law of Obligations* (Durban, Juta, 1996) 878–84.

[70] N Davrados, 'Demystifying Enrichment Without Cause' (2018) 78 *Louisiana Law Review* 1223, 1228.

[71] ibid 1230.

[72] Zimmermann, *The Law of Obligations* (n 69) 879.

[73] ibid 882–84. For a discussion of the French law and the problems generated by a fragmentary system, see P Letelier, 'Another Civilian View of Unjust Enrichment's Structural Debate' [2020] *CLJ* 531.

[74] *Edmonston v SA-Second Mortgage Co* 289 So (2d) 116 (1974).

[75] Honore (n 68) 246.

the action fell into disuse in South Africa, although occasionally it is referred to. In *ABSA Bank v Stander* for instance the court saw the extended action in *negotiorum gestio* as analogous to the *actio de in rem verso*,[76] while pointing out that there was no actual instance of the *actio* being available to an improver of property in modern South African law.

It is difficult therefore to find clear examples of the *actio* from which parallels can be drawn of use to English law. In German law, for example, the narrowing of the *versio*-claim occurred because during the drafting of the German Civil Code the original Drafting Commission thought that in the light of the breadth of their general (*sine causa*) principle the *versio*-claim was unnecessary, but also in principle undesirable. In short, they were concerned that in the scenario outlined above where A and B contract and C benefits, that C not be affected by a contract he had no part in.[77] The action is therefore not available, except in one narrow context in Germany. Section 816(1) BGB provides:

> If an unauthorised person disposes of an object and the decision is effective against the authorised person, then he is obliged to make restitution to the authorised person of what he gains by the disposal. If the disposition is gratuitous, then the same duty applies to a person who as a result of the disposition directly gains a legal advantage.

The provision deals with the case where non-owner B purports to transfer an asset, owned by A, to C. Since B is not the owner, the usual rules of *nemo dat* bar him from transferring good title to C, unless the rules on bona fide acquisition from a non-owner apply.[78] If property does not pass, the proper action is the *rei vindicatio*. If it does pass, B must hand back the purchase price received for the asset to A, or C must hand over the thing itself, if he received it as a gift. Note the property link in that ownership transfers from A to C (albeit via the action of B). Outside the link no claim lies, unless § 822 BGB applies. It provides:

> If the recipient bestows the gains on a third person at no charge, then that third person is obliged to make restitution as if he had received the disposition from the creditor without legal grounds, to the extent that as a result of the bestowal the duty of the recipient to make restitution of the enrichment is excluded.

D. Encroachment or Invasion Claims

These claims lie on the boundary of delict, property and unjustified enrichment. They are not the same as the imposed enrichment cases because the enrichment is caused by the act of the defendant – not that of the claimant. In German law this

[76] 1998 (1) SA 939, 950–54.

[77] J du Plessis and R Zimmermann, 'The Basic Features of the German Law of Unjustified Enrichment' [1994] *Restitution Law Review* 14.

[78] §§ 932–35 BGB.

is the *Eingriffskondiktion* and the reason why liability is dealt with in unjustified enrichment arises from the fact that there are no gain-based damages for delict in Germany. The most difficult question, however, is similar to one also asked in South Africa. Which wrongs give rise to a concurrent unjustified enrichment claim?[79] German law now applies the theory of attribution whereby if the infringed right attributes the defendant's gain to the claimant the *Eingriffskondiktion* applies, hence property wrongs – as in England – attract gain-based liability, because property rights contain within them the right to fruits from the property owned. In terms of 'at the expense' the claimant need not show any actual loss, just as in England.[80]

The division between delict and unjustified enrichment is more fluid in an uncodified system such as South Africa. The *condictio sine causa specialis* applies where the defendant has come into possession of the item and then consumes or alienates it. This transfer could be because of a *negotium*, but if the defendant receives gratuitously (*ex causa lucrativa*) there does not need to be a *negotium*.[81] South Africa therefore distinguishes between the party who receives gratuitously (in the absence of a *negotium*) and one who does not. The bona fide purchaser has no liability.[82] The meaning of *negotium* seems a little vague but refers to some form of dealings between the parties. That may be a contract but negotiations for a contract may suffice.[83] The aim of the requirement is clearly to restrict the range of parties from whom the owner of the property may claim; it is a proxy indicator that the defendant should have known he could not legitimately dispose of the property. Money is definitely recoverable,[84] and opinion – rightly – favours the same outcome in goods cases.

The delictual *actio ad exhibendum* is available as a claim for the value of the thing consumed or alienated[85] where the defendant had knowledge – actual or constructive – of the plaintiff's claim to the property at the time of the disposal. Although characterised as delictual and covering ground also covered by Aquilian liability,[86] which is equally delictual, quantum of relief is therefore identical to an enrichment action. The *condictio furtiva* was also originally in Roman law delictual, but hovers on the boundary line in South African law and has been used as an enrichment action,[87] although more recently described as delictual.[88] It is not just

[79] Dannemann (n 67) 91–92; D Visser, 'The Potential Role of a General Enrichment Action' (2009) 20 *Stellenbosch Law Review* 454, 463–64, discussing *National Media Ltd v Jooste* 1996 (3) SA 262.

[80] Dannemann (n 67) 102.

[81] Visser, *Unjustified Enrichment* (n 46) 655.

[82] *Van der Westhuizen v McDonald and Mundel* 1907 TS 933; *Commissioner of Customs & Excise v Bank of Lisbon International* 1994 (1) SA 205, 215.

[83] Visser, *Unjustified Enrichment* (n 46) 656–57.

[84] *Commissioner of Customs & Excise v Bank of Lisbon Intl Ltd* 1994 (1) SA 205; *Nissan South Africa (Pty) Ltd v Marnitz NO Ltd* 2005 (1) SA 441.

[85] Visser, *Unjustified Enrichment* (n 46) 660; *Alderson & Flitton (Tzaneen) Pty Ltd v EG Duffeys Spares (Pty) Ltd* 1975 (3) SA 41.

[86] *Frankel Pollak Vinderine Inc v Stanton NO* 2000 (1) SA 425.

[87] *Krueger v Navratil* 1952 (4) SA 405; *Clifford v Farinha* 1988 (4) SA 315.

[88] *Chetty v Italtile Ceramics Ltd* 2013 (3) SA 374.

available to the owner, but to anyone with a proven interest in the asset and is available not just against a thief, but one who uses the asset temporarily and the thief's heirs. It is also wider than the *actio ad exhibendum*, not just in that it is available to a wider class of plaintiffs, but also in that it applies where the defendant has not voluntarily disposed of the asset. It provides the claimant with the highest value of the asset between appropriation and the action being instituted and all the benefits derived from the property. There is an overlap with the *condictio sine causa* in that a thief acquires gratuitously and so is vulnerable to the *condictio*;[89] other mala fide possessors are also vulnerable to this action.

II. Common Law

One of the key objections made to unjust enrichment theory is overgeneralisation. Birks treated enrichment as one thing, asking what value had been transferred to the defendant.[90] That might be value in terms of money in which case it is incontrovertible. Money being the measure of enrichment it is impossible not to be enriched. Other enrichments – of things or services can be subjectively devalued. What this means is that the defendant can say that he would not have purchased the service at the market rate and so it is only worth a lesser sum to him. We do not need to go into details as to precisely how this works at the moment; what matters is that on the Birksian view there is a transfer of something of value which is enriching in the 'ordinary sense' of the word – ie, it provides the defendant with a quantifiable actual benefit and it is the actual benefit which is returned to a successful claimant. In the same way 'at the expense of' is treated as a single question to be answered prior to identifying an unjust factor, or in later work the absence of basis.

The wrong turn began here according to Stevens.[91] In essence he argues there are three errors in the Birksian view of unjust enrichment. The first is that if we are really interested in enrichment in this 'ordinary sense' of the word we should measure the quantum of recovery as being the amount by which we think the defendant is enriched at trial. If the defendant is disenriched between receipt and trial, we must reduce the quantum of recovery. Stevens points out correctly that this is not what English law does, although it is, with some qualifications, what South African law does. In explaining his second point, Stevens gives an example of the destroyed stamp. In that example you and I have the world's only examples of a rare stamp. You mistakenly destroy yours and mine triples in value. You do not have a claim against me. Concentration on mistake, however, means this must be explained. Another example of the same phenomenon is the 'rising heat' example.

[89] Visser, *Unjustified Enrichment* (n 46) 665.

[90] PBH Birks, *An Introduction to the Law of Restitution*, rev edn (Oxford, Clarendon Press, 1989) 109–32.

[91] R Stevens, 'The Unjust Enrichment Disaster' (2018) 134 *LQR* 574.

This derives from the decision in *Edinburgh Tramways v Courtenay*.[92] The owner of the downstairs flat put on his heating and since heat rises lowers the upstairs owner's heating bill. Is the upstairs owner enriched at his expense and can the downstairs owner claim part of his heating bill back? No. Proving this has given rise to some rather tortured explanations, however, such as that there is a gift of the heat or that it has been abandoned.[93] Stevens' third objection is that unjust enrichment claims as understood in the 'orthodox' account contains four or five different claims with 'no more in common' with each other than with the 'now excluded restitution for wrongs'.[94] He makes the point – which by now should be familiar as a critique of unjust enrichment – that while contract is unified by a commitment to the binding nature of promissory agreement, there seems nothing similar binding unjust enrichment together and indeed that the books often admit as much.[95]

These errors are all, at bottom, caused by the 'four questions' approach. Proponents of unjust enrichment, it is said, make two flawed assumptions first that because all claims in z have feature x, any claim that does not feature x is not z and that because some claims in z have feature y, all claims in z should.[96] Neither is true; to think they are true is to make the essentialist error and is avoided by thinking about unjust enrichment as an ideal type concept picking out significant features of empirical cases rather than common features. Stevens' simple answer to why the downstairs owner has no claim against his neighbour or why the owner of the (now destroyed) stamp has no claim against his fellow collector is that there is no performance. Performance requires that the claimant do something, that he intended it to be for the defendant and that it was accepted by the latter. This means the defendant who receives a performance does so either on the basis that there is a justified basis or that there is not.[97] The upstairs owner does not accept the heating and so even if the downstairs owner mistakenly believes there is a contract for him to crank up the heating to warm the upstairs flat no relief is possible. It is not merely that acceptance is required or there is no payment[98] – tender is not payment – but that there must be some normative reason why the defendant should care. This implies that the defendant must accept the basis on which the claimant has made the transfer. Stevens denies therefore that we can have any purely unilateral reason for restitution. To rely purely on the claimant's mistake is, he argues, immoral. It uses the defendant as a means to an end when he is not

[92] *Edinburgh Tramways v Courtenay* 1909 SC (HL) 99; see R Stevens, *The Laws of Restitution* (Oxford, OUP, 2023) 30–31.

[93] For discussion, see D Sheehan, '"At the Expense of": Linking Claimant and Defendant in the Law of Unjust Enrichment' (2020) 20 *Oxford University Commonwealth Law Journal* 235, 237–38; Stevens, *The Laws of Restitution* (n 92) 32; for the way this is dealt with in the civil law, see S Meier, 'Enrichment at the Expense of Another and Incidental Benefits in German Law' [2019] *Acta Juridica* 453.

[94] Stevens, 'The Unjust Enrichment Disaster' (n 91) 574–75.

[95] ibid 575–76.

[96] ibid 577.

[97] ibid 581.

[98] ibid 582; see, on acceptance, Stevens, *The Laws of Restitution* (n 92) 46–50.

implicated. While it is a step too far to require the defendant's acceptance of the purported basis, the defendant does need to accept the receipt itself.[99] This means that in the performance cases 'at the expense of' is built in. Performance also solves Stevens' enrichment problem. We reverse the performance; the enrichment is merely the value of that performance.[100] Stevens' critique is a powerful one and we see that the notion of performance has an important role to play in structuring the law of unjust enrichment – and allows us to exclude claims inappropriately included by Birks. However, two points need to be made. First, neither in his article nor his book, does Stevens look in detail at non-performance claims in an unjustified enrichment claim in civil law or mixed systems. Second, as we see in chapter three, it is not correct to say that mistake as a 'unilateral' reason for relief is immoral and unjustifiable.

This section therefore sketches out an understanding and framework of unjust enrichment that is not dependent on the four questions analysis seen at the beginning of chapter one. It is a framework, which draws on the civilian experience. The power of the 'four questions' approach was in part the coherence of the system explaining restitutionary claims for vitiated intention, but this meant that cases were classified together as mistake cases which a German lawyer would see as wholly distinct – payments under a liability mistake and improvements of property mistakenly believing he is the owner for instance.[101] The rules of attribution, for example, are different in these cases, and this is obscured by the four questions analysis.

A. Performance Claims

To demonstrate that English law has a set of claims which can usefully be distinguished as performance claims we examine its rules as to 'expense'. English law does not start from the same premises as the civilian systems but arrives at approximately the same position, albeit without ever explicitly talking about performance claims. In the South African context, Visser describes a performance in the same terms I will use for English law. It is a deliberate transfer of money, chattels or services from one person to another.[102] The general rule in English law requires a transactional link. This entails an intentional transfer by the claimant to the defendant in a single transaction, or a series of transactions so closely related that they were intended as a single mechanism of transfer. Leapfrogging is generally not allowed,[103] although there are exceptions to this general rule, such as where

[99] Smith (n 5) 112.

[100] Stevens, 'The Unjust Enrichment Disaster' (n 91) 581; he now denies that talk of enrichment is useful even in this context. Stevens, *The Laws of Restitution* (n 92) 70.

[101] Meier, 'Restitution of Undue Transfers in the Civil Law and the Common Law' (n 22) 535.

[102] Visser, *Unjustified Enrichment* (n 46) 223.

[103] *Uren v First National Home Finance* [2005] EWHC 2529.

all three parties make the same mistake and there would be unnecessary circuity of action if the short cut were not permitted.[104] Where a performance is reversible it is then the value of the performance made to the claimant which is recoverable. This is easiest to see in services cases where it is the (market) value of the services that is claimable not the value of any realised gain and we discuss this in more detail in the context of quantum meruit in chapter five;[105] indeed there does not need to be any marketable residuum at all. Pure services with a market value are enriching. This is not evidence that talk of enrichment is misleading and we should talk about performance instead. The fact of the performance having been requested or accepted is proof of its being of value to the defendant. Alternatively, its necessity disentitles the defendant from saying he is not enriched. Even if the result of the performance is destroyed, it was enriching, and the question now is a separate one of risk allocation; who should take the risk of the end-result being destroyed?

Another pointer to the importance of performance is that where a performance is successful – ie, a debt is discharged – no restitution is possible. This is sometimes referred to as a defence of good consideration, but is not properly a defence in the sense that it does not exculpate a defendant.[106] It should simply prove that the cause of action has not been made out and indeed Burrows (now Lord Burrows) now argues that it is for the claimant to prove there was no debt.[107] The location of the burden of proof is instructive; it is not right to say that the unjust factors approach starts with a mistaken payment and assumes relief until a defence is introduced. This rule about the burden of proof must be the same in cases of unenforceable or natural obligations.[108]

Our starting point to establish the attribution rules is *Investment Trust Companies v HMRC*.[109] Importantly, although the test there is expressed as being the test for attribution in unjust enrichment, it is not. It is one of the tests, not the singular test, for attribution in unjust enrichment. It is, though, **the** test for attribution in performance cases. The facts were that the claimants received services from different fund management companies. They mistakenly believed that VAT was due and were charged and paid accordingly. The managers accounted to HMRC for the money paid to them as output tax. Output tax is the VAT charged by the HMRC on the services provided by the fund management companies. The

[104] *Khan v Permayer* [2001] BPIR 95.

[105] Stevens, *The Laws of Restitution* (n 92) 65–70.

[106] *Barclays Bank v WJ Simms, Son & Cooke (Southern) Ltd* [1980] QB 677.

[107] AS Burrows, 'Is there a Defence of Good Consideration?' in C Mitchell and WJ Swadling (eds), *The Restatement Third: Restitution and Unjust Enrichment* (Oxford, Hart Publishing, 2013) 183. On South African law, see du Plessis, 'Labels and Meaning' (n 24) 103.

[108] On natural obligations, see D Sheehan, 'Natural Obligations in English Law' [2004] *Lloyds Maritime & Commercial Law Quarterly* 172; M McInnes, 'Natural Obligations and Unjust Enrichment' in E Bant and M Harding (eds), *Exploring Private Law* (Cambridge, CUP, 2010), but for a sceptical view, Tang Hang Wu, 'Natural Obligations and the Common Law of Unjust Enrichment' (2006) 6 *Oxford University Commonwealth Law Journal* 133.

[109] *Investment Trust Companies v HMRC* [2017] UKSC 29, [2018] 2 AC 275.

managers deducted sums payable on supplies made to themselves as input tax. Input tax is the VAT charged by HMRC on goods and services received by the fund management companies – it is the tax paid on what they bought in. The managers paid over the balance. That balance represents the tax on the value added by the managers and ensured that HMRC did not receive VAT twice. It was the output tax that was invalidly demanded by the Revenue because of the incorrect transposition of the relevant EU Directive. The managers were able to recover part of the sums paid to HMRC, and those recoveries were paid to the claimants. The fund managers had been unable to recover all the money paid over and the claimants sued HMRC for that irrecoverable money. The Supreme Court held that HMRC was not enriched at the expense of ITC, although it was rescued by the operation of sections 80, 80A of the VAT Act 1994 and the VAT Regulations 1995. The Supreme Court argued that there was a transfer of value to the managers, which was defective. Another transfer of value was made between the managers and HMRC.[110] The transfers were not, the Supreme Court held, a sham, nor were they a single scheme of transactions, nor were the managers agents for the claimants in paying HMRC. The Supreme Court saw two separate payments and two separate mistakes, one about a contract and the other about a statutory obligation.[111] While the Supreme Court did not deny that in economic terms HMRC was enriched at the expense of the claimants, they insisted that was insufficient to found the claim.[112]

Talk of transfer of value is unhelpful. Value is not a thing capable of transfer; it is a characteristic of something. Value, for our purposes in this book, is relational value. Value can take many forms; my friendships are of value to me, but they are not of relational value. I cannot exchange my friendship for something else. For our purposes in the law of unjust enrichment, money, chattels and services are of value because they can be exchanged. Rights as well can be (generally at least) exchanged and this sits at the heart of the contention that proprietary claims too can be based on unjust enrichment.[113] Nonetheless, the Supreme Court was right that there was no transaction between the claimants and HMRC. Lord Reed continued that to describe English law in terms of a direct provider rule was consistent with a composite transaction test where coordinated transactions are involved. A coordinated transaction provided, along with the interposition of an agent, or the possibility of a sham,[114] examples of cases where the dealing was not direct but should be treated as if it were.

[110] ibid [71].
[111] ibid.
[112] ibid [32].
[113] A Lodder, *Enrichment in the Law of Unjust Enrichment and Restitution* (Oxford, Hart Publishing, 2012) 16–19.
[114] [2017] UKSC 29, [2018] 2 AC 275, [47]–[50]; tracing, assignment and discharge of a debt are also mentioned. See *Tecnimont Arabia Ltd v National Westminster Bank* [2022] EWHC 1172, [110]–[113].

The next (albeit not chronologically) case, *Menelaou v Bank of Cyprus*,[115] was a subrogation case. It involved the discharge of a liability; these cases need to be treated with some care. The first point is that we need to view a discharge of liability as an enrichment to be reversed *in specie*. The effect of such reversal is that the defendant is put back *in statu quo ante*, even though the claimant may receive rights he never previously had.[116] It does not matter therefore – consistently with the absence of a double cap rule in English law limiting recovering to the lower of the defendant's gain or the claimant's loss – that there is no corresponding loss to the claimant. The second point is that there are broadly three key, but not exhaustive, categories of subrogation.[117] The first is the 'misappropriation' cases, dealt with in chapter seven. The second is the 'common liability' cases, dealt with in chapter six; these latter cases are not unjust enrichment cases. The third is the 'lending cases,' where C pays (A who pays) X, who discharges D's debt to X. Alternatively C pays A, who pays X who discharges D's liability to X. *Menelaou* is such a lending case. The bank had two charges over Rush Green Hall to secure debts owed by the Menelaou parents. The parents wanted to downsize and since the sale of Rush Green Hall would not produce a sum great enough to pay off the debts, the bank agreed to release the charges on condition that it would be granted a charge on Great Oak Court, which was to be purchased by the parents for Melissa Menelaou, the daughter, who was unaware of the charge. That charge was registered but turned out to be invalid. The bank claimed that, since the lien which had arisen in favour of the vendors of Great Oak Court when contracts had been exchanged, had been extinguished when the purchase money was paid, it was entitled to be subrogated to that lien. It succeeded.

The decision has been heavily criticised for the justices' rather vague references to sufficiency of link and failure to make clear whether a direct link is necessary or if an indirect link will suffice[118] and the coordinated transactions test has been more generally criticised as being unclear.[119] However, Lord Neuberger argued that the link between the bank and Melissa was direct and did so by recharacterising what had happened as one composite transaction.[120] Lord Neuberger doubled down on this in *ITC v HMRC* where the idea of the composite transaction was confirmed, although, as seen above, one was not present on the facts of that case. However, the view Lord Neuberger took of the tripartite nature of the transaction in *Menelaou* flies in the face of the initial conclusion

[115] *Menelaou v Bank of Cyprus* [2015] UKSC 66, [2016] AC 176.
[116] S Watterson, 'Subrogation' in GJ Virgo and S Worthington (eds), *Commercial Remedies: Resolving Controversies* (Cambridge, CUP, 2017) 440–42.
[117] ibid 452–54.
[118] Stevens, 'The Unjust Enrichment Disaster' (n 91) 599.
[119] S Watterson, 'Subrogation as a Remedy for Unjust Enrichment' [2016] *CLJ* 219; contra R Shah, 'Indirect Enrichment in the Supreme Court' [2017] *CLJ* 490.
[120] [2015] UKSC 66, [2016] AC 176, [72].

that Melissa was not privy to the agreement.[121] The bank did know it was dealing with Melissa's parents in *Menelaou*, however, and, as Lord Reed said in *ITC*, it mistakenly authorised the use of the funds to purchase the second property instead of requiring its use to discharge the debt owed to itself.[122] Unlike in *ITC v HMRC* there was a causal and tracing link[123] between the bank's payment and Melissa's enrichment by discharge.[124] 'Lending' cases can be performance claims[125] but with C, having paid X, taking advantage of the now-extinguished liability of D to X rather than having a direct claim against the payee, X. As Lord Reed said, 'Although it is [X] who receives the payment from [C], [D] is directly enriched since the enrichment … is the discharge'.[126] This is said not to explain *Menelaou*, however,[127] because a fourth party paid or enriched X. The pattern is C pays A who pays X who discharges D's debt to X. X can drop out, but A cannot. The coordinated transactions test, however, prioritises the intention of the relevant participants and whether D's enrichment was the intended result of the sequence of transactions. Goff and Jones explain *Menelaou* in this way.[128] This distinguishes *ITC* where the customer just pays the bill to discharge their liability; there is no intention on his part that VAT be paid through to the state. Explaining *Menelaou* like this, however, is difficult given that Melissa received the second property, Great Oak Court, a month prior to charges being released on the first (Rush Hall Green), which renders it difficult to see a coordinated sequence in the way claimed. It is in any case probably impossible to explain every fourth-party case in this way.[129] It is important, therefore, to remember that the *ITC* test is not one of attribution for unjust enrichment, but only for performance claims. It may be better to recognise that *Menelaou* and the four-party cases are not performance claims, but relief is grounded on tracing and the fact the money was not at the free disposal of the parents.[130]

Probably the coordinated transactions test goes further than in civilian jurisdictions, and so performance claims are slightly more expansive than in such

[121] T Cutts, 'Modern Money Had and Received' (2018) 38 *OJLS* 1, 23.

[122] [2017] UKSC 29, [2018] 2 AC 275, [65]; see *Esben Finance Ltd v Neil Wong Hou-Liang* [2022] SGCA (I) 1, [151]–[153]; see also WJ Swadling 'In Defence of Formalism' in A Robertson and J Goudkamp (eds), *Form and Substance in the Law of Obligations* (Oxford, Hart Publishing, 2019) 116–17.

[123] [2015] UKSC 66, [2016] AC 176, [140].

[124] Sheehan, '"At the Expense of"' (n 93) 253.

[125] *ITC v HMRC* [2017] UKSC 29, [2018] 2 AC 275, [49] (Lord Reed); *Lowick Rose LLP v Swynsons Ltd* [2017] UKSC 32, [2018] AC 313, [30] (Lord Sumption).

[126] *ITC v HMRC* [2017] UKSC 29, [2018] 2 AC 275, [49]; contrast *Prudential BS v HMRC* [2018] UKSC 39, [2019] AC 929, [68] (Lord Mance).

[127] R Gregson, 'Is Subrogation a Remedy for Unjust Enrichment?' (2020) 136 *LQR* 481, 494; see also *Butler v Rice* [1910] 2 Ch 277.

[128] C Mitchell, P Mitchell and S Watterson (eds), *Goff & Jones: The Law of Unjust Enrichment*, 10th edn (London, Sweet & Maxwell, 2022) para 6.63.

[129] *Butler v Rice* [1910] 2 Ch 277 being an example.

[130] [2015] UKSC 66, [2016] AC 176, [137] (Lord Carnwath).

jurisdictions; however, this turns out to be a matter of taste rather than anything else.[131] An important implication of this concentration on intention is that where money or chattels are transferred intentionally there is a transfer of the asset's value, but no additional transfer of the use value. Rights to interest are not therefore based on unjust enrichment.[132] A second implication is that unintentional side-effects[133] cannot count. The lack of liability in the heat-rising or destroyed stamp cases is explicable. We do not need a tortured explanation in terms of grudging gifts or abandonment – just to say the requirements are not met for any cause of action. No protected interest is at stake. The fact that English law relies on positive reasons for restitution – the unjust factors of Birksian parlance – does not alter this. It does, however, mean, and we go into this in more depth in chapter four, that the unjust factor must be tied in some way to the intentional transfer in question. This is most likely to be an issue with mistake, but importantly means that it is not true that any old causal mistake will count. The claim failed therefore in *Lowick Rose LLP v Swynson Ltd*.[134] Swynson lent EMSL £15 million over a 12-month period in 2006 on the strength of negligent due diligence undertaken by Lowick Rose (or HMT as it was called). Another loan was made in 2007 but, deciding that there was no point in Swynson having two large non-performing debts, Hunt, who owned Swynson Ltd, made a personal loan to EMSL of £18.7 million used to pay Swynson. This negated any loss that Swynson had suffered from Lowick Rose's negligence; the claimants sought to be subrogated to the discharged right to sue in negligence. Lord Mance referred to the need for a single or composite transaction,[135] and noted that the deliberately structured transfers from Hunt to EMSL and EMSL to Swynson had unforeseen effects on the relation with Lowick Rose.[136] Lord Mance argued that a 'but for connection' was insufficient. Any enrichment of Lowick Rose by discharge of its liability was indirect and there was no appropriate unjust factor.[137] The performance Hunt had rendered was to Swynson, and so a mistake other than about that performance or transaction was irrelevant. We might say either that Lowick Rose's enrichment was an entirely unintentional side-effect or that Hunt's mistake in making the loan was insufficiently connected to the transaction itself.[138]

[131] B Haecker, 'Fog on the Channel: Six Comparative Lessons in Unjust(ified) Enrichment' [2017] *Restitution Law Review* 61, 70; Andrew Burrows also refers to the civil law in propounding his distinction between conferral (ie, essentially performance) and taking '"At the Expense of": A Fresh Look' [2017] *Restitution Law Review* 167.

[132] *Prudential BS v HMRC* [2018] UKSC 39, [2019] AC 929, [77]–[78]; *Test Claimants in the FII Litigation v HMRC* [2021] UKSC 31, [2021] 1 WLR 4354, [107].

[133] On which, see J Knobe, 'Intentional Action and Side Effects in Ordinary Language' (2003) 63 *Analysis* 190.

[134] [2017] UKSC 32, [2018] AC 313.

[135] ibid [58].

[136] ibid [68].

[137] ibid [89].

[138] ibid [34] (Lord Sumption), [83]–[89] (Lord Mance); [117]–[119] (Lord Neuberger); Cutts (n 121) 24; Burrows, *The Law of Restitution* (n 6) 181; Gregson, 'Is Subrogation a Remedy for Unjust

Another linkage is between 'at the expense of' and enrichment. One of the advantages of the performance idea in civil law jurisdictions is said to be that it also takes care of enrichment. We cannot go quite so far here because performance cannot take care of enrichment in non-performance cases. However, specifically focusing on 'at the expense of' allows us to be more precise in our conception of enrichment. It allows us to say it is the defective performance that constitutes the enrichment.[139] It also allows us to say in those cases where the defective transaction leads to the unjust acquisition of the right itself[140] that right was acquired as part of a defective performance. It also allows us to identify the relevant enrichment in non-performance claims more easily, and we return to this in chapter four.

Those deliberate transfers must be accepted, but this is a relatively weak requirement.[141] It is the acceptance of the transfer, not the basis on which it was made, that is usually important.[142] This indeed is also true of the receipt of rights, because we cannot be forced to take ownership of an item. It can always be disclaimed. Services are rather different in that the acceptance requirement is more stringent. Services cannot be rejected ex post so normally the rule is that for a defendant to be liable there must be a request of some sort.[143] If there is no request, the defendant can legitimately reply that he would not have agreed to pay for these services. Sometimes the defendant might claim he is enriched only to a lesser level than market value. This is a process of subjective devaluation accepted as legitimate by Lord Clarke in *Benedetti v Sawiris*.[144] The request is not necessary in every case. If the services are factually or legally necessary such that someone would have had to provide them anyway, they might be 'incontrovertibly enriching' and this justifies saying that the defendant is enriched.[145] This is a principle equally found in civil law and mixed systems,[146] and protects the defendant's freedom of choice.

The second aspect of identifying a performance claim is to identify the correct transaction. Who is performing to whom? The lack of performance to the defendant lies behind the barring of a claim in leapfrogging cases where the claimant tries to recover from a defendant benefited by his doing work on the latter's property under a contract with a third party.[147] In *Aiken v Short*, the defendant, who was entitled to the repayment of a £200 loan made by the testator and secured by an

Enrichment?' (n 127) 488 suggests this demonstrates subrogation does not follow the same rules on mistake as direct claims, but it in fact indicates a restriction on all mistake claims. See Burrows (n 6) 180–81.

[139] Lodder (n 113) 46.

[140] ibid 104.

[141] AS Burrows, 'In Defence of Unjust Enrichment' [2019] *CLJ* 521, 533–34.

[142] Smith (n 5) 112–13.

[143] *Falcke v Scottish Imperial Insurance* (1886) 34 Ch D 234.

[144] *Benedetti v Sawiris* [2013] UKSC 50 [2014] AC 938, [26].

[145] Which might be the best explanation of *Upton on Severn RDC v Powell* [1942] 1 All ER 220.

[146] South African law, for example, accepts a threefold distinction between necessary, useful and luxurious expenditure. See Visser, *Unjustified Enrichment* (n 46) 593–94.

[147] See, eg, *McDonald Dickens & Macklin & Costello* [2011] EWCA Civ 930; *Uren v First National Home Finance* [2005] EWHC 2529 (Ch); Sheehan, '"At the Expense of"' (n 93) 247–48.

equitable mortgage applied to the debtor for payment.[148] The debtor – Carter – referred her to a bank which had purchased the mortgaged property. The bank paid in order to discharge the mortgage. It later transpired that Carter had had no title to the property (and so neither did the bank) and that the defendant had had no valid security. It was held the bank could not recover, because the defendant had had a perfect right to the money – to discharge the debt owed. We can analyse this as the bank rendering valid performance to the defendant on behalf of the debtor. *Barclays Bank v WJ Simms, Son & Cooke (Southern) Ltd* illustrates the converse case where a stopped cheque was paid by the bank in error.[149] The bank had no authority to make the payment and so could recover from the payee. There was no valid performance to the payee. Where conversely there is a valid instruction, the bank cannot recover from the payee and must debit its customer instead, because there has been a valid performance vis-a-vis the customer – even if there has been no such vis-a-vis the payee. The effect of this is much the same as in the German distinction between the value relation, the relationship between customer and payee, and the cover relation between bank and customer. If the value relation is defective, the customer recovers from the payee; if the cover relation is defective, the bank recovers from the customer.[150] The rule holds in Germany even if both relations are defective; there the paying bank recovers from the 'customer' who recovers from the payee. The reason for this is that we choose our counterparties. The rule in England is probably different to avoid circuity of action. There are other differences. German law – and South African law – allow no claim by the bank against the payee in countermanded cheque cases, except that a payee who knows of the countermand cannot discharge the debt[151] and it is only in that case where the bank has a claim against the recipient. This may change in Germany following the reversal of the rule in the context of cancelled electronic transfers,[152] in a decision where the bank was held to have a non-performance claim (*Nichtleistungskondiktion*) irrespective of the recipient's knowledge.

B. Non-Performance Claims for Improvement and Encroachment

Matching civil law actions to English law has two effects. The first, as we see in greater detail in chapter six, is to exclude some 'unjust factors' from unjust

[148] *Aiken v Short* (1856) 1 H&N 210, 156 ER 1180.

[149] *Barclays Bank v WJ Simms, Son & Cooke (Southern) Ltd* [1980] QB 677; contrast *Lloyds Bank Plc v Independent Insurance Co Ltd* [1999] 2 WLR 986 where the bank rendered performance to the customer and discharged the debt and where no recovery was possible; PBH Birks, 'At the Expense of the Claimant: Direct and Indirect Enrichment in English Law' [2000] *Oxford University Comparative Law Forum* 1, fn 30.

[150] S Meier, 'Mistaken Payments in Three Party Situations: A German View of English Law' [1999] *CLJ* 567, 571.

[151] Visser, *Unjustified Enrichment* (n 46) 349; Haecker (n 131) 71.

[152] BGHZ 205, 334.

enrichment. The second, is that it forces us to recognise that the unjust factors are not causes of action. 'Mistake' is not a cause of action because not all mistake claims are performance claims. In chapter four, for example, we map mistake claims into several different causes of action depending on the test for mistake or whether it is a performance claim. South African courts see the *condictiones* as distinct causes of action.[153] However, taking the definition of cause of action in chapter one as a description of – at the right level of generality – the necessary and sufficient conditions of relief the South African *condictio indebiti* may not be a single cause of action, because it can be satisfied by mistake, duress or incapacity all of which have different rules[154] and different rules apply again when the *condictio* is raised as a result of a representative's action.[155]

Two claims are relevant here. The first is the improvement claim. Here there is no purposive, intended transfer. An example is *Greenwood v Bennett* where the claimant made repairs to a car – which turned out to be the defendant's – believing it to be his own.[156] The defendant's enrichment is still as a result of the claimant's action, but the transactional approach of *ITC v HMRC* cannot work. The transfer to the defendant was totally unintended as the typical error is that the claimant thought the asset improved was his – or one he was entitled to work on. 'At the expense of' is established by showing simply that the improvement would not have occurred but for the efforts and expenditure by the claimant. In chapter four, we examine how enrichment is calculated. It is not – or at least not always – the market value of the services as opposed to the increased sale value of the improved asset. This is not problematic. Just because a question is answered in one way in one set of cases does not entail its needing to be answered in the same way in a different context; different approaches to 'at the expense of' are, for instance, not ruled out by *ITC v HMRC*.[157] While for Stevens the defendant's acceptance is vital for the justification of a performance claim, questions of the defendant's acceptance do not really come up in this type of case. There is something of a Hobson's choice in saying, 'You can only have your property back if you pay for the work'. This is why both civil law and English law restrict recovery in general terms to improvements and expenditure that was necessary, or 'incontrovertibly enriching', or discretionarily in the civil law to useful expenditure.

The second is the encroachment claim where the defendant's enrichment is as a result of the defendant's action. Assuming unjust enrichment claims lie in the context of tort and concurrently with the tort claim, we can be certain that they are not performance claims. There is no intentional transfer by the claimant

[153] *Willis Faber Enthoven v Receiver of Revenue* 1992 (4) SA 202, 224.

[154] See also G Glover, 'The *Condictio Indebiti* and Unjust Factors' (2006) 69 *Tidskrif vir Hedendagse Romeinse Hollandse Reg* 419, 435; du Plessis, 'Labels and Meaning' (n 24) 129 notes that undue influence might be added to the list.

[155] du Plessis, 'Labels and Meaning' (n 24) 120.

[156] *Greenwood v Bennett* [1973] Ch 195 (CA).

[157] [2017] UKSC 29, [2018] 2 AC 275, [50] (Lord Reed); see also P Letelier, 'Attribution in Unjust Enrichment' in C Mitchell et al (eds), *New Directions in Private Law Theory* (London, UCL Press, 2023).

to the defendant. There is a taking by the defendant, or an appropriation of something rightfully to be attributed to the claimant. 'At the expense of' must therefore be established differently by showing that the defendant has had the (factual) benefit of an entitlement properly belonging or legally attributable to the claimant. This is essentially the approach in the German *Eingriffskondiktion* and South Africa.[158] Importantly this is different again from 'expense' in the imposed enrichment cases.

Mitchell and Rostill have analysed the availability of mesne profits as a gain-based remedy in this type of case.[159] They argue that such profits are sometimes founded on a tort claim, sometimes in contract and sometimes in unjust enrichment. In terms of a claim in unjust enrichment, they have suggested that the appropriate cause of action is failure of consideration.[160] They illustrate this by reference to the 'tolerated trespasser' who is enriched by the ability to occupy and make use of the land; 'at the expense of' is proven by each time period in which the defendant can use the property as an independent transfer of value – that value being the ability to use the land. The failure of basis comes about because the parties will have had a common understanding as to the need for payment.[161] To justify the use value of the land being at the expense of the landowner, Mitchell and Rostill rely on the reformulation of the *ITC v HMRC* directness principle by Foxton J in *School Facilities Management Ltd v Christ the King College*[162] where he stated that the *Prudential BS v HMRC*[163] rule that there was no separate transfer of the time value (or use value) of money did not apply to the use of value of land, at least where that is the only benefit claimed. Mitchell and Rostill concede that secondary benefits where the defendant uses profits to buy an asset that then generates income may not be covered by the 'direct transfer' rule;[164] although they do not say so, these gains should be recoverable in a wrongs claim. Yet, understood in terms of intentional transactions, the rule Mitchell and Rostill extract from *SFM* could only apply to a performance claim. There is no intentional transfer of the right to occupy to a trespasser. If there were, he would not be a trespasser. Second, it is hard to see why the logic of *Prudential* that a transfer of money is not accompanied by a separate transfer of the right or ability to use it does not apply to other forms of asset.[165] On the facts of *SFM*, however, seeing the enrichment as the ability to use the building – as opposed to the building itself which had, due

[158] Visser, *Unjustified Enrichment* (n 46) 653.
[159] C Mitchell and L Rostill, 'Making Sense of Mesne Profits: Causes of Action' [2021] *CLJ* 130.
[160] ibid 150.
[161] ibid 151–52.
[162] *School Facilities Management Ltd v Christ the King College* [2020] EWHC 1118 (Comm).
[163] [2018] UKSC 39.
[164] C Mitchell and L Rostill, 'Making Sense of Mesne Profits: Remedies' [2021] *CLJ* 552, 578–79.
[165] There may be an exception. Where a claimant seeks the value of an asset that value includes the ability to use already and so there would be double recovery to allow a use claim as well. Where the claimant seeks specific proprietary restitution, the value of any potential use is not included in the claim and so use claims are combinable with, for example, rescission claims. See Lodder (n 113) 129–30 and discussion in ch 7.

to the practical impossibility of its removal, acceded to the College's land – would mean the parties could not get a clean break.[166] The benefit in *SFM* is therefore best understood as the building itself.

Two other examples follow. In *Lewisham LBC v Masterson*, the parties had pursued ultimately fruitless and rather half-hearted negotiations over several years for a lease.[167] The rent did seem to be agreed, however, and that agreement was used as evidence of the value of the use of the land. However, this is a performance claim for the value of a performance (allowing occupation) rendered by the owner in anticipation of a contract that never arose. In *Ovidio Carrideo Nominees (Pty) Ltd v The Dog Depot (Pty) Ltd*,[168] the parties thought they had an agreement, but it was in fact void; the landlord's counter-claim to the tenant's claim for repayment of rent was in the nature of a performance rendered (allowing occupation) to discharge a void contract, and was not knocked out by the policy behind the statute.[169] The claims were set off and the tenant denied relief.

Mitchell and Rostill argue that the reasoning is outdated,[170] but *Morris v Tarrant* concluded in effect that if a wrongs claim was available, unjust enrichment claim should not lie alongside it.[171] There is in any case little benefit to such a concurrent encroachment claim in unjust enrichment, although some unjust enrichment claims should clearly lie concurrently. If I pay you £100 because of your lies, I can sue either for the tort of deceit or for a mistaken payment. Under the German *Eingriffskondiktion*, the attribution requirement is met by saying that the gain should be awarded to the claimant because on a purposive analysis the right legally attributes the gain to him. English law seems to take this view also,[172] and in the absence of a performance link would need to use this test in both tort and the encroachment action. In both cases the action is probably also vulnerable to change of position. Waiver of tort is an example of a scenario where switching causes of action might bring (or might have brought) a tangible benefit.[173] Typically an item is taken and sold, and the claimant seeks the sale price. The old *actio personalis* rule, abolished by the Law Reform (Miscellaneous Provisions) Act 1934, that a tort action died with its defendant did not apply to all the claims at issue in *Phillips v Homfray (No 2)*.[174] In that case, three defendants had operated a colliery on land next to the claimant's. They had extracted coal from underneath

[166] R Gregson, 'Building Unexpectedly Accedes to Land' [2021] *CLJ* 449.

[167] *Lewisham LBC v Masterson* (2000) 80 P&CR 117.

[168] *Ovidio Carrideo Nominees (Pty) Ltd v The Dog Depot (Pty) Ltd* [2006] VSCA 6; see Mitchell and Rostill, 'Making Sense of Mesne Profits: Remedies' (n 164) 574–78 for a discussion of these decisions.

[169] ibid [22] (Chernov JA); [38]–[41] (Nettle JA); this is sometimes referred to as a defence of good consideration, but is really a set-off; see Bant and Edelman (n 15) 365–66.

[170] Mitchell and Rostill, 'Making Sense of Mesne Profits: Causes of Action' (n 159) 147–48.

[171] *Morris v Tarrant* [1972] 2 QB 143.

[172] Stevens, *The Laws of Restitution* (n 92) 303; see Dannemann (n 67) 94; the German action in unjustified enrichment is needed because of the German law of tort's failure to provide gain-based remedies.

[173] On waiver of tort see, eg, *Lamine v Dorrell* (1705) 2 Ld Raym 1216, 92 ER 303; *Oughton v Seppings* (1830) 1 B&Ad 241, 109 ER 776; *Powell v Rees* (1837) 7 Ad&E 426, 112 ER 531.

[174] *Phillips v Homfray (No 2)* (1883) 24 Ch D 439 (CA); *Chesworth v Farrar* [1967] 1 QB 407.

the claimant's land and sold it, but two of the defendants died. The claim to the proceeds of sale survived so the action to recover the proceeds was, Stevens argues, not tortious,[175] but an action based on a superior right to property. Bowen and Cotton LJJ refer, however, to the claim for proceeds as based on a wrongful act,[176] although they also state it is in substance brought to recover property; with the abolition of the *actio personalis* rule it is difficult to see an advantage in not resting the action squarely on the wrong.

C. Intermediary Cases

Intermediary cases are rare in civilian systems, but much more common in English law and other common law systems. In common law systems claims by beneficiaries to recover from third-party recipients from misapplying trustees are proprietary in character and follow the same sort of pattern as the residual German *actio de in rem verso* in § 816 BGB. In South Africa, despite the *versio*-patterning of the action, the claim is a *condictio indebiti*.[177]

We return to this in detail in chapter seven, but proprietary claims contingent on tracing and rescission claims against third-party transferees provide similar cases in English law. It is therefore at best, with respect, misleading for the Supreme Court to describe tracing as 'equivalent' to the direct transfer. The trustee (T) for instance transfers the asset without authority to B; legal title is transferred to B and if B is a bona fide purchaser the beneficiary (C) has no claim against B, but naturally retains one against T.[178] A donee third party is proprietarily liable to C, as is a 'mala fide purchaser'. Some subrogation cases, the so-called 'misappropriation' cases, follow this pattern and we see details of this in chapter seven. Another English example of the *actio* is *Lipkin Gorman v Karpnale*,[179] where Cass transferred wealth from the firm to the defendant club. The firm then sued the club for the money in an action for money had and received. The club received the money via an intermediary and was liable to the firm. Another similar triangular claim, fitting the pattern of the *versio*-claim would be the proprietary claim in *Re Diplock*.[180] We have seen another possibility earlier in this chapter. These are a subcategory of the 'lending cases' in subrogation, where, as with the 'misappropriation'

[175] Stevens, *The Laws of Restitution* (n 92) 330–31.

[176] (1883) 24 Ch D 439 (CA) 454–55; WJ Swadling 'The Myth of Phillips v Homfray' in WJ Swadling and G Jones (eds), *The Search for Principle* (Oxford, OUP, 1999) 288–90.

[177] E Cameron et al (eds), *Honoré's South African Law of Trusts*, 6th edn (Durban, Juta, 2018) 454–55.

[178] See D Sheehan, 'Equitable Remedies for Breach of Trust' in R Halson and D Campbell (eds), *Research Handbook on Remedies* (Cheltenham, Edward Elgar, 2019).

[179] *Lipkin Gorman v Karpnale* [1991] 2 AC 548 (HL), which would not have supported a claim under §816(I) BGB. See Dannemann (n 67) 131–32.

[180] *Re Diplock* [1948] Ch 465 (CA); the strict liability personal claim fits a different pattern. See D Sheehan, 'Disentangling Equitable Personal Liability for Receipt and Assistance' [2008] *Restitution Law Review* 48.

cases, a tracing link may be needed. C lends to A who pays X who discharges D's debt to X. In such cases, C is subrogated to X's rights against D.

It is worth pointing out parenthetically that this category of intermediary claims is not the entirety of the category of proprietary claims. The presence of an intermediary is not needed for a proprietary claim. Rescission claims, as we see in chapter seven, are proprietary but they can also be performance claims where, as we discuss in chapter four, I rescind a voluntary instrument for mistake or rescind an executed contract for undue influence. Rescission claims therefore cut across the *condictio/versio* distinction drawn in civil law systems and we need to be mindful of this in our analysis. In rescissory performance cases I have transferred money or chattels[181] under a putative contract or deed of gift which I have then avoided. I have performed. As Lodder has pointed out, a proprietary claim is available when it is the right itself that is unjustly acquired by the defendant. What matters on Lodder's view is that the law recognises the defective intention of the claimant with regard to a specific right.[182]

III. Conclusion

This chapter has done a lot. We have attempted to show that English law follows a broadly similar pattern of claims to the civil law. This does not mean that English law recognises a pure absence of basis approach in its performance claims. It does not, as we see in chapter five, and so the pattern of performance claims looks similar to that in South African law. There too causes of action in unjustified enrichment are split into different performance claims, requiring proof of an unjust factor. The pattern of non-performance claims is slightly different and probably more limited in English as compared with South African law. There is probably (say) no enrichment claim for mala fide improvers in English law. In chapter three, we take this proposed structure and defend it using the methodology suggested in chapter one.

[181] Or services, but no proprietary claim can be available here. Indeed, some argue no (legal) proprietary claim is available in money claims either. See D O'Sullivan, S Elliott and R Zakrzewski (eds), *The Law of Rescission*, 3rd edn (Oxford, OUP, 2023) para 16.05.

[182] Lodder (n 113) 218–19.

3

Unity and Difference in Unjust Enrichment

Introduction

Chapter one set out a defence of the view that causes of action and other legal concepts are Weberian ideal types. As such they are interpretive concepts in a Dworkinian sense and both dynamic and historically situated. The chapter defended a view that the way in which we collect and categorise legal concepts is by means of an examination of their normative underpinnings and identification of significant family resemblances. This allows for law to draw on principles and ideas from across its breadth while maintaining what Dworkin referred to as local priority. Chapter two set out the structure of the law of unjust enrichment defended in this book in which the law knows both a series of performance claims and some non-performance claims. The claims grouped together in that chapter are different in many respects and do in fact draw on principles from across the law. This is important because it rapidly becomes clear that while unjust enrichment as a category and a Weberian ideal-type concept has an underlying theme or **function,** it overlaps with contract and property law. That is not a problem in the common law or in civilian or mixed systems. Some authors, however, argue on this basis that unjust enrichment has no independent existence. Hedley argues that much of the subject is best explained as implied contract. Jaffey sees it as a combination of (at the very least) contract, imputed contract and property law. We examine the views of these two theorists in the second part of the chapter.

The first section of this chapter provides a more positive case for the coherence of the area, bearing in mind the purpose for which we are classifying. Unjust enrichment, I claim, concerns cases of the reversal of defective enrichments (whether by performance or some other way). This chapter's first subsection examines the internal similarities of unjust enrichment. We see that a robust system of unjust factors, including mistake, can provide, at least part of, the normative glue of the area. In other words, unjust factors, understood as broad reasons for restitution demonstrating the presence of a relevant defect, exist across both performance and non-performance claims. We leave proprietary claims and any relevant similarities there might be justifying including these within unjust enrichment to chapter seven. As we saw in chapter one, Stevens has challenged the legitimacy of unjust enrichment as a category, arguing that there are multiple types of claims with little if anything in common. In one subset of claims he raises a further point as to the illegitimacy of relying on mistake,[1] because a claim relying on mistake does not exhibit the required bilaterality. We leave Stevens' doctrinal arguments to later chapters and discuss here the related Kantian/Hegelian critique of mistake claims and the requirement that the enrichment be accepted in some way to establish the necessary bilaterality. The second subsection provides a defence of multipolar reasoning in unjust enrichment law. It shows how drawing on different principles from different areas need not destroy the utility of unjust enrichment. We should remember here my description of unjust enrichment from chapter one as **functional**, **normatively pluralistic** and **historically and morally contingent**.

I. The Utility of Unjust Enrichment

A. Internal Similarities: The Importance of Unjust Factors

At the end of chapter one, we introduced the analogy with a rope which Barker, drawing on Wittgenstein, uses to show that not every element we point to in grouping cases together need be shared by all. While we can usefully group rules and rights together on analytic similarities (eg, *in rem* versus *in personam*), the way in which we classify depends critically on our purpose in doing so; why do we classify? Our purpose here is explaining the rationale for causes of action in unjust enrichment. To do this, the similarities by which we group causes of action should be moral and normative in character. Care is needed here. Unjust factors are not causes of action. We see in chapter four that there are several different 'mistake' actions. However, they can be seen as broad reasons for restitution and, as morally and normatively significant reasons, impacting on our autonomy, they are eligible characteristics to assist us in grouping causes of action together as part of unjust enrichment.

This section deals with a preliminary problem. In order to use unjust factors and 'mistake' as a normative glue we must justify why mistake provides any good reason for a claim. This is important because mistaken payments are often seen as the central claim (or cause of action) of unjust enrichment; if our theory cannot explain the core case we would seem to be in trouble.

i. The 'Problem' with 'Mistake'

In cases of mistake, I have a belief that X. Reality is not-X. In acting on my plans I accept the proposition X and by doing so my substantive plans do not turn out the way I expected. A condition of my intention is falsified, and my free choice

[1] R Stevens, 'The Unjust Enrichment Disaster' (2018) 134 *LQR* 574; R Stevens, *The Laws of Restitution* (Oxford, OUP, 2023) 80.

is not actualised properly in terms of my intentions and plans.[2] But why do you care? You are surely within your rights to say, 'Well, you shouldn't make mistakes; it's your fault. Go away'. No system does this.[3] Stevens, however, claims that reliance on mistake to justify the claim is simply immoral. It treats the defendant as a means to the claimant's ends. In essence, his normative position is that a mistake which leads to the defendant's factual enrichment cannot by itself plausibly justify the defendant's coming under any obligation at all. To impose an obligation on the basis of mistake does not respect bilaterality in the law; mistake is not a reason in the correct form, respecting both claimant and defendant.[4] It is to meet the requirement that the action be that of both claimant and defendant that the law requires a request or acceptance on the latter's part. The best example of this is services because, unlike payment, services can be rendered independently of the legal system and normally there is no liability without a request. Mistake is not therefore important as a vitiating factor, demonstrating that the claimant's intention was flawed in some way. Rather, English law provides relief because the defendant was not entitled to the money and mistake plays one of several different roles, such as a heuristic demonstrating that no gift was intended. We return to Stevens' doctrinal argument that mistake was never seen as vitiating intention in English law in chapter four, and to the question of whether English law recognises a pure absence of basis approach to performance claims in chapter five.

In this section we focus on the theory behind the proposition that some form of acceptance of the performance is required to establish the necessary bilaterality. Stevens' work is primarily doctrinal rather than theoretical, but a corrective justice theory, drawing on Kant, which explains the necessity for bilaterality is that of Ernest Weinrib. While Weinrib's theory is not the only way to explain the need for bilaterality in private law, it, and like theories, have been very influential in recent theoretical work in private law and Stevens' doctrinal work is consistent with Weinrib's theory. It is therefore worth examining in some detail. For Weinrib, private law's bilaterality is its key feature and a critical dividing line between private and public law. Weinrib holds that for any claim to be justified between private parties, both need to be implicated in some way consistent with corrective justice. In a private law action, the claimant's loss and defendant's gain are correlative because they are occasioned by the same injustice or breach of duty.[5] If that is so, the reason for the action accords with corrective justice. It applies equally to both parties,[6] and to no other party. It is bilateral.[7] Weinrib puts meat on these bones

[2] See D Sheehan, 'Mistakes, Failure of Consideration and the Planning Theory of Intention' (2015) 28 *Canadian Journal of Law & Jurisprudence* 155.

[3] See P Gallo, 'Unjust Enrichment: A Comparative Analysis' (1992) 40 *American Journal of Comparative Law* 431, 442–45.

[4] R Stevens, 'Private Law and the Forms of Reasons' in A Robertson and J Goudkamp (eds), *Form and Substance in the Law of Obligations* (Oxford, Hart Publishing, 2019) 119.

[5] E Weinrib, *The Idea of Private Law* (Cambridge, MA, Harvard University Press, 1995) 33.

[6] E Weinrib, 'The Gains and Losses of Corrective Justice' (1994) 44 *Duke Law Journal* 277, 289.

[7] LD Smith, 'Corrective Justice: The Heart of Restitution' (2001) 79 *Texas Law Review* 2115, 2134.

by reference to Kantian right. For Kant, action is permissible if consistent with the freedom of those it affects; the claimant suffers an actionable injury when the defendant acts inconsistently with his freedom.[8] In the context of unjust enrichment, Weinrib argues that the normative significance of the transfer consists in the legal nexus it establishes between the transferee and the transferor.[9] If the transfer is defective, the subject matter of the transfer – value – has not rightfully moved and corrective justice requires the transferee to return it.[10] The transfer links the parties correlatively and the obligation-creating conditions that render this unjust are themselves correlatively related through the lack of the claimant's donative intent and the transferee's acceptance of the transfer as being non-gratuitous and non-donative. It is a requirement of liability that the parties' purposes in relation to each other should converge in that neither treats the transfer as a gift.[11] It is this acceptance of the transfer that renders it a bilateral transaction,[12] and the bilaterality that allows the claim to be morally justifiable. Without this aspect of the claim, the claimant is using the defendant as a means to his own ends; he is not respecting the defendant as an autonomous entity entitled to freedom from interference by others. As Weinrib expresses it, the claimant's 'lack of donative intent' is insufficient and untrue to 'liability's relational character'.[13]

Weinrib's idea of acceptance, however, crumbles on contact with the law. The defendant's acceptance of the transfer as non-donative is key, but the defendant is not, he argues, 'entitled to assume'[14] that the claimant made a gift. The view that it was non-donative can be imputed to a defendant who did not advert to the question. Indeed, the implication is stronger. Even if the defendant positively believes it is a gift, this can presumably be ignored and acceptance of the transfer as non-donative imputed. While it is undoubtedly necessary for a payment to be accepted to be a payment – leaving an envelope of money on my doorstep is not the same thing as paying me; at best it is tender – this imputation that I not only accept the payment but accept that it was not a gift is in the end fictional, as is Stevens' suggestion that such acceptance is implicit in the payment of money.[15]

Other strategies to argue that mistaken payments are recoverable consistently with the reciprocal demands of respect for independence include that of Brudner and Nadler. They develop a distinctive view of private law based on Hegelian methodology, which they call dialogic community.[16] They argue that the immanent

[8] Weinrib, 'The Gains and Losses of Corrective Justice' (n 6) 290–91.

[9] E Weinrib, 'The Normative Structure of Unjust Enrichment' in C Rickett and R Grantham (eds), *Structure and Justification in Private Law: Essays for Peter Birks* (Oxford, Hart Publishing, 2008) 29.

[10] ibid 43–44.

[11] E Weinrib, 'Correctively Unjust Enrichment' in R Chambers, C Mitchell and J Penner (eds), *Philosophical Foundations of the Law of Unjust Enrichment* (Oxford, OUP, 2009) 42.

[12] ibid 40.

[13] E Weinrib 'The Corrective Justice of Liability for Unjust Enrichment' in E Bant et al (eds), *Research Handbook on Unjust Enrichment and Restitution* (Cheltenham, Edward Elgar, 2020) 176.

[14] ibid 178.

[15] Stevens, *The Laws of Restitution* (n 1) 81.

[16] A Brudner and J Nadler, *The Unity of the Common Law*, 2nd edn (Oxford, OUP, 2017) 59–62.

unity of the common law requires a synthesis of both goal-based accounts and rights-based accounts of the law.[17] These are not exclusive. The atomistic standpoint of private law, seeing each person as having individual agency and the worth of that individual agency as being fundamental, must be combined with the communitarian. The atomism of private law is required by community because a community cannot exist without the atomistic individual. Community is required by the atomistic individual as a means to protect his liberty and acquisitions. The individual self is also incapable of sustaining projects; it needs others to give itself meaning.[18] This can be in several different ways, so the forming of habitual dispositions of character based on inner impulses and the recognition of our social role can each be constitutive of ourselves. Social freedom realised in institutional reality or ethical life (*Sittlichkeit*) is an actualisation of free will. A legal paradigm based on individual agency is required by community. Community is necessary for assessing the individual's independent worth and reciprocally recognising that independent worth becomes a matter of the common good.[19] Both individual agency and community are required, and the legal paradigm generated maintains the distinction between community and individual that is essential for a liberal vision, and the dominant modern view is that Hegel was essentially a liberal.[20]

Nadler argues that mistaken payments cannot be explained as protecting parties' ability to choose.[21] Freedom of choice is not affected by a mistaken choice to pay; a mistaken choice simply does not affect our capacity to make choices.[22] In fact, our ability to make mistakes is predicated on our having a capacity to make the mistaken (or correct) choice in the first place. The first step to explain liability is to accept that the success of self-authored plans, goals and projects is a common good. After all we are all members of a social union which supports itself, its collective ends and equally the ability of individuals to express themselves fully.[23] However, if that is right, we are entitled to a system of law that is supportive of our ability to lead a life we can see and shape as our own,[24] because not implementing such a common good would itself entail our being reduced to another's interest. The recognition of our ability to shape our own lives necessarily means

[17] ibid 47–48.

[18] L Disley, 'Hegel, Autonomy and Community' in T Brooks and S Stein (eds), *Hegel's Political Philosophy: On the Normative Significance of Method and System* (Oxford, OUP, 2017) 240; A Laitinen, E Mayr and C Sandis, 'Kant and Hegel on Purposive Action' (2018) 21 *Philosophical Explorations* 90, 100.

[19] Brudner and Nadler (n 16) 58–61; for T Brooks, 'Between Natural Law and Legal Positivism: Dworkin and Hegel on Legal Theory' (2007) 23 *Georgia State University Law Review* 513, 553 there is an analogy here with Dworkin.

[20] D Cornell, 'Towards a Modern/Postmodernist Conception of Ethics' (1985) 133 *University of Pennsylvania Law Review* 291, 363; P Rosenberg, 'Hegel's Political Philosophy' (2021) 33 *Critical Review* 392, 393.

[21] Brudner and Nadler (n 16) 250.

[22] ibid 242–43.

[23] A Patten, 'Hegel's Alternative to Nationalism' (2021) 33 *Critical Review* 359, 369–72.

[24] Brudner and Nadler (n 16) 255.

that the link between outcome and intention and whether our plans succeed or fail comes into play – mistakes as defined in the common law. This takes us right back to the objection that there is no duty on anyone to shape their activity by reference to someone else's goals. If there were, that person's own rights would be violated.[25] Nadler accepts that it is wrong for one party to use another as a means to her own ends. The way she avoids the conclusion that mistaken payments must be left where they are is an appeal to the court as a public institution. If property law – by saying title has passed – is undermining self-determination in the thicker sense of being able to action our self-determined plans, the court as a public institution has a duty to set it aside.[26] The complaint is not that the defendant has done something, but about the law's effect. The claim is a petition, in Nadler's expression, as to what the court ought to do as a public institution of justice. Not to suspend property law, when enforcing it subverts the claimant's autonomy and suspension, does not affect the defendant's freedom of choice, would violate the common good of freedom as the actualised potential to live according to our own ends, and it is the state (and the court as an emanation of the state) that has the obligation to act.[27]

This is a rather tortured explanation. As far as the defendant is concerned, the niceties of whether the claimant has a right exercisable against him requiring the money to be repaid or against the court, requiring the court to suspend property law so that it can order the defendant to repay, seem irrelevant. The defendant is still being required to pay and the reason still appears to be that repayment supports the claimant's autonomy, and importantly that it supports the claimant's autonomy in the thick sense I defend below.

Nadler denies that we can do the same thing with other forms of enrichment; there can be no suspension of contract law or anything like it to provide relief for mistakenly provided services. Nadler denies therefore that unintended improvements to property or mistakenly provided services can be dealt with in the same way,[28] except in unusual cases where the asset is sold or for sale, such as in *Greenwood v Bennett*.[29] In those cases we can treat the realised value of the improved asset as the equivalent of a mistaken payment. This is inconsistent with the view that incontrovertible enrichments, such as necessary services that would have had to be provided in any event, are recoverable. In *Craven-Ellis v Canons Ltd*, for example, Greer LJ commented that the services provided by the directors to the company were such that 'if they had not been performed by the plaintiff, they would have had to get some other agent to carry out'.[30] While it is difficult to find cases where the necessity of the services, as opposed to their acceptance, was the sole reason for recovery, it must be right and is also true in civil law that the

[25] J Nadler, 'What Right does Unjust Enrichment Protect?' (2008) 28 *OJLS* 245, 251.
[26] Brudner and Nadler (n 16) 256–57.
[27] ibid 262–64.
[28] ibid 260–61.
[29] *Greenwood v Bennett* [1973] Ch 195 (CA).
[30] *Craven-Ellis v Canons Ltd* [1936] 2 KB 403, 412.

necessity of the services means the defendant need not request them. Weinrib does allow for incontrovertible benefit. Necessary expenditure, he suggests, is expenditure that the defendant has no reason not to accept,[31] and so can be taken to have accepted. Yet if we are true to the bilateral structure of corrective justice, as he describes it, it surely matters that the defendant would not have accepted it from the claimant as opposed to a third party. This, however, is precisely what happened in *Upton on Severn RDC v Powell*.[32] The Court of Appeal decided the case on the basis that there was a valid contract, but this seems wrong. The problem in short was that everyone involved thought the services free. There was no offer to pay which the fire brigade believed it was accepting.[33] It is better explained as unjust enrichment. The defendant phoned Upton police station and asked them to send the fire brigade. They sent the Upton brigade, but the defendant was in the Pershore fire district (and the Upton police district). Pershore would have been obliged to put out the fire for free, but Upton claimed payment, as it was entitled to do for out-of-area services. The mistake that everyone made at first was that the farm was in Upton (and the services free), which negatived any offer to pay by the defendant or any free acceptance of (paid-for) services by him and indeed any acceptance of an offer to pay by the fire brigade. None of this matters, however. The fire brigade's actions were factually necessary, and the defendant was not entitled to deny that.

ii. *Justifying Mistake*

What then is happening in mistake claims? I have in the past set out a structure for understanding a mistake claim, drawing on the work of Michael Bratman, based on the workings of our intentions and whether the intention we acted upon covered the facts to hand. There are three aspects to intention. I act intentionally (intentionality); I act with the intention of finishing this book (intention 'with which'); I intend to act tomorrow (future intention).[34] On this view, when we act, we do so with a given intention. I pay with the intention of discharging a debt. That is necessarily a conditional intention. Those conditions may be background conditions (ie, not ones I consciously advert to) or foreground conditions (which I do advert to). Either way, the intention is valuable to me because it enables me to put together coordinating plans that determine my actions over time and fulfil my end goals. We are all planning creatures and plans enable me to coordinate with myself in the future. My plan to write this book is constant over time. I begin by reading cases and articles and end by putting the footnotes into house style and

[31] Weinrib, 'The Corrective Justice of Liability for Unjust Enrichment' (n 13) 180.

[32] *Upton on Severn RDC v Powell* [1942] 1 All ER 220.

[33] *TTMI Sarl v Statoil ASA (The Sibohelle)* [2011] EWHC 1150, [2011] 2 Lloyds Rep 220, [44] (Beatson J); E Peel (ed), *Treitel on the Law of Contract*, 15th edn (London, Sweet & Maxwell, 2020) para 2.049; see also PBH Birks, *An Introduction to the Law of Restitution*, rev edn (Oxford, Clarendon Press, 1989) 120.

[34] Sheehan, 'Mistakes, Failure of Consideration and the Planning Theory of Intention' (n 2) 157–58.

adding the contents page.[35] I pay you therefore on the condition that I owe the money.[36] This is also important because the condition (in this case at least) is based on a higher order policy. These policies have agential authority in that they determine the types of desires that I consider should be incorporated into my practical reasoning. These higher order policies should be stable over time, or they will fail to be useful in guiding our intentions in a stable and predictable manner. We end up changing our minds all over the place.

Back to my intention to pay you to discharge a debt. In fact, I do not owe you the money, so, having paid, I discover the condition on which I did pay is false. If the law did not permit recovery, it disrespects me as a self-legislating autonomous agent.[37] I am not acting in accordance with my rationally determined norm to pay what I owe (and not what I do not). It is this norm that guides my decision-making and counts as the higher order policy mentioned earlier. It is also the norm which the law would force me to violate if it did not allow me to recover. The mistake is unilateral, but unwinding it is based on a respect for me as an autonomous agent able to carry my substantive plans through to fruition. That requires a thicker and more substantive sense of our autonomy than Weinrib's. One way of expressing this consistently with how I have expressed the concerns of mistaken payments law is that the law should treat people as substantively free – able to make meaningful choices and therefore to be able to expect to carry their plans through to fruition – rather than simply being free from others' choices. It also appears likely that there is a chilling effect to refusing relief for mistake, which makes it less likely that we will pay or transfer chattels, just in case there is a mistake, and we cannot recover the payment.[38]

This is not to deny the need to take the defendant's position into account. Acceptance does provide a bilateral link; without your acceptance, or perhaps the bank's acceptance on your behalf, no payment occurs. When I drop the envelope of money through your letter box, and you later (knowing the story) pick it up and put the cash in your wallet, you accept the payment; until then it is at best tender. However, you cannot possibly accept the basis on which it is made because you do not know what that is. The facts as you know them are equally consistent with my intending a gift and intending to pay a non-existent debt. Nonetheless, you have the possibility to reject the money.[39] Services, on the other hand, can be rendered without my accepting them, but as Pollock CB famously said, 'One cleans another's shoes … what else can he do but put them on?'[40] Acceptance or request

[35] ibid 160–62.

[36] ibid 163–64.

[37] ibid 165.

[38] H Dagan, 'Autonomy, Relational Justice and the Law of Restitution' in E Bant et al (eds), *Research Handbook on Unjust Enrichment and Restitution* (Cheltenham, Edward Elgar, 2020) 221; H Dagan, 'Mistakes' (2001) 79 *Texas Law Review* 1795, 1798–1802.

[39] LD Smith, 'Restitution: A New Start?' in P Devonshire and R Havelock (eds), *The Impact of Equity and Restitution on Commerce* (Oxford, Hart Publishing, 2018).

[40] *Taylor v Laird* (1865) 25 LJ Ex 329, 332.

is therefore needed here as well, subject to one narrow exception. That narrow exception relates to the necessity of the services and is one also found in civilian and mixed systems.[41] Essentially the justification is precisely as Weinrib puts it, although as noted to accept this we must drop the strictness of the requirement for bilaterality. There is always an opportunity to reject rights (in chattels, money, etc). This is not so for services which cannot be ex post rejected, and this means that there is a good reason to treat the latter differently.

There is a second important reason for accepting mistake in the context of this book. Dworkin requires a judge to divide departments of law to match popular opinion.[42] In chapter one, we saw that there is a tension between this and Hercules' general methodology of examining the whole of private law. However, this method of matching local priority to generally accepted categories is nonetheless important for establishing the law's legitimacy. Dworkin's actual example contrasts careless and intentional harm which are much smaller categories than 'tort' or 'unjust enrichment'. 'Mistake' is arguably such a smaller category of local priority, and our conventional morality does ascribe importance to mistake. All things considered, our law should, and does, track this. The intuition is morally defensible on the basis of a substantive principle of autonomy, the need for private law to aim to enhance our autonomy and mutual respect for each other's self-determination. We can appeal to this justification in ranking cases according to our moral intuitions of where liability should begin and end. Property mistakes rank quite highly in our intuitions that something should be done. Services mistakes rank lower, although at least some services mistakes seem – contrary to Penner's view, who also engages in this moral ranking – to count in English law.[43] Unjust enrichment is, as seen in chapter one, historically and morally contingent. To tear it up and shift to a different system pulls against the republican goals of local priority and risks confusion in our understanding of the law.

iii. The Utility of 'Mistake'

The utility of classing cases like *Greenwood v Bennett*[44] and *Barclays Bank v WJ Simms, Son & Cooke (Southern) Ltd*[45] together is obscured by civilian systems' treatment of mistake. In the former case, Bennett handed over a car to Searle to be repaired. Searle turned out to be a rogue and having caused considerable damage to the car sold it to Harper who repaired it and sold it on. The police sought in an interpleader to determine who had the better right to the car. Lord Denning

[41] On necessary and useful enrichments, see D Visser, *Unjustified Enrichment* (Durban, Juta, 2008) 543–45.

[42] R Dworkin, *Law's Empire* (Cambridge, MA, Harvard University Press, 1986) 252.

[43] J Penner, 'We All Make Mistakes: A Duty of Virtue Theory of Restitutionary Liability' (2018) 82 *MLR* 222, 225–28.

[44] [1973] Ch 195 (CA).

[45] *Barclays Bank v WJ Simms, Son & Cooke (Southern) Ltd* [1980] QB 677.

stated the principle rather broadly that whether the claimants (Bennett) recovered the car with or without the aid of the courts the innocent purchaser should recover the value of the improvements.[46] The latter case involved the recovery of a mistaken payment. While *Greenwood* does not involve a claim; the purchaser was not suing for the value of improvements but obtaining payment as a condition of being made to give up the car, the logic applies to support a free-standing claim. South Africa has historically treated mistake as central to the *condictio indebiti*, although some recent cases, as seen in chapter two, have awarded the *condictio* with no reference to mistake at all. Despite mistake being occasionally cited in the improvement cases,[47] the logic of the action under the extended action in *negotiorum gestio* is not – and has never been thought to be – dependent on mistake.[48]

While we see the detailed doctrinal details in chapter four, the essential reason for relief **is** dependent on mistake in each case in English law. In the absence of the Roman back story, it provides English law an intuitive positive reason for restitution which is easier to accept and to introduce in a case-based common law system.[49] There are important distinctions to be drawn between the performance and improvement cases, such that they cannot be seen as the same cause of action. However, if we see an unjust factor as a broad reason for restitution, explaining why the defendant's enrichment is recoverable as defective, the same broad reason applies across these cases. It is that the claimant's acts are at variance with his intention and the intended outcome. The intention 'with which' he acted was flawed. In practical terms, therefore, the essential reason for the claim is the same, and the thick substantive view of autonomy outlined above can account for mistaken payments, mistaken provision of services and mistaken improvement of another's property cases.

This allows us to see robust family resemblances between the cases. This is a real benefit of a system of unjust factors. The rules on attribution and 'at the expense of' differ between these cases, as we see in more detail in chapter four. Enrichment is not quantified in the same way either. In the performance claims the claimant recovers the value of his performance; the value of that performance is the enrichment received by the defendant. It does not matter if the result has no objective value – Stevens has the example of painting coal white – because if requested the defendant has stated that the performance itself is of value and if the services are necessary, he is disentitled from the objection that he does not accept them. In the improvement cases there may be relevance to the increased potential sale value of the asset. These differences, which reflect the importance of different

[46] [1973] QB 195 (CA) 202.

[47] See *McCarthy Retail v Shortdistance Carriers Ltd* 2001 (3) SA 482; in Scotland see *Newton v Newton* 1925 SC(HL) 925; D Sheehan, 'Unjust Factors or Restitution of Transfers Sine Causa' [2008] *Oxford University Comparative Law Forum* 1.

[48] J du Plessis, 'Towards a Rational Structure of Liability for Unjustified Enrichment' (2005) 122 *South African Law Journal* 142, 163.

[49] H Scott and D Visser, 'The Impact of Legal Culture on the Law of Unjustified Enrichment: The Role of Reasons' in E Bant and M Harding (eds), *Exploring Private Law* (Cambridge, CUP, 2010).

principles and their impact on the question of relief, need to be matched up with the important similarity that the broad reason for recovery is the same. Without an acceptance of unjust factors this is obscured. This is simply an example of the law classifying cases together based on their relevant functional normative similarity. However, the fact that different principles are in play as well simply illustrates the normative pluralism of the area.

B. Multipolar Legal Reasoning in Unjust Enrichment

Unjust enrichment is normatively pluralistic, but the idea still has a normative developmental weight. The idea is intrinsic to the law in that – consistently with Dworkin's idea of theoretical ascent – it can be abstracted upwards from the case to provide normative resources that can be used elsewhere in the law.[50] One specific example of this is the recent acceptance by the High Court of Australia that services can be dealt with under the rubric of failure of basis just like money payments.[51] Other cases also refer to the developmental role that unjust enrichment plays.[52] In the context of our discussion from chapter one, courts deploy the concept of unjust enrichment in the same way as any other ideal type. The theme of unjust enrichment – its **function** – is the reversal of defective enrichments (whether that be by way of performance or some other way). We take the case law and sort through it identifying how and where and why the ideal type's themes manifest themselves and how and why the case law diverges from them,[53] identifying the family resemblances and dissimilarities as we do so. This, as we saw, allows us both to identify whether we have a case of unjust enrichment and to develop the law of unjust enrichment through a constant dynamic interpretive process. It has a distinct advantage over what we might call the prescriptive approach in that it is rooted in our past legal and political practice. It avoids egregious examples of overreach such as Birks' description of the whole law on knowing receipt as in effect wrong because it did not instantiate the strict liability, he believed unjust enrichment required of it,[54] when in fact the area is better explained and more consistently with its history in terms of wrongdoing.[55] This type of prescriptive

[50] K Barker, 'Theorising Unjust Enrichment: Being Realist(ic)' (2006) 26 *OJLS* 609, 616.

[51] *Mann v Paterson Construction (Pty) Ltd* [2019] HCA 32, (2019) 267 CLR 560, [78], [168]–[169].

[52] See, eg, *Lipkin Gorman v Karpnale Ltd* [1991] 2 AC 548 (HL); *Bofinger v Kingsway Group Ltd* [2009] HCA 44, (2009) 239 CLR 269; *Pavey & Matthews Pty Ltd v Paul* (1987) 162 CLR 221.

[53] A Kedar, 'Ideal Types as Hermeneutic Concepts' (2007) 1 *Journal of the Philosophy of History* 318, 341–42; S Brewer, 'Exemplary Reasoning: Semantics, Pragmatics and the Rational Force of Legal Argument by Analogy' (1996) 109 *Harvard Law Review* 923, 962–63; in the unjust enrichment context, see E Sherwin, 'Restitution and Equity: An Analysis of the Principle of Unjust Enrichment' (2001) 79 *Texas Law Review* 2083, 2104–08.

[54] See PBH Birks, *Unjust Enrichment*, 2nd edn (Oxford, OUP, 2005) 156; TT Arvind and D Sheehan 'Reframing Private Law Taxonomy' (2015) 35 *LS* 480, 487.

[55] D Sheehan, 'Disentangling Equitable Personal Liability for Receipt and Assistance' [2008] *Restitution Law Review* 48.

approach has been the ultimate cause of many of the deficiencies in unjust enrichment theory. On the view taken here, however, the ideal type of unjust enrichment can draw on, as part of its intension, principles from other areas of law and this is no problem in and of itself. This is because unjust enrichment, like any similar area of law, such as tort for example, is **normatively pluralistic**. Overlaps are inevitable even as we might strive to minimise them. Too much overlap can destroy the possibility of sensitive normative recommendations,[56] but some overlap need not destroy the family resemblances holding categories together. The overlaps can even be said to enrich and inform our understanding of the different categories.

Two areas that unjust enrichment draws on extensively, as we have already noticed, are property and contract. Some claims could be part of public law as well as unjust enrichment. We explore the linkages between public law and unjust enrichment further in chapter six. Here we concentrate on property and contract. Even they are multipolar. Take private property law first. While property can be defined in terms of the form rights take as opposed to being a source of rights, the question can still be asked: why do we have (these) property rights at all? The definition of a category depends, as we have seen, on the question we want answering. Dworkin refers to three types of argument: rights-based, duty-based and goals-based arguments.[57] Goal-based arguments might include instrumental goals about how society should be organised; rights-based argument might identify certain moral or ethical rights and duties. The institution of property is justified not merely by moral rights between individuals: the right to exclusive use of a thing vis-a-vis others for example, but also by what we think a distributively or economically just distribution of resources looks like, and what just methods of acquiring those resources might be.[58] This requires us to delineate the limits, design and social function of the institution. That we cannot explain property (or the reason why we have property rights at all) through one justificatory principle lends support to the view we cannot explain unjust enrichment this way either. Equally, Saprai has demonstrated that the unipolar promise principle cannot explain contract law and introduces other bottom-up principles to demonstrate contract's normative plurality.[59]

How then do property and contract impact unjust enrichment? Penner has argued that at property's heart lies a liberty to decide what to do with our assets, or to decide the use of those assets. He argues that such a liberty contributes to the 'good life' or to our wellbeing.[60] He argues therefore that giving assets away can contribute to my wellbeing in that, for example, I take my wife's interests as

[56] H Dagan, 'Legal Realism and the Taxonomy of Private Law' in C Rickett and R Grantham (eds), *Structure and Justification in Private Law: Essays for Peter Birks* (Oxford, Hart Publishing, 2008) 164–65.

[57] R Dworkin, *Taking Rights Seriously* (London, Duckworth, 1977) 171.

[58] D Lametti, 'Property and (Perhaps) Justice' (1998) 43 *McGill Law Journal* 663, 670–83.

[59] P Saprai, *Contract Law Without Foundations: Towards a Republican Theory of Contract* (Oxford, OUP, 2019) chs 3, 7.

[60] J Penner, *The Idea of Property* (Oxford, Clarendon Press, 1997) 206–07.

my own and so giving her a necklace which she likes serves my interests as well; making her happy makes me happy. The liberty to give is included in the idea of a property right. We can also see property and contract in terms of their interaction with each other. Sale, as an exchange, is different from gift in that I deny that the asset is of value to me when I exchange it.[61] As Penner puts it, the asset once I have exchanged it for another asset or a service is no longer in any position to serve my interests and my relationship with it is the same as any asset I have never owned.[62] I give it up precisely because my interests are served by having something else instead. The right of sale is therefore dependent on our right to contract. The reason is that sale is on any view at the intersection between contract and property. A justification for contract must explain contracts to clean people's shoes, but sale is simply a different type of exchange from the 'money for shoe-cleaning' exchange that is the contract to clean shoes. The right to contract is a right to exchange. If the right to make a gift is explicable differently from that to make an exchange, rights to reverse a gift, sale or any putative exchange are explicable differently in that the latter cases engage principles of contract.[63] Yet we may still be trying to fully respect the claimant as a person actualising their own ends. It is simply not possible to justify the underlying putative transaction except in terms of property, contract, or both, which makes it difficult to deny those principles' relevance if the transaction is defective.

This implies that some claims consequent on transactional defects can be both contract and unjust enrichment. In South African law rescission claims – claims for the equitable remedy of *restitutio in integrum* – for (say) fraud are said to be contractual, but some cases refer to the underlying principle as one against unjust enrichment,[64] and the *restitutio* remedy has had a clear impact on the development of the *condictio indebiti*.[65] In English law, Saprai discusses duress and undue influence under the heading of passive exploitation in his book on contract theory, but the fact that rescission responds to the same unjust factors points to clear normative similarities with unjust enrichment law. Chen-Wishart, however, identifies a plurality of other values that affect the result, including substantive unfairness, public policy and the enforcer's conduct and argues, consistently with the thrust of this book, that only by creating the conceptual space to integrate these other values into our account can we fully understand the law.[66]

[61] J Penner, 'Ownership, Co-Ownership, and the Justification of Property Rights' in T Endicott et al (eds), *Properties of Law: Essays in Honour of Jim Harris* (Oxford, OUP, 2006) 182–83.

[62] ibid 183.

[63] D Sheehan, 'The Property Principle and the Structure of Unjust Enrichment' [2011] *Restitution Law Review* 138, 152.

[64] *Johnson v Jainodien* 1982 (4) SA 599; *Hall-Thermotank Natal (Pty) Ltd v Hardman* 1968 (4) SA 818, 832; *Feinstein v Niggli* 1981 (2) SA 684.

[65] H Scott, *Unjust Enrichment in South African Law* (Oxford, Hart Publishing, 2013) 39–54.

[66] M Chen-Wishart, 'The Nature of Vitiating Factors in Contract Law' in G Klass, G Letsas and P Saprai (eds), *Philosophical Foundations of Contract Law* (Oxford, OUP, 2014).

Examples can be multiplied, but we will give only two more. One of the most obvious practical consequences of accepting contract principles into unjust enrichment in the common law is in the case of restitution within the confines of a valid contract, for example, on termination for breach, examined in detail in chapter five. In this context, the question arises as to whether the contract price can be seen as a ceiling to a *quantum meruit* or *valebat* claim. High Court of Australia authority is now that it is a ceiling. Gageler J endorsed a hard ceiling while the plurality (Nettle, Gordon and Edelman JJ) endorsed a softer ceiling, suggesting sometimes it would be unconscionable to confine the claimant to the contract price, but without really explaining when.[67] This is a natural extension of the realisation that the unjust enrichment claim is derived from a particular combination of property and contract principles. The right to contract is dependent on the right to exchange and what is vital is that that exchange be a free exercise of autonomy. In the same way that it would disrespect the claimant's autonomy in exchange to fail to allow restitution where the exchange relevantly fails, so it disrespects the defendant's autonomy in exchange to fail to respect an agreed price and require a higher payment.[68] We cannot conclude from this that these are only contract claims and nothing else. That fails to recognise the similarities that exist with other performance claims. It fails to properly abstract upwards the rationales behind each of these specific cases and recognise the normative similarities. It fails to appreciate significant family resemblances.

Stepping outside performance claims, the relevance of property is equally apparent in non-performance claims. A comparative examination shows that cases of mistaken improvements of another's property cases (believing the asset to be one's own) engage property principles. German law has distinctive principles regarding the position of bona fide possessors and occupiers which are located in property law. We could (if we wanted to) locate *Greenwood v Bennett* in property law, but this would obscure the similarities (the relevance of mistake) with some performance claims as well as presumptively (and wrongly) barring change of position. It is also worth pointing out that treating these cases in property law has given rise to significant problems in both mixed jurisdictions.[69]

All of this illustrates two points. First, we may not even have to choose between property and unjust enrichment principles. A principle could be a principle of different areas,[70] depending on the question being asked and the purpose for

[67] *Mann v Paterson Construction (Pty) Ltd* [2019] HCA 32, (2019) 267 CLR 560, [101]–[102] (Gageler J), [205] (Nettle J et al); see, more generally, S Waddams, 'Contract and Unjust Enrichment: Competing Categories or Complementary Concepts?' in C Rickett and R Grantham (eds), *Structure and Justification in Private Law: Essays for Peter Birks* (Oxford, Hart Publishing, 2008).

[68] As notoriously happened in *Boomer v Muir* 24 P 2d 570 (1933).

[69] R Evans-Jones, 'Seeking Imposed Enrichment in Improvements: Classification and General Enrichment Actions in Mixed Legal Systems – Scotland and South Africa' [2008] *Restitution Law Review* 18, 35–38.

[70] Sheehan, 'The Property Principle and the Structure of Unjust Enrichment' (n 63) 155; a point also made in the South African context of unjustified enrichment by J du Plessis, 'Long Live Unjustified Enrichment: A Reply to Nils Jansen' [2019] *Acta Juridica* 371, 383–84.

which we are classifying. I have previously suggested that unjust enrichment, as a doctrinal – and inevitably a normative developmental – category, draws on substantive property rights and principles and contract rights principles bound together as an instantiation of a form of justice – corrective justice in a broad (and non-Kantian) sense.[71] That still seems largely right. Secondly, the cleavage found between performance and non-performance claims, although a deep one, does not dictate that the latter be left out of our subject.

C. A Formal Postscript

There is one final important point that unjust enrichment claims seem to have in common. It is not a normative but a formal analytic similarity. In unjust enrichment there is no duty. There is merely a Hohfeldian liability. The defendant is liable to have their relationship with the claimant altered by which a duty of repayment is imposed;[72] the claimant in turn holds a reciprocal Hohfeldian power. The first reason for thinking I do not have a duty not to receive money or chattels is that this is completely passive. I can be under a liability to repay the money even though I did not know the payment had occurred.[73] It is an objection to this that I must have accepted the payment and that requires some action by me or on my behalf (maybe by the bank), but a duty not to accept a mistaken payment or to repay one can only exist from the point you know there is a problem. Prior to that point I cannot know that there is a duty. The workings of your mind are a mystery to me. There is quite literally no being guided by any duty to return or not to accept;[74] since part of the point of a duty is to do precisely this, that is a good reason to think there is no duty. Knowledge of the defendant of the mistake is not, however, as a matter of positive law a requirement of the cause of action. The defendant is liable to make restitution from the moment the money is paid. Moreover, such a duty could be quite onerous for the defendant. Most of the time the demands may be modest, but we can imagine cases where they are not.[75] Taking these as liabilities instead reduces the burden of unjust enrichment law; one objection might be that the court imposes the duty instead when it orders repayment; the order is, however, as Stephen Smith explains, free-standing.[76] In other words, the duty to repay is imposed by the court, invoking directive authority – the authority to be obeyed.[77]

[71] Sheehan, 'The Property Principle and the Structure of Unjust Enrichment' (n 63) 158–59.

[72] S Smith, 'A Duty to Make Restitution' (2013) 26 *Canadian Journal of Law & Jurisprudence* 157.

[73] ibid 172.

[74] S Smith, *Rights, Wrongs and Injustices* (Oxford, OUP, 2019) 243–245; see contra, S Steel and R Stevens, 'The Secondary Legal Duty to Pay Damages' (2020) 136 *LQR* 283.

[75] S Smith 'Justifying the Law of Unjust Enrichment' (2001) 79 *Texas Law Review* 2177, 2187–88.

[76] Smith, *Rights, Wrongs and Injustices* (n 74) 101–02.

[77] ibid 233–34.

A second reason for thinking that there is no duty to make restitution is that there are no damages for failure to do so and it is pretty much obligatory in English law to impose damages for failure to comply with a duty. Even where there is no loss, the law imposes nominal damages. There are, to be fair, exceptions but a strong argument would need to be put as to why there was a duty to make restitution that when breached did not sound in damages.[78] There is no award of damages for failure to pay damages either,[79] and Stephen Smith has therefore suggested that restitutionary obligations and obligations to pay damages are of the same form.[80] They are both Hohfeldian liabilities.[81]

II. Replies to Critics

Having set out a positive case for the normative pluralism of unjust enrichment, it is now time to turn to two prominent critics of unjust enrichment, who in their different ways fail to understand how categories and concepts of law actually operate.

A. Steve Hedley

Hedley is a long-standing sceptic of unjust enrichment.[82] His criticisms of unjust enrichment theory have been quite steady and consistent over many years. His writings provide both a negative criticism and a more positive proposal. The negative criticism revolves around what Hedley sees as the 'interpretive' bent of unjust enrichment and its concentration on conceptual theory. This 'negative' strand of Hedley's work is valuable and reveals an important truth about how we do law. The 'positive' strand, however, ends up rather more problematic and unrealistic in nature. We take these in turn.

In his early work, Hedley attacked the series of 'grids' that Birks used to illustrate his views.[83] This strand of Hedley's work has been further developed since Birks' death into a wider critique of unjust enrichment theorists' attempts to set

[78] Smith, 'A Duty to Make Restitution' (n 72) 170.

[79] *The Lips* [1988] AC 395 (HL).

[80] S Smith, 'Unjust Enrichment: Nearer to Tort than to Contract' in R Chambers, C Mitchell and J Penner (eds), *Philosophical Foundations of the Law of Unjust Enrichment* (Oxford, OUP, 2009).

[81] Smith, *Rights, Wrongs and Injustices* (n 74) 236–37.

[82] See, eg, S Hedley, 'Unjust Enrichment: A Middle Course?' (2002) 2 *Oxford University Commonwealth Law Journal* 181, S Hedley, 'Unjust at Common Law: So Many Concepts, So Little Clarity' (2006) 3 *European Review of Private Law* 399.

[83] See, for an earlier critique of Hedley's views, D Sheehan, 'Implied Contract and the Taxonomy of Unjust Enrichment' in P Giliker (ed), *Re-Examining Contract and Unjust Enrichment* (Leiden, Brill, 2007).

out and develop the theory in ever greater detail and theoretical rigour.[84] It started, however, with criticism of the grid. The grid was admittedly a moving target. Each time Birks introduced the grid, it was subtly different, but generally Birks referred to a series of 'events'. These were things that happened, such as consent, wrongs or unjust enrichment (and for completeness 'other'). He then referred to 'responses'.[85] These were the things the law did as a result of the events that had happened. It might validate a contract, provide compensation or restitution or proprietary responses. Unjust enrichment could – logically, Birks said – only be found in the intersection of unjust enrichment and restitution. Compensation could not logically be a response to unjust enrichment.[86] Hedley quite simply asked where the logic came from. Birks never provided any further detail, simply appealing to logic. Hedley can be read, not as questioning the provision of restitution (as opposed to something else or nothing at all),[87] but as questioning whether this is **logically** determined – ie, whether it is unintelligible to deny its provision, as opposed to merely normatively undesirable. Birks never properly engaged with theoretical or normative issues, but one of the main points lying behind the argument in this book is that law does not work in a logical, geometric fashion. From a Dworkinian perspective, we would expect to see different areas of law drawing on different principles, some of which may have purchase elsewhere in the law. Principles overlap and they have different weights in different contexts, and this is a conclusion that is attractive to Hedley as well.[88] Deductive logic may have some part to play in the law, but legal rules are not deduced logically from premises.[89] The conclusion that the response to unjust enrichment is restitution – and nothing else – is therefore a normative conclusion not a logical one.

The practical consequences of the logical approach and its endeavour towards ever-greater conceptual and logical rigour has, however, become an ever-increasing divide from the legal doctrine that it attempts to explain.[90] After all, judges rarely apply the principles with the logical care and attention some authors would wish.[91] For Hedley, this simply proves the courts are not overly

[84] S Hedley, 'Justice and Discretion in the Law of Restitution' (2019) 48 *Common Law World Review* 94.

[85] See, eg, Birks, *Unjust Enrichment* (n 54) 21–28; PBH Birks, 'The Law of Restitution at the End of an Era' (1999) 29 *University of Western Australia Law Review* 13; PBH Birks, 'Equity Conscience and Unjust Enrichment' (1999) 23 *Melbourne University Law Review* 1.

[86] Birks, *An Introduction to the Law of Restitution* (n 33) ch 2.

[87] Hedley wrote a textbook on restitution, so is plainly not averse to gain-based relief per se. S Hedley, *A Critical Introduction to Restitution* (London, Butterworths, 2001).

[88] S Hedley, 'What is Unjust Enrichment For?' (2016) 16 *Oxford University Commonwealth Law Journal* 333.

[89] Sheehan, 'Implied Contract and the Taxonomy of Unjust Enrichment' (n 83) 194–95.

[90] S Hedley, 'Farewell to Unjustified Enrichment: A Common Law Response' [2016] *Edinburgh Law Review* 326, 332.

[91] See, for criticism of the Supreme Court for not taking due logical care and attention to the theory, GJ Virgo, 'All the World's a Stage: The Seven Ages of Restitution' (2016) University of Cambridge Faculty of Law Working Paper No 51/2016, available at: papers.ssrn.com/sol3/papers.cfm?abstract_id=2845462.

bothered with the theory[92] and this in turn suggests a basic failing of the logical approach. Hedley has written of a divide between externalists, who look at law from an external viewpoint – law and economics say – and internalists, who want to understand law as an autonomous, formalist, free-standing system. He describes what he calls a radical internalist strand of thought that dismisses the concerns of the externalists and extra-legal concerns altogether,[93] and which condemns externalist thinking as unprincipled and anti-theoretical when in fact it merely points out flaws in internalist theory.[94] To say that a proper understanding of law requires not just a concentration on the intension – the abstract idea of a concept – but its extension and context, not just on principles and justificatory rationales but policy too, should not be uncontroversial.[95] Coherence and abstract principle are not everything.[96] If, like Stephen Smith, we take interpretive theory to be about making sense of or revealing an intelligible order in law, it is compatible with most theories of law.[97] Such a view of interpretive theory does, as Hedley has suggested, draw on Dworkin and so the methodology of this book can be seen as interpretivist in this looser sense and to support Hedley in his view that while formal structure is important – and all theorists of whatever bent agree on that – context is also important. The debate is about the extent of its relevance not about whether it is relevant.[98] Hedley's critique of the methodology of Birksian unjust enrichment theory has bite therefore. In reviewing Webb's book, *Reasons and Restitution*, Hedley applauds Webb's view that there is no unjust enrichment principle. Although the causes of actions we commonly think of as belonging to unjust enrichment do rest on principles these are in the main, Webb argues, property principles. Hedley, however, finds it odd that Webb is happy to group these causes of action together under the unjust enrichment head, despite the inability to outline a distinct principle.[99] An area of law should be 'for' something. Unjust enrichment is not, however, 'for' anything. What this means is that the disagreement with Birks was not merely methodological in that both Hedley and Birks had the same goal of finding a unified area but disagreed on how to get there. For Hedley (unlike Birks) restitution and unjust enrichment is a rubbish tip of material left over once contract, tort and other private

[92] Hedley, 'Justice and Discretion in the Law of Restitution' (n 84) 107; S Hedley, 'And so the Legal World Goes Round: The Search for a Meaningful Law of Restitution' (2016), available at: papers.ssrn.com/sol3/papers.cfm?abstract_id=2854292.

[93] S Hedley, 'Looking Outwards or looking Inwards: Obligations Scholarship in the Early Twenty-First Century' in A Robertson (ed), *The Goals of Private Law* (Oxford, Hart Publishing, 2009) 206.

[94] ibid 208–09.

[95] Arvind and Sheehan (n 54) 489–90.

[96] See also, S Hedley, 'The Shock of the Old: Interpretivism in Obligations' in C Rickett and R Grantham (eds), *Structure and Justification in Private Law: Essays for Peter Birks* (Oxford, Hart Publishing, 2008); S Hedley, 'The Rise and Fall of Private Law Theory' (2018) 134 *LQR* 214.

[97] S Hedley, 'Is Private Law Meaningless?' [2011] *Current Legal Problems* 89.

[98] Arvind and Sheehan (n 54) 495–96.

[99] Hedley, 'What is Unjust Enrichment For?' (n 88) 343.

law categories were developed which engages no single normative principle and should not be expected to do so either.

In the 'positive' strand of his work, Hedley therefore treats many restitutionary claims in terms of implied contract but is equally happy to say parts of restitution involve new property rights, rights under a trust, the law of torts or equitable wrongs 'and so on'.[100] At the same time, unjust enrichment ideas crop up across the law.[101] For reasons of space we concentrate on Hedley's view of contract here. It is an expansive view, with a wide penumbra. Hedley has – as we might expect – never claimed to expound implied contract with the same level of logical rigour as Birks claimed for unjust enrichment theory.[102] However, he does not expound it with much rigour at all, commenting that 'contract is a flexible and permeable notion' and that the 'metaphorical "implied contract"' is a tool for dealing with its outer edges.[103] He goes further, saying that contract law is just the law of what benefits need paying for and that it is the law of the market.[104] As we have seen, it would be unfair on Hedley to say that he rejects all theory or that he rejects all formal structure in the law. He comments that legal concepts have 'a degree of flexibility but are not infinitely flexible'.[105] This is right. Legal concepts are Weberian ideal types and relate to each other and to their empirical extensions by means of Wittgensteinian family resemblances. This makes them inevitably malleable. That being so, concepts are not as malleable as Hedley makes them out to be. Hedley leans too heavily on context or extension and not enough on intension.[106] Importantly, this does not entail the extreme claim that context is irrelevant. The claim here is much more modest. It is just that Hedley has the balance wrong.

We can illustrate the reach of Hedley's proposed concept of implied contract with a selection of examples that he himself puts forward. Hedley's first example in an article from 2004 of an almost-contract is that of a 17-year-old child's contracting in a supermarket.[107] In some cases, he will be contracting to buy food – a necessary – and the contract will be valid. But let us imagine he is not. Such contracts for goods other than necessaries are invalid but may be ratifiable when the child turns 18. Aside from that, the child will be able to recover if there has been a total failure of consideration,[108] or presumably a mistake, even one of law. It is clear, however, that the rules differ only in some respects from those relating to fully valid contracts.[109] There is, however, little if anything that connects this to

[100] Hedley, *A Critical Introduction to Restitution* (n 87) 2.
[101] S Hedley, 'Unjust Enrichment as the Basis of Restitution: An Overworked Concept' (1985) 5 *Legal Studies* 56.
[102] S Hedley, 'Implied Contract and Restitution' [2004] *CLJ* 435, 436.
[103] ibid 436.
[104] ibid 439.
[105] S Hedley, 'The Rise and Fall of Private Law Theory' (2018) 134 *LQR* 214, 225.
[106] Sheehan, 'Implied Contract and the Taxonomy of Unjust Enrichment' (n 83) 201–04.
[107] Hedley, 'Implied Contract and Restitution' (n 102) 439.
[108] *Steinberg v Scala (Leeds) Ltd* [1923] 2 Ch 452 (CA).
[109] Hedley, 'Implied Contract and Restitution' (n 102) 442.

the case of my taking Hedley's bicycle and riding it around the Irish countryside. This is his example of 'wrongful failure to contract' and is much further away from the traditional view of a valid contract.[110] It assumes something we know did not happen; to imply a contract which we know was not concluded tells us nothing about why we 'imply the contract'. There is therefore no plausible normative principle explaining the existence of liability that links these cases. Hedley might reply that he does not seek to state his position with the same degree of logical rigour as Birks.[111] Nor does he need to, but his analysis must have sufficient rigour to be useful. If legal concepts are as vague and have quite the wide penumbra that Hedley claims for contract, right answers become impossible. Accepting a Dworkinian perspective, Hedley's position on implied contract is difficult to defend.[112]

We can therefore turn Hedley's attack on unjust enrichment back on him. Essentially the criticism he raises against unjust enrichment is that it is not useful. However, the truth is that it is his analogy with implied contract, which is not useful, or more precisely, is not useful for the purpose of classifying causes of action and justifying rationales for relief. It may of course be useful for other purposes. Recognising an analogy with contract in the failure to contract cases might usefully inform the calculation of quantum of damages but does not address the question why liability for damages exists in the first place. More broadly, Hedley's approach to implied contract is not useful because, although it might pick out some resemblances between the cases, we need – as we saw in chapter one – to look not just at similarities, but also dissimilarities. By concentrating on the similarities, Hedley risks his categories getting away from him and expanding infinitely. It is a problem of under-determination. An old critique of Wittgenstein[113] is that you can always find a family resemblance; in the private law field we might say there is always a claimant. That criticism of Wittgenstein, discussed in chapter one, was misguided,[114] but applies to Hedley's theory of implied contract.

B. Peter Jaffey

Jaffey has, like Hedley, been a long-standing critic of unjust enrichment theory. Despite his division of the cases into two sets of case governed by either a property principle or by contract and imputed contract,[115] his theory is quite different from Hedley's. Jaffey argues that each area of law must be a justificatory category.

[110] Sheehan, 'Implied Contract and the Taxonomy of Unjust Enrichment' (n 83) 201.

[111] Hedley, 'Implied Contract and Restitution' (n 102) 436.

[112] Sheehan, 'Implied Contract and the Taxonomy of Unjust Enrichment' (n 83) 200–04.

[113] See, eg, JE Bellaimy, 'Family Resemblance and the Problem of Under-Determination of Extension' (1990) 13 *Philosophical Investigations* 31.

[114] See H Andersen, 'Kuhn's Account of Family Resemblance: A Solution to the Problem of Wide-Open Texture' (2000) 52 *Erkenntnis* 313, 314–15.

[115] P Jaffey, *The Nature and Scope of Restitution* (Oxford, Hart Publishing, 2000); P Jaffey, *Private Law and Property Claims* (Oxford, Hart Publishing, 2007).

By this he means that there must be a unique justificatory rationale that justifies all claims within the category and critically no claims that arise outside the category should be justified by reference to it. On this basis, he argues that unjust enrichment shows no such justificatory principle. If anything, the category is purely remedial. He has distinguished between the weak theory of unjust enrichment, which merely asserts the existence of the claim and the strong theory which asserts the existence of a principle of (or against) unjust enrichment,[116] observing that it is not easy to identify arguments in the literature in favour of the latter or explaining what it might be.[117] He therefore argues 'the strong theory must be established or refuted by a careful analysis of the unjust enrichment claims in the weak sense to see what their justification is'.[118] For Jaffey there is no commonality and no single justificatory principle.

Jaffey constructs the same type of geometric edifice as Birks and his theory can be criticised in the same way. Jaffey may object to this characterisation on the basis that Birks' scheme was not based on any justificatory rationales but was formalistic in character by contrast. However, each author produces a rather geometric map which could in principle be reduced to diagrammatic form, although, unlike Birks, Jaffey never attempts this diagrammatic exposition. Jaffey does, however, demand that each area of law be a justificatory category with a single unique justificatory rationale. In other words, no rationale is relevant to a claim outside 'its' category and all claims in the category are justified by the same justification. He insists that a historical understanding of an area cannot assist with a principled explanation of it.[119] Not only are Jaffey's categories, like Birks', hermetically sealed boxes on this view, he fails to give sufficient weight to the development of an area.[120] Birks was equally guilty of this, claiming, as we have seen, that the entire law on knowing receipt was misconceived. Birks' expression was 'history cannot justify the muddle it has made'.[121] The criticism levelled at both authors therefore is a failure to appreciate that legal reasoning is always multi-causal and multilayered. Principles are always drawn from different places and applied according to the context in which they find themselves. Different principles will have different weights in different scenarios, and this is to be expected. It is impossibly purist for Jaffey to demand that all areas of law be founded on unique justificatory rationales. Although unjust enrichment has a particular **function** – the reversal of defective enrichments (whether by performance or in some other way) – that does not preclude a degree of normative pluralism and recognition of principles drawn from other areas.

[116] P Jaffey, 'Two Theories of Unjust Enrichment' in J Neyers et al (eds), *Understanding Unjust Enrichment* (Oxford, Hart Publishing, 2004).
[117] ibid 143.
[118] ibid 144.
[119] P Jaffey, 'Explaining the Trust' (2015) 131 *LQR* 377, 378.
[120] D Sheehan, 'Express Trusts, Private Law Theory and Legal Concepts' (2022) 35 *Canadian Journal of Law & Jurisprudence* 511.
[121] Birks, *Unjust Enrichment* (n 54) 156–57.

Jaffey separates out restitutionary claims into property claims, contract and imputed contract claims. We take these in turn. For Jaffey, the reason why mistaken payments must be returned is that the money belonged to the claimant. The power to transfer property is derived from property law and that power is invalidly or ineffectively exercised. It follows therefore from the principle of remedial consistency that the defendant-recipient must return it. The principle of remedial consistency is also known as the monist principle. It states in essence that the remedy we provide must give the same benefit to the claimant as the infringed right – unless to do that would be unduly burdensome on the defendant.[122] I have criticised the monist principle elsewhere,[123] and will not do so again here, but one point should be made. Jaffey argues that unjust enrichment as commonly understood by its proponents is in fact a remedial category. It tells us what remedy we obtain and notes similarities between these remedies, but this does not tell us why those remedies are appropriate.[124] It is a fallacy, Jaffey says, to think that because the remedy is the same, we can group the claims together. This is true. Not all claims for compensatory damages are justified the same way. On Jaffey's view, the private property principle provides the required justification for restitutionary claims. Jaffey describes that justification in the following terms. 'O should have the benefit allocated to him by a property right … because he has acted in reliance on the assumption … that he has or will have the property right'.[125] This is the reliance principle of private property and empowers O (the owner) to exploit resources for his own benefit, until there is a valid transfer of those resources. The invalidity of the transfer as a matter of property law necessarily means O still has the benefit and a proprietary claim against the defendant's general estate for the 'value' of the asset transferred.[126]

Jaffey argues that failure to put the restitutionary obligation within property creates an ugly inconsistency where property law says the transfer is valid and unjust enrichment law says it is not.[127] However, it would be equally something of an ugly contradiction to say on the one hand that property law validates the transaction – and gives the transferee legal title – but that property law requires it to be returned because of the invalidity of the transaction.[128] Jaffey does avoid this latter contradiction by arguing in effect that it is valid in law, but invalid in equity. The transferor retains ownership of the 'value' of the property which is separate from the ownership of the specific items. As explained elsewhere, this

[122] Jaffey, *Private Law and Property Claims* (n 115) 40; P Jaffey, 'Remedial Consistency in Private Law' (2022) 72 *University of Toronto Law Journal* 216.

[123] Sheehan, 'The Property Principle and the Structure of Unjust Enrichment' (n 63) 140–43.

[124] Jaffey, *Private Law and Property Claims* (n 115) 16–18.

[125] ibid 79.

[126] P Jaffey, 'Proprietary Claims to Recover Mistaken or Unauthorised Payments' in P Devonshire and R Havelock (eds), *The Impact of Equity and Restitution in Commerce* (Oxford, Hart Publishing, 2019) 86–87.

[127] P Jaffey, 'Restitution, Property and Unjust Enrichment' [2013] *Restitution Law Review* 17, 20.

[128] Sheehan, 'The Property Principle and the Structure of Unjust Enrichment' (n 63) 152.

idea of owning value is misconceived and produces some bizarre consequences. Jaffey is, for example, required to appeal to a hitherto unacknowledged property right, which allows a restitutionary claimant to own value in another's assets, but without owning any particular assets.[129]

Jaffey argues that in cases where a defendant requests that work be done there is an implicit promise to pay. In most services cases there is in fact a request and these cases must be treated as contractual – rather than as an imputed contract. If the normal conditions for contractual liability are not satisfied it is best to see the court as relaxing those requirements.[130] Pre-contractual claims where work is done in anticipation of a contract that never arises can be seen as contractual on this view. Jaffey argues that to link the contract and property cases together actively undermines the contract-oriented regime for services.[131] The undermining of the contractual regime is most obvious where there was a valid contract. In cases of restitution after termination for breach, therefore, Jaffey insists the claim lies within the area of contract law and is based on an actual existing contract.[132] Jaffey characterises the failure of consideration view of these cases as saying that the claimant's performance was provided on the basis (on condition) that the reciprocal counter-performance would be provided. It was not provided, so a claim lies. Jaffey's objection to this is simple. If the condition were part of the contract, the claim is contractual. If it is not, it is not binding.[133] If we accept – and Jaffey does not – that a claim can be both contract and unjust enrichment, these claims can be accepted as being guided in part by contractual principles (such as on quantum and contract price ceilings) but also as being sufficiently similar to other claims to reverse performances as to be a type of unjust enrichment claim. In other words, it simply proves that principles from one area of law have a cross-cutting relevance in others. On a Dworkinian analysis – and Jaffey has in fact claimed to be Dworkinian[134] – this is to be expected.

Jaffey describes imputed contracts as addressing the question 'whether, without having made an agreement, the plaintiff can do work or incur expenditure that benefits the defendant … and then claim payment for it from him'.[135] In such cases, Jaffey posits two conditions for liability under an imputed contract. The first is that it must be certain the defendant benefited from the claimant's actions, so that any reasonable party in the defendant's position would have contracted for the benefit at an acceptable price. This is the benefit condition. There should be no claim, however, where there was no good reason for the claimant's failure to

[129] For comment see Sheehan, 'Express Trusts, Private Law Theory and Legal Concepts' (n 120) 522–25.

[130] Jaffey, *The Nature and Scope of Restitution* (n 115) 77–78.

[131] P Jaffey, 'Unjust Enrichment and Contract' (2014) 77 *MLR* 983.

[132] Jaffey, *The Nature and Scope of Restitution* (n 115) ch 2.

[133] Jaffey, 'Unjust Enrichment and Contract' (n 131) 987–88.

[134] P Jaffey, 'Authority in the Common Law' (2011) 36 *Australian Journal of Legal Philosophy* 1, 22–24.

[135] Jaffey, *The Nature and Scope of Restitution* (n 115) 77.

enter an actual express agreement[136] – the officiousness condition. Jaffey rejects the idea that these imputed contract claims are restitutionary claims to reverse unjust enrichment. Doing work, he argues, does not necessarily entail a loss – although there will be an opportunity cost – and if there is a loss there need not be a correlation with the defendant's gain. The claim imposes an exchange rather than reversing a transfer.[137] He argues that it is therefore a false analogy to classify any of these cases involving work or services – whether contract or imputed contract – with the property cases, as the law of unjust enrichment does. Exchanges and reverses of transfers are simply different things. This points, however, to a critical cleavage between our views. I maintain that what matters is the performance by provision of services, chattels or money. That performance (whatever form it takes) can be reversed. Jaffey denies this. Jaffey also has a second argument. Imputed contract claims should be classed with contract because they protect the claimants' reliance interest.[138] This proposition is difficult to accept because it is hard to see what the claimant relies on. The key to contractual liability, if founded on reliance, is that you rely on the defendant's actions in instigating the belief that he will perform. Here the claimant has nothing to rely on; the best we can say is that the claimant did not intend a gift.

One important further criticism is that the category of imputed contract does not provide a normative reason for the claim. It is rather something of an example of an approach that we might call 'restitution unless'. Given that there was a benefit to the defendant he must pay a sum for that benefit, unless there is a good reason why he should not (eg, that the claimant acted officiously). We start therefore from the position that all such benefits are returnable/attract restitutionary remedies without identifying a positive reason for that. In a case-based non-codified system – like English law or South African law – it is easier to develop the law by identifying such a positive reason,[139] and actually, for Barker, it is a morally more attractive way to go about things than the alternative.[140] Not only does Jaffey's position not identify a positive reason for restitution, it goes in the face of the common law method in doing so.

The concern – that the claimant not be acting officiously – does crop up across the law and Jaffey is right to draw attention to this. Further, Jaffey is right to point to different examples of imputed contracts and, in many cases of imputed contract, quite right to criticise the explanation in terms of unjust factors. It is worth asking, however, if his category (like Hedley's) is not in danger of escaping control. It may be that, if it is escaping control, one reason is Jaffey's failure to sort through the

[136] ibid 78–79.
[137] ibid 9–10.
[138] ibid 79.
[139] Scott and Visser (n 49) 165–66.
[140] K Barker, 'Responsibility for Gain: Unjust Factors or Absence of Legal Ground? Starting Points in Unjust Enrichment Law' in R Grantham and C Rickett (eds), *Structure and Justification in Private Law: Essays for Peter Birks* (Oxford, Hart Publishing, 2008).

positive reasons for restitution. For example, in cases of necessitous interventions we are told that the claimant must not have intended a gift and that he must have intended to advance the defendant's interests not his own. The requirement that the intervention be necessary is present to counter any suggestion of officiousness,[141] but it also implies that the defendant has received a benefit. Jaffey rightly points out that it is unhelpful to call a policy of encouraging necessitous interventions an unjust factor.[142] These cases of necessitous intervention are known as cases of *negotiorum gestio* in civilian systems and are not there classed as cases of unjustified enrichment;[143] nor should they be in English law as we discuss in chapter six. However, Jaffey has mixed some cases of performance claims – mistaken rendering of services that the defendant would have had to pay for elsewhere – in with necessitous intervention claims.[144] Yet mistake is much more easily referred to as an unjust factor than 'a policy of encouraging necessary or useful interventions in another's affairs'. The latter really does not relate to a defect of any sort. Another example of imputed contract which is relevantly different in terms of the claim-norm underlying relief is the compulsory discharge of another's debt. It is not officious, because it is compulsory and it provides a benefit because the debt is discharged.[145] We examine these claims in more detail in chapter six, but for now it is best to note – as Stevens does – that the reason the defendant is liable in such cases is simply that he was liable before. The defendant is **primarily** liable:[146] no further justification is needed. There is certainly no defect as such in the claimant's payment. To group these mistaken provision of services claims with necessitous intervention and compulsory discharge obscures two things. First, it groups performance claims with non-performance claims. A clear theme of this book is that we must treat performance and non-performance claims separately. Second, and this is simply the flipside of the earlier point, by ignoring the clear similarities – the role of mistake – between the mistaken provision of services claims and mistaken payments it separates cases that should be treated together. It is an example of both the false assimilation and false differentiation Jaffey warns against.[147]

III. Conclusion

This chapter concludes the outline of the book's main argument. In chapter one we established that areas of law like unjust enrichment have a **function**, are **historically contingent** upon a certain conventional morality embedded in the society it

[141] Jaffey, *The Nature and Scope of Restitution* (n 115) 79.
[142] ibid 82.
[143] D Sheehan, '*Negotiorum Gestio*: A Civilian Concept in the Common Law' (2006) 55 *ICLQ* 253.
[144] Jaffey, *The Nature and Scope of Restitution* (n 115) 84–85.
[145] ibid 93–96.
[146] Stevens, 'The Unjust Enrichment Disaster' (n 1) 587–89.
[147] Jaffey, *Private Law and Property Claims* (n 115) 6–9.

serves and are inevitably **normatively pluralist**. We suggested that legal causes of action were Weberian ideal types and Dworkinian interpretive concepts and that they were related to their factual extensions and to each other by means of picking out morally significant family resemblances. Chapter two outlined a structure for the law of unjust enrichment which combines elements of the civilian systems with unjust factors and this chapter has done several things. First, it has defended the importance of mistake. Second, it has shown how unjust enrichment is **normatively pluralist** and illustrates that unjust enrichment is a good example of how the type of legal categorisation defended in chapter one operates in practice. Third, it has shown how unjust enrichment, in reversing defective enrichments, including both performance and non-performance cases, applies in cases where there can be no duty to return or duty 'not to receive'. Unjust enrichment gives rise to Hohfeldian liabilities not duties. Last, it has provided a reply to two theorists who in different ways deny unjust enrichment's function and existence. Chapter four begins the important task of fleshing out how all of this is reflected in the details of the different causes of action that exist within our law of unjust enrichment.

4

Intent-Based Causes of Action I: Mistakes, Duress, Undue Influence and Unconscionable Bargains

Introduction

The book so far has made a claim that English law can be usefully understood as following a type of civilian split between performance and non-performance claims, albeit one that makes extensive and, as we see in this chapter, cross-cutting use of unjust factors. The advantage of this is that it allows us to restructure and properly understand the 'at the expense of' requirement in the context of different causes of action. Mistaken transfers are not the same cause of action as mistaken improvements of others' property for example. This is true even if we wish to explain them under the rubric of mistake. The continuing English preference for unjust factors, however, means that there is not one single overarching performance claim as exists in Germany and we return to this significant point in chapter five.

This chapter is divided into two main sections. The first examines mistake – the classic 'claimant-sided' unjust factor – and the second the 'defendant-sided' factors such as duress. We divide and categorise these into several distinct causes of action.

I. Mistakes

This section is divided into three main parts. The first part aims to clear the ground somewhat, by defining what we mean by a mistake. The second looks at mistaken performance claims, and the third at non-performance claims, primarily mistaken improvement of property.

A. What is a Mistake?[1]

A mistake claim can be seen as responding to a flaw in the claimant's decision-making process caused (usually) by incorrect inputs. This is not strictly necessary; the mistake is an element in the decision-making process that at some point may have involved all true premises. We use systematically error-prone heuristics – one of which is that vivid, concrete and easily remembered data is preferred. In the mistake of law context that might mean seeing some cases as more important (wrongly so).[2] We must allow both types of mistakes – incorrect premises and incorrect processing – to count. Any other view can lead us to the impossible task of having to decide what brought the claimant to the belief he had. This leads us to the conclusion that *Kleinwort Benson v Lincoln City Council*[3] was correct that payment based on a case later overruled was a mistaken payment, although this has caused problems for limitation periods which can be extended under section 32(1)(c) of the Limitation Act 1980 so that time runs from the point the mistake was reasonably discoverable. The standard criticism here is that nothing prevents the limitation period from being extended indefinitely.[4] On a Dworkinian view of law,[5] as adopted in this book, however, the payer incorrectly deduced that the case on which he relied was correct and the Supreme Court, despite criticising *Kleinwort Benson*, in the end rightly did not depart from it in *Test Claimants in the FII Litigation v HMRC*.[6] The payer's judgment as to 'fit' and 'justification' was wrong, and this could have been known at the time. Certainly, we do not need to wait until after the overruling decision to make an argument that the earlier decision was wrong. Given this, what matters is that the claimant has decided to do x on the basis that the facts (or law) are y when he would otherwise have made a different decision.[7] As we noted in chapter three, the importance of my higher order beliefs and motivations is that they form self-governing policies which I consider in my practical reasoning. A mistake involves a condition on my intention; I intend to pay if I owe the money (and I believe that I do). The law would disrespect me as an autonomous agent if it did not allow relief when I do not owe the money. To refuse relief would be to force me to pay in the teeth of my higher

[1] D Sheehan, 'What is a Mistake?' (2000) 20 *Legal Studies* 538; E Allan Farnsworth, *Alleviating Mistakes: Reversal and Forgiveness for Flawed Perceptions* (Oxford, OUP, 2004) chs 2–4.

[2] MA Eisenberg, 'The Limits of Cognition and the Limits of Contract' (1994) 47 *Stanford Law Review* 211, 218–22.

[3] *Kleinwort Benson v Lincoln City Council* [1999] 2 AC 349 (HL).

[4] *Test Claimants in the FII Litigation v HMRC* [2020] UKSC 47, [2022] AC 1, [155] (Lord Reed); see D Sheehan, 'Mistakes of Law and Limitation Periods' [2021] *CLJ* 446.

[5] Sheehan, 'What is a Mistake?' (n 1) 546–49, 558–60, but see contra, eg, R Stevens, 'Restitution and Time' (2021) 137 *LQR* 368.

[6] [2020] UKSC 47, [2022] AC 1, [221] (Lord Reed). See also *AXA General Insurance Ltd v Lord Advocate* [2011] UKSC 46, [2012] 1 AC 868, [121] (Lord Reed) accepting the retroactive nature of judgments on the declaratory theory.

[7] D Sheehan, 'Mistake, Failure of Consideration and the Planning Theory of Intention' (2015) 28 *Canadian Journal of Law & Jurisprudence* 155.

order policy to pay if (and only if) I owe. This is true whether the mistake is one of fact or law.[8]

A mistake can then be seen as a belief in something that can, at the time it is acted upon, in principle be proven not to be the case and forgetfulness or ignorance can lead to false beliefs recognised as mistakes.[9] This necessitates the corresponding idea of correctness. In principle there must be a method by which we can discover what the correct answer is; at the very least it must be possible to prove that the answer is incorrect.[10] Mispredictions create something of a problem. Authority is that a misprediction does not ground relief.[11] Mistakes justify relief because they represent a dissonance between the world as it is and our plans. Our intention (with which) simply does not cover the case. Since planning is always future-oriented it is hard to see why mispredictions should not count as there too exists a dissonance between plans and reality.[12] Some have referred to the mispredictor taking a risk,[13] but this is flawed and conclusory.[14] The answer may be prosaic in that it will be practically impossible to tell the difference between a misprediction and a change of mind.

An example of relief for misprediction, however, is *Kerrison v Glyn, Mills, Currie & Co.*[15] On its face, Kerrison lodged £500 with the defendant based on a misprediction. Kerrison believed future liabilities to pay would accrue; the ratio is that a misprediction as to future liability suffices for relief. This seems reasonable. A court ought to be able to assume that an actor will not change his mind about paying money he expects to owe (if he does indeed end up owing it). Mispredictions can in some cases be reinterpreted as mistakes.[16] *Kerrison* is no exception. The mistake, properly understood, was that Kessler & Co was a 'living commercial entity'.[17] Kessler was the banker to a Mexican mine co-owned by Kerrison and which had put up credit for the mining undertaking but had become

[8] ibid 164–67; see against this view, A Nair, '"Mistakes of Law" and Legal Reasoning: Interpreting *Kleinwort Benson v Lincoln City Council*' in R Chambers, C Mitchell and J Penner (eds), *Philosophical Foundations of the Law of Unjust Enrichment* (Oxford, OUP, 2009).

[9] For a mistake of fact this includes cases where the technology to prove it has not been invented because in principle it was provable (just not in practice at the time). See R Sutton, 'Mistake, Symbol, Metaphor and Unfolding' [2002] *Restitution Law Review* 9, 14.

[10] Sheehan, 'What is a Mistake?' (n 1) 539.

[11] *Dextra Bank v Bank of Jamaica* [2002] 1 All ER (Comm) 193 (PC) 202; C Mitchell, P Mitchell and S Watterson (eds), *Goff & Jones: The Law of Unjust Enrichment*, 10th edn (London, Sweet & Maxwell, 2022) paras 9.07–9.17.

[12] Sheehan, 'Mistake, Failure of Consideration and the Planning Theory of Intention' (n 7) 170–72.

[13] W Seah, 'Mispredictions, Mistakes and the Law of Unjust Enrichment' [2007] *Restitution Law Review* 93; PS Davies, 'Risk in Unjust Enrichment' [2012] *Restitution Law Review* 57.

[14] F Wilmot-Smith, 'Replacing Risk-Taking Reasoning' (2011) 127 *LQR* 610.

[15] *Kerrison v Glyn, Mills, Currie & Co* (1912) 81 LJKB 465 (HL).

[16] *Re Griffiths* [2008] EWHC 118, [2009] Ch 162 (misprediction as to anticipated future lifespan versus mistake that he was not suffering from cancer); *Dextra Bank v Bank of Jamaica* [2002] 1 All ER (Comm) 193 (PC) is arguably materially identical to *Kerrison* (misprediction that a loan would be forthcoming, and a liability would accrue); Farnsworth (n 1) 55 describes the process as involving substantial discretion.

[17] (1912) 81 LJKB 465, 469–70.

insolvent itself prior to the payment. Without the mistake as to credit worthiness, there could have been no misprediction. That said, the law is entitled to assume there will be no change of mind about paying sums believed to be accruing due in the future, justifying the ratio decidendi of the decision.[18]

B. Mistaken Performance Claims: Money

i. The General Rule

What then are the elements of the cause of action to recover mistaken performances? It should make no difference what form the performance takes – whether money, services or chattels.[19] In general, services must be requested for the defendant to be liable for their provision and usually this means that something will have been promised in return. If that reciprocity is not forthcoming, the claimant will generally have a claim in failure of consideration. It is only where the services are unrequested but necessary that a mistake claim will be needed. The task of a performance claim is to reverse the performance, which is quantified as the value of the money, chattels or services rendered at the time of performance – not the time of trial. The first requirement therefore is that we show there was an intentional transaction as discussed in chapter two. Second, we must decide what types of mistake count. In the past the question has been whether the action should be only available for liability mistakes or something wider. In *Kelly v Solari* the relevant insurance policy had lapsed, but the insurer mistakenly treated it as continuing and valid and paid out.[20] For Stevens, the proper interpretation is that it is the lack of entitlement that justifies recovery, and he quotes a segment at the end of Parke B's judgment in support.[21]

> If, indeed, the money is intentionally paid, without reference to the truth or falsehood of the fact, the plaintiff meaning to waive all inquiry into it, and that the person receiving shall have the money at all events, whether the fact be true or false, the latter is certainly entitled to retain it; but if it is paid under the impression of the truth of a fact which is untrue, it may, generally speaking, be recovered back, however careless the party paying may have been, in omitting to use due diligence to inquire into the fact. In such a case the receiver was not entitled to it, nor intended to have it.[22]

This seems an implausible reading of the passage. In context, Parke B is contrasting the case where the claimant just pays without reference to the truth or falsity of the facts and the defendant is entitled to keep the money and the mistake case where he is not paying without regard to truth and falsity and the defendant must

[18] Sheehan, 'Mistake, Failure of Consideration and the Planning Theory of Intention' (n 7) 172.
[19] J du Plessis, *The South African Law of Unjustified Enrichment* (Durban, Juta, 2012) 102.
[20] *Kelly v Solari* (1841) 9 M&W 54, 152 ER 24.
[21] R Stevens, *The Laws of Restitution* (Oxford, OUP, 2023) 71.
[22] *Kelly v Solari* (1841) 9 M&W 54, 152 ER 24, 26.

repay. The mistake is (part of) the reason why the defendant must repay. As is well known, at the time there was still a mistake of law bar.[23] If the mistake had been one of law, recovery would have been barred, as is clear from Lord Abinger CB. The point was that at the time we needed lack of entitlement to the money (ie, no valid obligation on the payer to pay) and a mistake of fact as to liability.

There was also no defence of change of position at the time of *Kelly v Solari*. We return to the defence in chapter eight, but for now the lack of this feature limiting the potential liability of an innocent payee who had relied on the receipt required a limited range for the cause of action itself.[24] A test of fundamental mistake has therefore also been aired but rejected as too vague. In *Australia & New Zealand Banking Group Ltd v Westpac Banking Corporation*, the High Court of Australia suggested that arguably it meant no more than that the mistake caused the payment.[25] In *Norwich Union Fire Insurance Society Ltd v WH Price Ltd*, the mistake was a liability mistake and Lord Wright ran the two ideas together, calling the mistake a 'fundamental one'.[26]

In the modern era – particularly after the recognition in *Lipkin Gorman v Karpnale*[27] of the change of position defence – the test seems to be one of causation except that where there is a valid obligation to pay no liability lies. That case connotes no cause of action because the obligation is still present. This was acknowledged in the main case cited for the sufficiency of causation, *Barclays Bank v WJ Simms, Son & Cooke (Southern) Ltd*,[28] and referred to as the good consideration defence, although strictly, as we saw in chapter two, it is not a defence. The absence of an otherwise valid obligation to pay is part of the cause of action. In that decision, a housing association drew a cheque for about £24,000 on its account with the bank in favour of a building company, the defendant. The following day a receiver was appointed to the company, and instructions were given to the bank to stop the cheque. Nonetheless, the cheque was inadvertently paid. It was therefore a type of liability mistake, although the liability about which the bank was mistaken was as to its customer – not the cheque's payee. Robert Goff J embarked on a survey of the cases. He concluded, 'If a person pays money to another under a mistake of fact which causes him to make the payment, he is prima facie entitled to recover it as money paid under a mistake of fact'.[29] The test, as he laid it down, is ambiguous between a counterfactual test and a test requiring the mistake to be merely 'a contributing cause';[30] the former is likely the law, is more consistent with

[23] Ascribed to *Bilbie v Lumley* (1802) 2 East 469, 102 ER 448.

[24] *Barclays Bank v WJ Simms, Son & Cooke (Southern) Ltd* [1980] QB 677.

[25] *Australia & New Zealand Banking Group Ltd v Westpac* (1988) 164 CLR 662, 670–71.

[26] *Norwich Union Fire Insurance Society Ltd v WH Price Ltd* [1934] AC 455 (PC).

[27] *Lipkin Gorman v Karpnale Ltd* [1991] 2 AC 542.

[28] [1980] QB 677.

[29] ibid 695.

[30] R Grantham and CEF Rickett, *Enrichment and Restitution in New Zealand* (Oxford, Hart Publishing, 2000) 126–27.

the law's usual approach,[31] but arguably requires us to delve in the metaphysics of causation and necessary and sufficient (or multiple sufficient) causes in a way that Bant suggests is impossible when confronted with the workings of the human mind.[32]

Most cases will in practice be liability mistakes. The debate above has been as to whether the causative nature of the error should be a sufficient condition for relief in the absence of belief in a putative non-existent liability. We argued above that the reason we give relief in mistake cases is because the payer is not acting in accordance with his rationally determined norms. In chapter two, however, we saw a further limit on the type of mistake that can count. The mistake must be tied to the alleged performance. If it is not, liability would be indefensibly wide and take in purely incidental enrichment, as illustrated by *Lowick Rose v Swynson Ltd*.[33]

In *Nurdin and Peacock Plc v DB Ramsden and Co Ltd*, the claimant was the assignee of a lease granted by the defendant in 1990 for 25 years.[34] The initial annual rent was set at X. In the fourth and fifth years of the lease the rent rose to X+Y. Although there was provision for an upwards only rent review at the end of the fifth year, that never took place. The rent ought to have fallen back to X. The claimants, however, carried on paying at the rate X+Y. They discovered their mistake and informed the landlord that they would be deducting overpayments from future rent. However, their solicitors advised them to carry on paying at the higher rate until the matter was settled in court, claiming the overpayments could then be recovered. Nurdin and Peacock claimed repayment on the basis that they believed mistakenly that the overpayments were recoverable when they were not. They knew the payments – or some of them at least – were not due. There is a paradox of sorts; if relief was allowed there was no mistake and therefore no relief. Neuberger J chose to cut the knot in favour of relief. *Nurdin & Peacock* accepts that the causal mistake test applies to mistaken payments in the absence of mistaken belief in liability to pay. However, it also foreshadows the suggested limit above that not every causal mistake counts with references to whether the mistake was 'directly connected to the overpayment or … to the relationship between payer and payee'.[35] Strictly *Nurdin & Peacock* is not a *causa solvendi* case because the payments were not made to discharge a debt, but nor were they made to make a gift.

The narrower requirement of liability mistake in the *condictio indebiti* in the mixed systems means that any liability for cases like *Nurdin & Peacock* must be placed elsewhere. Grouping all these mistaken payment cases together seems

[31] *Colonial Bank v Exchange Bank* (1886) 11 App Cas 84 (PC); *Kleinwort Sons & Co v Dunlop Rubber Co* (1907) 97 LT 263 (HL); *RE Jones Ltd v Waring and Gillow Ltd* [1926] AC 670 (HL) and *Kerrison v Glyn, Mills Currie & Co* (1912) 81 LJKB 465 (HL); see *Goff & Jones* (n 11) para 9.63 and cases cited.

[32] E Bant, 'Causation and Scope of Liability in Unjust Enrichment' [2009] *Restitution Law Review* 60.

[33] *Lowick Rose LLP v Swynson Ltd* [2017] UKSC 32.

[34] *Nurdin and Peacock Plc v DB Ramsden and Co Ltd* [1999] 1 WLR 1249.

[35] ibid 1272; for contemporary criticism, see G Jones, 'Lord Goff's Contribution to the Law of Restitution' in WJ Swadling and G Jones (eds), *The Search for Principle* (Oxford, OUP, 1999) 224–25.

preferable and there are cases where mixed systems inappropriately divide recovery of seemingly similar mistake cases between the different *condictiones*. We see this in mistaken payments by banks where the bank (B) pays the recipient (R) purportedly on behalf of the customer (P). If there was no underlying debt, P has the *condictio indebiti* against R on proof that P made a mistake as to liability to pay. If the payment or cheque is countermanded by P but B renders it in any case, there is no performance between P and R, but none between B and P either. In England, the bank recovers against R, but in South Africa if the underlying debt was valid, the inadvertent payment will discharge the debt (in the absence of R's knowledge of the countermand) and no action lies against R.[36] It is only if there was no underlying debt that there is an action, but it seems that in South Africa B recovers from R under the *condictio sine causa specialis*.[37] The explanation for the use of the *condictio sine causa specialis* is that while B makes a liability mistake (of sorts) it is not the same type of liability mistake as P makes in paying R believing he is discharging a liability of P to R. Rather in paying R, B thinks that it is discharging its (B's) liability to P (not B's liability to R). It is only if B pays in its own right that the *condictio indebiti* lies.[38] This makes an important difference in that mistake need not be proven for the *condictio sine causa* but must be proven for the *condictio indebiti*. Indeed, it must be proven that the error was excusable. The difference in treatment seems indefensible. Yet many civilian lawyers will argue the English approach allows for success by undeserving claimants.[39] Imagine a party who is in doubt as to whether the money is owing or not (so is not mistaken as to liability) but pays believing that there will be beneficial tax consequences. The tax consequences are in fact adverse. The logic of a pure causation test is that recovery should lie. Whether the mistake is insufficiently tied to the alleged performance – the *Lowick Rose* and *Nurdin & Peacock* limitation – to preclude this result has not yet been, but will need to be carefully worked out. Some guidance may, however, be had from the gift cases, discussed below.

ii. Deutsche Morgan Grenfell v IRC

Deutsche Morgan Grenfell v IRC provides a possible exception to the rule that the enrichment must not have been owed.[40] The taxpayer was caught out by a rule of English corporation tax that, under EU law, unlawfully discriminated between UK-based and EU-based companies. Had DMG been based in the UK, it would

[36] *B&H Engineering v First National Bank of South Africa* 1995 (2) SA 279; *Natal Bank v Roorda* 1903 TH 298; this is the opposite of English law in *Barclays Bank v WJ Simms, Son & Cooke (Southern) Ltd* [1980] QB 677.

[37] *B&H Engineering v First National Bank of South Africa* 1995 (2) SA 279; *Govender v Standard Bank of South Africa Ltd* 1984 (4) SA 392.

[38] *Firstrand Bank Ltd v Absa Bank Ltd* 2001 (1) SA 803.

[39] S Meier, 'Restitution of Undue Transfers in the Civil Law and the Common Law' (2017) 27 *New Zealand Universities Law Review* 528, 539.

[40] *Deutsche Morgan Grenfell v IRC* [2006] UKHL 49, [2007] 1 AC 558.

have been able to elect to defer the payment of advance corporation tax (ACT) by making a group income election, but the bank believed that it was not allowed to do so. After the decision in *Hoechst v IRC*,[41] that this failure to allow deferral was contrary to EU law, the bank sought relief. The House of Lords found that the bank had made a mistake in believing that no election could be made. Without that finding, time would have run out for the claim. One problem was that since no income election had in fact been made, the tax was actually due.[42] This meant that no *Woolwich* claim could lie and explains why the principal was not recoverable. It explains why Lord Scott argued the claimant should only recover if the ACT were unlawful;[43] in his view it was not, which in turn led to the argument that the claim should be one for compensation for breach of EU law. The bank in fact recovered compound interest for HMRC's use of the money. This is only possible by relying on the mistake to argue that the disallowance of an income election created an effective interest free loan. Repayment of that was then justified on the grounds that DMG would undoubtedly have successfully challenged the rule and then exercised the consequent right to delay payment. Lord Scott rejected this characterisation[44] but it lies, for example, behind Lord Walker's comment, 'DMG paid the ACT because it mistakenly thought it had to'.[45] The majority and minority both regarded the absence of any liability as an element of the claim. The majority then attempted to show the absence of liability on the facts. The case as regards limitation has been overruled,[46] and Stevens describes it – correctly – as clearly wrong.[47] The tax was due. The objection to recovery in restitution is not met by saying that the taxpayer would have used the machinery to avoid liability if they knew the rule that they could not do so was disapplied under EU law. They did not use the machinery. The tax was due and the fact that the claimant's intention to pay might be vitiated is not to the point.

C. Mistaken Performance Claims: Gifts and Deeds

There are two ways in which a gift could be made. I could make it via a formal deed under seal, which I will describe as a voluntary instrument, or more commonly, I could make an informal gift by simply handing the donee the money.

[41] *Hoechst v IRC* [2001] ECR I-1727, [2001] Ch 620.

[42] R Stevens, 'Justified Enrichment' (2005) 5 *Oxford University Commonwealth Law Journal* 145; R Chambers 'Deutsche Morgan Grenfell v IRC' (2006) 6 *Oxford University Commonwealth Law Journal* 227; D Sheehan, 'Mistaken Overpayments of Tax' in S Elliott et al (eds), *Restitution of Overpaid Tax* (Oxford, Hart Publishing, 2013) 58–60; contrast R Williams, *Unjust Enrichment and Public Law* (Oxford, Hart Publishing, 2010) 80–82.

[43] *Deutsche Morgan Grenfell v IRC* [2006] UKHL 49, [2007] 1 AC 558, 589–93.

[44] ibid 592.

[45] ibid 609 (Lord Walker).

[46] *By Test Claimants in the FII Litigation v HMRC* [2020] UKSC 47.

[47] R Stevens, 'The Unjust Enrichment Disaster' (2018) 134 *LQR* 574, 593–95.

A deed may therefore be a performance *causa donandi*, but it need not be. It could be *causa solvendi* as where land is transferred in, for instance, purported conveyance to the incorrect legatee under a will. The rescission of a deed gives rise to a proprietary claim. The claimant is either able to take back title to the asset or he is not.[48] We do not value the asset, and if we did it would not matter if we thought it valueless.[49] It will suffice for our purposes that where the claimant is able to rescind the deed he has a power *in rem* to revest title to the asset.[50] In the informal gift cases, I simply seek to recover the value paid over without seeking to revest title. There is an intentional execution of the deed even if the intention with which it was done was defective. Equally, there is in the more informal cases an intentional payment. In each case, therefore, the intentional act counts as performance, although the law characterises what is performed – and therefore what is reversible – differently. In proprietary cases it is the defective transfer of a right; in personal claims the defective transfer of (a thing of) value.[51] Lodder puts it that, if the defendant is enriched by the receipt of rights, a proprietary claim is appropriate if the law allows for that claim.[52] That formulation seems unhelpful, but he goes on to say that a proprietary claim may be available when it is the right itself that is unjustly acquired by the defendant.

In *Pitt v Holt*[53] the Supreme Court reviewed the case law.[54] There were two conjoined appeals. Both involved discretionary trusts. In the first case the claimant's husband suffered brain injuries and needed significant care. Damages were paid to the claimant in respect of the incident causing the injury and settled on trust. However, inheritance tax liability arose as a result of the failure to comply with section 89 of the Inheritance Act 1984. The Supreme Court allowed the appeal on the grounds of an equitable jurisdiction to set aside a voluntary disposition for mistake. Lord Walker (giving judgment for the whole court) invoked a seriousness criterion with the express aim of protecting the donee against too ready availability of restitution. He concluded that the donor must make a mistake as to the legal character of the transaction or a matter of law 'basic to the transaction'.[55] This is the same type of requirement as that discussed earlier in the context of

[48] R Chambers, 'Two Kinds of Enrichment' in R Chambers, C Mitchell and J Penner (eds), *The Philosophical Foundations of the Law of Unjust Enrichment* (Oxford, OUP, 2009) 243.

[49] *Blacklocks v JB Developments (Godalming) Ltd* [1982] Ch 183.

[50] D Sheehan, *The Principles of Personal Property Law*, 2nd edn (Oxford, Hart Publishing, 2017) 179–81.

[51] D Sheehan, '"At the Expense of": Linking Claimant and Defendant in the Law of Unjust Enrichment' (2020) 20 *Oxford University Commonwealth Law Journal* 235, 244–46.

[52] A Lodder, *Enrichment in the Law of Unjust Enrichment and Restitution* (Oxford, Hart Publishing, 2012) 218.

[53] *Pitt v Holt* [2013] UKSC 26, [2013] 2 AC 108.

[54] See, eg, *Gibbon v Mitchell* [1990] 1 WLR 1304; *Lady Hood of Avalon v Mackinnon* [1909] 1 Ch 476; *Ogilvie v Littleboy* (1897) 13 TLR 399.

[55] [2013] UKSC 26, [2013] 2 AC 108, [122] (Lord Walker); *Kennedy v Kennedy* [2014] EWHC 4129, [36] (Etherton C); *Proudman v Freedman* [2015] EWHC 1457; *Co-operative Bank plc v Hayes Freehold Ltd* [2017] EWHC 1820, [130–141] (Henry Carr J).

Nurdin & Peacock v DB Ramsden & Co that my mistake be related in some way to the transaction I am purporting to engage in. What is needed is a mistake 'as to the effect of the transaction and not merely … advantages to be gained by entering into it'.[56] Lord Walker also referred in *Pitt v Holt* to the mistake's 'degree of centrality to the transaction in question and the seriousness of its consequences' and the need to 'make an evaluative judgment whether it would be unconscionable or unjust to leave the mistake uncorrected'.[57]

Even though gifts are unilateral, the institution of gift giving deserves respect and allowing all causative mistakes to count might undermine the institution and there is little sign therefore of movement to a causation test alone, despite criticism that the *Pitt* test is vague.[58] In *Morgan v Ashcroft*,[59] Scott LJ applied the 'fundamental' test to restitution of mistaken gifts. The context was special in that it was restitution of a money mistakenly paid by a bookmaker to settle gambling debts (at a time when these were legally gifts). In *Pagel v Forman*[60] it was assumed that a mistaken informal gift attracted the *Pitt v Holt* test, and the distinction is also referred to in *Deutsche Morgan Grenfell v IRC*.[61] It is also referred to in the case of *Re Magarey Farlam Lawyers Trust Account (No 3)* where partners in the law firm reimbursed eight clients for losses sustained as a result of an employee's fraud.[62] They expected no further defalcations to appear, although more did. The partners were unable to recover in mistake. The payments were voluntary, made under what they thought was a moral obligation, but also with an eye to the clients' not taking legal action. The moral obligation the judge referred to would have to be one about the existence of which the firm's partners were mistaken for relief to apply.[63] Debelle J points, however, to several scenarios where mistaken gifts can be recovered,[64] including the possibility of a serious mistake, but suggested there were multiple reasons for non-recovery on the facts.

In *Moses v Moses*[65] two questions came up. The first was whether a personal unjust enrichment claim should lie if rescission of a deed was not possible. The second was whether the *Pitt v Holt* test is a test for gifts or for rescission. Jude Moses had transferred land to Selwyn Moses, wrongly believing that he was entitled to it under a will. Selwyn sold the land on for $300,000. The majority led by Lord Sales allowed a personal unjust enrichment claim despite rescission being barred. The deed had transferred title to Selwyn, and he was enriched as a result.

[56] *Gibbon v Mitchell* [1990] 1 WLR 1304, 1309 (Millett J).

[57] [2013] UKSC 26, [2013] 2 AC 108, [128].

[58] Tang Hang Wu, 'Restitution for Mistaken Gifts' (2004) 20 *Journal of Contract Law* 1; *Goff & Jones* (n 11) para 9.145.

[59] *Morgan v Ashcroft* [1938] 1 KB 49; see *Goff & Jones* (n 11) para 9.154.

[60] *Pagel v Forman* [2013] EWHC 2210 (Comm).

[61] [2006] UKHL 49 [2007] 1 AC 558, [87].

[62] *Re Magarey Farlam Lawyers Trust Account (No 3)* [2007] SASC 9, (2007) 96 SASR 337.

[63] As in *Larner v London County Council* [1949] 2 KB 683 (CA).

[64] [2007] SASC 9, (2007) 96 SASR 337, [170]–[183].

[65] *Moses v Moses* [2022] UKPC 42; J English, 'Deeds, Rescission and Restitution' (2023) 139 *LQR* 363.

This seems right. We do not need in other circumstances to rescind title to assets transferred because of a liability mistake to recover in unjust enrichment. They are different causes of action. However, the mistake had been one as to whether Jude was obliged to transfer the land. What if it were a gift? The Privy Council seems to have thought that *Pitt v Holt* was a test as to rescission only and not to gifts more generally, but if gift is, as suggested above, an institution worth respecting then despite characterisation of the performance being different the claim-norm justifying relief is the same – that my mistake was as to a matter basic to the transaction. Even if different causes of action, the test for relief should be the same to avoid one claim undercutting the other.

D. Mistaken Performance Claims: Services and Chattels

The restitution of services is often seen as requiring a different justification from that of money. Jaffey, as we saw in chapter three, discusses the distinction between a property principle, explaining restitution of money (or chattels) and an imputed contracts principle, explaining restitution in services cases. Traditionally as well the South African *condictiones* have presupposed that there has been a transfer of ownership – *a datio*. The *condictio* claim therefore includes both a claim for repayment of money and restitution of chattels. It does not – traditionally – include services. If services are, however, to be treated more like money cases, as Visser suggests they should, work will be needed on the scope of relief. Some South African law cases show how this might be possible, treating the recovery of the value of services in the same way as a transfer of property under a *condictio indebiti*.[66]

This is right in principle. If I provide services to you that are not owing, because the contract is void that ought to be treated in the same way as if I pay you money under a void contract. In each case we might most commonly say I made a mistake as to liability. In such cases I have putatively rendered a performance, the only difference being that it was services not payment or transfer of a chattel. These cases can be treated as being the same cause of action as mistaken payments. It is true that in most such cases of void contracts the defendant will have freely accepted or otherwise requested the services. In turn this means that such actions where services are provided are most often pleaded as failure of basis cases. *Rover International v Cannon Film Sales Ltd* is an example.[67] The contract was void because it was entered into prior to the incorporation of one of the parties. EMI would provide films for dubbing and distribution in Italy and the gross receipts would be split in an agreed proportion and advances would be paid for EMI.

[66] See, eg, *Frame v Palmer* 1950 (3) SA 340; on the need for *a datio*, see D Visser, *Unjustified Enrichment* (Durban, Juta, 2008) 222–23, although this is not so of the *condictio furtiva* or all the guises of the *condictio sine causa specialis*.

[67] *Rover International v Cannon Film Sales Ltd* [1989] 1 WLR 912.

The advances were paid before the mistake that Rover – the incorporation of which was necessary to deal with Italian tax law – had not been incorporated until after the contract was formed was discovered. Those mistaken payments were recoverable and a quantum meruit was awarded with respect to the work done.[68] There is little benefit to pleading a mistake claim in these cases, except to take advantage of section 32(1)(c) of the Limitation Act 1980 which allows for the extension of time where the claimant could not previously reasonably have discovered the error.

i. Services

It is typical when examining services cases to insist on an objectively apparent choice by the defendant to accept them on a particular given basis. Such cases – like *Rover International* – are typically treated as failure of basis rather than mistake. We return to these in chapter five. As might be guessed, cases where such a choice is legally unnecessary for the defendant to be liable are uncommon. They are uncommon because to render an innocent (non-wrongdoing) defendant liable for an enrichment he would not have chosen and may not want is to infringe his autonomy and his freedom of choice. The services must be proven to be incontrovertibly enriching – ie, no one could reasonably deny they were enriched. Just as in civil law jurisdictions, the easiest way to show this is that the services were necessary.

An example is *Craven-Ellis v Canons Ltd*.[69] In that case the claimant was appointed managing director of the company but failed to acquire his qualifying quantity of shares in the company. The contract of employment was therefore void, but the claimant recovered under a quantum meruit. The case has been controversial as potentially undermining the invalidating rule; however, the plaintiff undertook work under a mistake that the contract was valid and did so deliberately. He provided a performance to the defendant. It was important to the result of the case that the services had in fact been accepted[70] and if the claimant had not performed them someone else would have had to do so.[71] This was therefore a case of factually necessary expenditure or work. Another case of mistaken provision of services is *Upton on Severn RDC v Powell*.[72] That case involved the fire brigade attending an out-of-area blaze and then seeking reimbursement. Had it been in-area no charges could have been levied. The appellant whose farm was in the Upton police area, but Pershore fire district, called the Upton police to request the fire brigade and they in turn informed the Upton brigade. Lord Greene

[68] ibid 925–28.
[69] *Craven-Ellis v Canons Ltd* [1936] 2 KB 403.
[70] ibid 409.
[71] ibid 412.
[72] *Upton on Severn RDC v Powell* [1942] 1 All ER 220.

MR held that there was a contract,[73] although, as we saw in chapter three, this is incorrect as nobody initially thought the services were chargeable. Nonetheless, the appellant was unable to say, 'I didn't mean Upton if I had to pay'. The work done to extinguish the fire was factually necessary. The brigade's mistake as to their obligation to act coupled with the fact that no reasonable person could have rejected the services gave rise to a mistaken provision of services claim.[74] Such cases are cases of incontrovertible benefit.[75] Legally necessary expenditure was considered in *Canadian Automatic Data-Processing Services Ltd v Bentley*[76] which involved the question whether the claimant had relieved the defendant of liability to make certain severance payments. The majority said not, McKenzie J giving the reasoned judgment argued that the benefit to Bentley was not incontrovertible because it was not inevitable that he would have been legally obliged to pay. ADP had argued that if it had not paid, Bentley would have been obliged to do so as part of his obligations as a director of the defaulting employer – Syntecor. McKenzie J said that the primary liability was that of the company and the directors' liability was secondary. Corporate officers are not generally liable for corporate debts. Although the Employment Standards Agency had a discretion as to whether to pursue the director, that discretion could not be replicated by unjust enrichment jurisprudence. Consequently, McKenzie J argued the directors might not have been liable[77] and were not in fact enriched.

ii. Chattels

In principle there is little difference between mistaken services cases, mistaken payments and mistaken transfer of chattels. To reiterate, all three can be performance claims. The only question in services and chattels cases is the relative extra difficulty in calculating quantum. The claimant must therefore generally prove that the chattel was requested or accepted by the defendant, allowing either for a failure of basis or mistake claim.

Whether the defendant was incontrovertibly enriched tends to revolve around the chattel's ready returnability or realisability in money. Returnability and incontrovertible enrichment are often run together but are better seen as separate. In *Weatherby v Banham*,[78] Lord Tenterden decided that by retaining periodical

[73] ibid 221, but see *TTMI Sarl v Statoil ASA (The Sibohelle)* [2011] EWHC 1150, [2011] 2 Lloyds Rep 220, [44] (Beatson J); E Peel (ed), *Treitel on the Law of Contract*, 15th edn (London, Sweet & Maxwell, 2020) para 2.049.

[74] PBH Birks, *An Introduction to the Law of Restitution*, rev edn (Oxford, Clarendon Press, 1989) 120.

[75] See also *Peel (Regional Municipality) v Canada* [1992] 3 SCR 762, 795 (McLachlin J); *Re Berkeley (Applegate) (Investment Consultants) Ltd* [1989] Ch 32, 50–51.

[76] *Canadian Automatic Data-Processing Services Ltd v Bentley* 2004 BCCA 408, (2004) 242 DLR (4th) 250.

[77] ibid [65]–[70], [72].

[78] *Weatherby v Banham* (1832) 5 Car & P 227, 172 ER 950.

magazines that could have been returned the defendant had rendered himself liable for the price in an action for goods sold and delivered. In modern law, the way this would be put is in terms of readily returnable items and liability in unjust enrichment;[79] importantly retaining something readily returnable was seen in *Weatherby* as evidence of acceptance of the periodicals. If this is right, there will be few (if any) cases where a claimant will need to rely on incontrovertible benefit. Modern debate has referred to two related cases. In *Harrison v Madejski*, Harrison purchased a car from Madejski.[80] Madejski had not intended to sell a personalised number plate with the vehicle, but Harrison had formed the mistaken view that it was included. The trial judge decided that the car was sold without the registration mark. The Court of Appeal affirmed this but said that Harrison had freely accepted the mark when he procured registration of the car with the DVLA. The Court of Appeal relied on the decision of *Cressman v Coys of Kensington (Sales) Ltd*,[81] which involved almost identical facts. The Court of Appeal said McDonald was incontrovertibly enriched because the licence plate he had received in facts almost identical to Harrison was a readily returnable item. He had chosen not to return this asset, readily realisable in money and had obtained use of it in the meantime. The upshot of *Cressman* is that if a chattel is returnable and readily realisable in money, the benefit is incontrovertible although it would be preferable to say that the failure to return such a chattel was good evidence it had been accepted by the defendant and that the market value (ie, what it would be realised for) is the starting point for determining quantum of enrichment. Questions revolve in academic commentary as to what counts as ready realisability and whether it is normatively justified to charge the defendant for a benefit that he would never have sold. Bant and Edelman have favoured an approach, considering the nature of the benefit and the characteristics of the defendant.[82] Matters are easier where the item has been realised in money already. Here, because the function of money is to value assets and services, the defendant who is now enriched by money is unable to deny the quantum of that enrichment.

A different view is simpler. If the chattel is readily returnable it should be returned and failure to do so is evidence of acceptance. That is the position in Germany, and until the controversial decision of *Kudu Granite Operations (Pty) Ltd v Caterna Ltd*[83] was the position in South Africa.[84] If the thing is not returnable *in specie* its surrogate or value can be recovered.

[79] E Bant and J Edelman, *Unjust Enrichment*, 2nd edn (Oxford, Hart Publishing, 2016) 71.

[80] *Harrison v Madejski* [2014] EWCA Civ 361.

[81] *Cressman v Coys of Kensington (Sales) Ltd* [2004] EWCA Civ 47, [2004] 1 WLR 2775; see also, *Marston Construction Ltd v Kigass* (1989) 46 Building LR 109.

[82] Bant and Edelman (n 79) 73.

[83] *Kudu Granite Operations (Pty) Ltd v Caterna Ltd* 2003 (5) SA 193 (SCA); Visser (n 66) 162–63; J du Plessis, 'Determining the Moment when Enrichment Liability is Quantified: The Curious Case of *Paschke v Frans*' [2016] *Journal of South African Law* 281, 284–85.

[84] *Tellurometer (Pty) Ltd v PDC (Pty) Ltd* 1978 (3) SA 563.

E. Mistaken Non-Performance Claims

These cases are often cases where there has been a mistaken improvement to property, believing it to be your own, or mistaken provision of services believing yourself obliged to provide them for a third party. Generally English law is reluctant to allow such claims except in circumstances of incontrovertible benefit. This makes sense; given the circumstances under which the enrichment is conferred, free acceptance is impossible. We examine two scenarios and how they differ from performance cases before asking if they are all examples of one cause of action – mistaken improvement of another's chattels or land and mistakenly discharging another's obligations.

i. Improvement to Property

An example of mistaken improvements to chattels is *Greenwood v Bennett*.[85] Only one type of mistake will suffice in most cases. That is the mistake that the property was the claimant's – or at least was property he was entitled to work on, perhaps as an agent. In *Greenwood v Bennett* a car was stolen, crashed by the thief and sold to a garage owner (Harper) who in the mistaken belief that he owned the car spent £226 on repairs and £75 on the car itself. He then sold the car for £450 to a finance company. A similar Canadian example involving mistaken improvements to a canoe is *Gidney v Shank*.[86] In interpleader proceedings in *Greenwood*, the buyer (Harper) claimed that the legal owner (Bennett) – whose title was not disputed – should refund at least the amount spent on improving the car. Bennett recovered the car and sold it. The garage owner had made a mistake in believing that the car was his and expended money on the factually necessary repair of someone else's car, leading to an incontrovertible benefit to the car's owner. It should therefore have been a condition of the owner recovering the car that he pay the cost of the repairs (ie, £226). The Court recognised a passive claim of equitable set-off,[87] although Lord Denning put it in language of unjust enrichment.[88] In principle there is no difference between a passive claim and an active claim,[89] and the logic of Lord Denning's dicta extends to active claims although he did not himself express it so widely. Indeed, the car had reached Bennett's hands without an order that he give credit for the improvements. An order was therefore made that £226 be paid by Bennett. Dicta by Lord Denning are unclear, however, in that he refers to the value of the improvements;[90] the repairs had increased the

[85] *Greenwood v Bennett* [1973] QB 195.

[86] *Gidney v Shank* [1995] 5 WWR 385, incorrectly overturned on appeal because the lack of relationship between the parties counted as a juristic reason [1996] 2 WWR 383.

[87] [1973] QB 195 (CA) 202 (Phillimore LJ).

[88] ibid 201.

[89] P Jaffey, *The Nature and Scope of Restitution* (Oxford, Hart Publishing, 2000) 92.

[90] [1973] QB 195 (CA) 202.

actual sale price of the car by £325, but the order was for the lower amount. Some Canadian cases will, however, allow a claim up to the amount of this realised value even if greater than the cost of the work.[91] An important objection in principle to the wide view articulated here is that the true owner of the car never accepted the benefit. There are two answers to this. First, it is difficult to see a meaningful acceptance on the behalf of the car owner. The choice that the car owner has is in effect to give credit for the improvements or give up the asset.[92] That is something of a Hobson's choice and in different circumstances we might call it economic duress or duress of property or chattels. What matters, however, is that the repairs were necessary and therefore there was no reason not to accept them. Related to this, Lord Denning is clear in *Greenwood* that when the purchaser repairs the car and honestly believes the car is his he does not take the risk of not being paid when undertaking such (in fact) unrequested services.[93]

The corresponding case in South Africa is *ABSA Bank v CB Stander* where a car dealer – Motortown – sold a car to Kent.[94] Kent lent it to Bezuidenhout, who crashed it and sent it to Stander to repair. Stander believed Bezuidenhout to be the owner. On realising his error, he tried to get Kent to pay for the repairs, but she refused. Title passed back to ABSA as Kent failed to pay instalments due and the bank claimed the car. Stander counter-claimed. The court said that he had acted mistakenly believing he was managing his own affairs by complying with obligations in terms of his agreement with Bezuidenhout.[95] In cases where a party improves a chattel – bona fide believing himself entitled to do so – and is in possession or occupation of that asset, a claim in property law as a bona fide possessor applies. Generally bona fide possessors are those who believe themselves the owners, and bona fide occupiers believe themselves to have a right to occupy, even though they do not own it.[96]

An alternative claim where a party undertakes to do acts, believing he is acting in his own interests and on his own business when he is not lies in the extended enrichment action of the *negotiorum gestor*. The latter claim is wider than the former in that it does not require the claimant to be improving the defendant's property. Stander had given up possession of the car, which rendered the bona fide possessor claim inapplicable, but recovery was allowed in the extended action. The closeness of the relation can also be seen in the decision of *McCarthy Retail v Shortdistance Carriers CC* which could have been argued and decided

[91] See, eg, *Conrad v Feldbar Constructions Ltd* (2004) 70 OR (3d) 298; *Van den Berg v Giles* [1979] 2 NZLR 111 also awards the increase in value of the property, but as we see – and wrongly, in a performance context.

[92] *Mayne v Kidd* [1951] 2 DLR 652 (SKCA) but see *Mutungih v Bokun* (2006) 40 CCLT (3d) 313 where credit was denied to the improver because he should have been suspicious that he was not acquiring good title. This seems wrong as excusability is not a prerequisite of relief for mistake.

[93] [1973] QB 195 (CA) 202.

[94] *ABSA Bank v CB Stander* 1998 (1) SA 939 (C).

[95] ibid 945.

[96] Visser (n 66) 602.

on either basis.[97] In that decision, the respondent's truck had been damaged and taken to the appellant's garage for repair. The garage was instructed not to repair the vehicle until the insurers agreed, but the truck was in fact repaired in the absence of that agreement. The court said that the appellant was a bona fide occupier who had repaired the truck under the mistaken view that there was agreement by the insurer.[98] The owner was enriched by the repairs and there was nobody other than the garage at whose expense he could have been enriched. The mistake that the asset is the claimant's own, lawfully in his possession, or that he is managing his own affairs with respect to it is explicitly raised.[99] That mistake is critical in England. It also seems critical in Scotland where the relevant case is *Newton v Newton*,[100] which is expressed in terms of mistake.

The line between these cases and the *condictio indebiti* can be fraught,[101] but it is an important one as the quantum of recovery may be different and indeed one good reason for accepting the split as part of English law is that it enables clarification as to when relief is based on the value of the services as opposed to the increase in sale value of the asset. Both are measures of real enrichment. In the non-performance claim, subject to the condition that the benefit be either realised or readily realisable[102] (and realisability may be difficult) the common law remains unclear as to whether the increased market value is recoverable. South Africa does clearly allow the increased market value of assets to be claimed after tangible improvements have been made.[103] South African law has adopted the Roman classification of necessary, useful and luxurious expenditures. Necessary expenditure preserves the property from destruction or deterioration. Useful expenditures raise the market value of the property.[104] The bona fide possessor can only recover useful expenditure up to the increased value of the asset, or the amount of his expenses – whichever is lower.[105] This is consistent with *Greenwood*, but also suggests that if the expenditure had been £325 and the raised sale price £226 (ie, the figures were reversed) recovery should still be limited to the lower value. In a performance claim, however, the value of the performance (ie, the market value of

[97] *McCarthy Retail v Shortdistance Carriers CC* 2001 (3) SA 482.
[98] ibid 491.
[99] A slightly different case epitomised by *ABSA Bank v CB Stander* 1998 (1) SA 939 (C).
[100] *Newton v Newton* 1925 SC(HL) 925; see *Shilliday v Smith* 1998 SC 725; and R Evans-Jones, 'Seeking Imposed Enrichment in Improvements: Classification and General Enrichment Actions in Mixed Systems – Scotland and South Africa' [2008] *Restitution Law Review* 18, 33.
[101] R Evans-Jones and M Fischer, 'Unjustified Enrichment's Evolution in Mixed Legal Systems: Confronting McCarthy Retail Ltd' [2019] *Acta Juridica* 395, 411–12, arguing it should be a *condictio indebiti*; *Newton v Newton* 1925 SC(HL) 25 might be seen as a *condictio causa data causa non secuta*. See R Evans-Jones, 'The Distorting Images of *Newton v Newton* and its Lessons for the Law of Property and Unjustified Enrichment in Scotland' [2005] *Edinburgh Law Review* 449.
[102] *McDonald v Coy's of Kensington* [2004] EWCA Civ 47, [2005] 1 WLR 2775, [35]–[40].
[103] Visser (n 66) 602–05; *Nortje v Pool NO* 1966 (3) SA 96; *Fletcher & Fletcher v Bulawayo Waterworks Ltd* 1915 AD 636.
[104] *United Building Society v Smookler's Trustee* 1906 TS 623.
[105] Visser (n 66) 604.

the services rendered) should be prima facie recoverable. Here that would be the higher figure of £325.

English law's consideration of mistake has advantages in this context.[106] In chapter three we saw that in England mistake, understood as a factor demonstrating a relevant flaw in my decision-making impacting on the exercise of my autonomy, justifies both performance and some non-performance claims. The fact of the mistake means that the garage owner's decision-making process was flawed, which is the key point in justifying a mistake claim, but also explains why it was impossible for him to engage in any sort of bargaining with the car's actual owner. To see mistake purely as a heuristic as Stevens does,[107] showing that no gift was intended, risks illegitimately merging improvement and performance claims. McInnes extends 'absence of juristic reason' to the non-performance cases for precisely this reason (there is no valid gift etc).[108] Stevens avoids this problem because he does not accept a free-standing claim in cases like *Greenwood*,[109] but as seen above this is not justified.

South African law rests its law on improvements on a different historical source from the *condictio* claims. Unlike in the *condictio indebiti*, where mistake is required, although its precise role is disputed,[110] no mistake is needed in the improver cases. Relief can be had even if – in some cases – the plaintiff knew that the property was not his and that he had no authority to deal with the asset. *Negotiorum gestio* may apply and the mala fide improver is able to recover in unjust enrichment in South Africa.[111] If the mala fide improver is awarded a remedy, awarding the bona fide improver a remedy must a fortiori be appropriate, although the opposite is plainly not the case. It is also worth pointing out that although a party mistaken as to his own existing title is bona fide, that is not the only way to prove bona fides. These are all reasons to think that the mistake is not the governing feature in South Africa. Mistake in English law cannot account for the mala fide improver's claim, but relief does not appear to be available in English law in these cases as the improver is likely acting 'officiously'[112] or 'voluntarily' for his

[106] D Sheehan, 'Unjust Factors or Restitution of Transfers Sine Causa' [2008] *Oxford University Comparative Law Forum* 1.

[107] Stevens, *The Laws of Restitution* (n 21) 72; Stevens has other roles for mistake as well which are not relevant to our point here.

[108] M McInnes, 'Revising the Reason for Restitution: Garland Ten Years After' (2015) 57 *Canadian Business Law Journal* 1, 14–15.

[109] Stevens, *The Laws of Restitution* (n 21) 264–65.

[110] J du Plessis, 'Labels and Meaning: Unjust Factors and Failure of Purpose as Reasons for Reversing Enrichment by Transfer' [2014] *Edinburgh Law Review* 416, 429–30; for a recent view of the role of error in the *condictio indebiti* like Stevens', see H Scott, 'Undue Transfer under Error (the *Condictio Indebiti*)' [2022] *Edinburgh Law Review* 403.

[111] J du Plessis, 'The Enrichment Claim of the *Mala Fide* Improver of Another's Property' in A Burrows, D Johnston and R Zimmermann (eds), *Judge and Jurist: Essays in Memory of Lord Rodger* (Oxford, OUP, 2013).

[112] *Falcke v Scottish Imperial Insurance* (1886) 34 Ch D 234; *Re Cleadon Trust Ltd* [1939] Ch 286; *Leigh v Dickeson* (1884) 15 QBD 60.

own benefit. Arguments might equally be made that South African law goes too far in providing the mala fide improver relief.[113] Whether that is right or not, local priority between performance and improvement cases must be justified by other similarities in South Africa. However, the distinction between England where the mistake directly grounds relief,[114] and South Africa where links are made with other areas of law, illustrates the historical contingency of how family resemblances work, and how classifications must be made. Given that a judge in a case-based system will have an eye to fit and justification this is unsurprising. The right answer need not be the same in both jurisdictions.

Land cases are sometimes treated differently from chattel cases in the common law. One difference is that improvements to land are not readily returnable. Realisability, therefore, takes centre stage. An important fear of commentators has been the prospect that the defendant be forced to sell the land to make good the claim. Tang is a good example of such a commentator.[115] For him, a forced sale of land (or a unique chattel) represents a severe disruption to the affairs of the defendant and should be avoided. McInnes describes the prospect of such sale as 'not an attractive prospect'.[116] There are suggestions that a mistaken improver of land not be able to take advantage of the principle of incontrovertible benefit therefore,[117] unless the land has already been sold at a profit.[118] A forced sale can also be avoided by the imposition of a charge over the land, enabling recovery when the defendant chooses to sell, which of course raises the question of what happens if he never chooses to sell.[119] The difficulty here, as in chattels, is ready realisability. Should the law say that a readily realisable benefit is incontrovertible in the context of land? Or should it require actual realisation? In an unjust enrichment context, is that sufficient protection for the defendant or should another requirement such as unconscionable behaviour be needed?

Two Canadian examples are instructive. In *Republic Resources Ltd v Ballen*, the plaintiff had mistakenly drilled a well for gas after the end of his lease and claimed that it had saved the defendant necessary expense or alternatively that the defendant could realise a financial gain by putting the well into production.[120] This was denied because it was impossible to see when such production might occur, and the drilling had saved no necessary expense. Contrast *Olchowy v McKay*,

[113] Scotland bars relief to the mala fide improver. See *Barbour v Halliday* (1840) 2 D 1279.

[114] J du Plessis, 'Towards a Rational Structure of Liability for Unjustified Enrichment' (2005) 122 *South African Law Journal* 142, 164.

[115] Tang Hang Wu, 'An Unjust Enrichment Claim for the Mistaken Improver of Land' [2011] *Conv* 8, 28–29.

[116] M McInnes, 'Improvements to Land, Equity, Proprietary Estoppel and Unjust Enrichment' (2016) 2 *Canadian Journal of Comparative & Contemporary Law* 421, 434.

[117] *Redland City Council v Kozic* [2022] QCA 158, [62] (McMurdo JA); *Roy v Lagona* [2010] VSC 250, [294] (Hansen J); *JS Bloor Ltd v Pavillion Developments Ltd* [2008] EWHC 724 (TCC); for criticism, see H Cooney, 'Restitution for Unrequested Improvements to Land' (2023) 139 *LQR* 179.

[118] *Conrad v Feldbar Constructions Ltd* (2004) 70 OR (3d) 298; *Sanderson v Campsall* 2000 BCSC 583.

[119] Tang, 'An Unjust Enrichment Claim for the Mistaken Improver of Land' (n 115) 28.

[120] *Republic Resources Ltd v Ballen* [1982] 1 WWR 692.

where recovery was denied, but for different reasons.[121] The claimant believing the land to be his had planted canola. The defendant, being completely aware of this acquired the land and harvested the canola taking the entire profit. He protested that he would have seeded alfalfa and was not enriched; the court accepted in principle the importance of the principle of subjective devaluation – if the improvement is made without the knowledge of the owner and is of no subjective benefit to him because he would have done something else he should not have to pay. The court said, however, that the receipt of an asset which has been realised in money or is readily realisable would be an incontrovertible benefit. The defendant was on this basis enriched. One might think that liability would be imposed therefore, but it was not. The defendant had not requested the benefit, there was no special relationship[122] between the parties, and the defendant was not subject to proprietary estoppel as he had not owned the land at the time of planting. While *Ballen* seems right, *Olchowy* seems wrong, particularly when it is remembered that the defendant knew exactly what the claimant was doing and cynically sat silent. Judicial attitudes have shifted in Canada over the last 20 years, however, away from *Olchowy*-style requirements of unconscionability and prior special relationships to a straightforward application of unjust enrichment criteria.[123] On enrichment, although for many years case law was sparse, Canadian law seems now to accept ready realisability as sufficient and allow the increase in the value of the land (and presumably chattels) to be recovered even if higher than the value of the expenses incurred.[124] This is a different and more generous rule than that in South Africa to the effect that relief should be limited to the value of the expenses if lower than the increased asset value and its appropriateness in policy terms will need to be decided. This will be difficult,[125] and many will argue the balance has been struck wrongly in Canada.

Resistance elsewhere in the common law world to such claims is quite fierce. *Blue Haven v Tully* is a non-Canadian example.[126] Tully contracted to sell the estate to Robinson who wanted to develop it into a coffee plantation, but a dispute broke out because the contract was for 130 acres, but the estate was in fact only about 95 acres. Tully then agreed to sell to Blue Haven, but ultimately Robinson obtained possession. The Privy Council held that Robinson was enriched at Blue Haven's expense. The latter had developed the estate as a coffee plantation and Robinson did not bear the cost of that.[127] The Privy Council accepted enrichment but denied relief. They appear to have believed the principles in unjust enrichment and

[121] *Olchowy v McKay* [1996] 1 WWR 36.

[122] M McInnes, *The Canadian Law of Unjust Enrichment and Restitution*, 2nd edn (Ottawa, Lexis, 2022) 463.

[123] ibid 448.

[124] *Love v Schumacher Estate* [2014] ONSC 4080; *Servello v Servello* [2014] ONSC 5035.

[125] See also McInnes, *The Canadian Law of Unjust Enrichment and Restitution* (n 122) 456–457; *Sherbeth v Sherbeth* [2007] MBQB 50.

[126] *Blue Haven v Tully* [2006] UKPC 17.

[127] ibid [20].

proprietary estoppel are essentially the same.[128] Robinson had not done anything to encourage Blue Haven to continue developing the plantation, was not guilty of unconscionable behaviour, and so could resist the claim;[129] however, the improvements to the land were necessary, enriching on that basis and the claimants were mistaken as to their title. The principles of proprietary estoppel and unjust enrichment are not the same and restitution should have been available. Contrast *Van den Berg v Giles* from New Zealand.[130] The defendant leased out a weekend house to the plaintiff who believed there was agreement to sell the house to him. He then proceeded to undertake renovations and improvements to the house, while the defendant failed to disabuse him of the notion that he was going to buy the house from her. The decision that the plaintiff should succeed in the unjust enrichment action was put as one of free acceptance but was in fact failure of basis. The difference lies in the way the parties' behaviour is considered. This insistence on unconscionability is an example of a contextual concern, relating to the importance of the asset in question modifying the principles otherwise applicable. It is probably wrong and unnecessary. Given the possibility of change of position and the need for the improvement work/services to be necessary, the requirement arguably over-protects defendants.

ii. Discharge of Another's Obligation

Mistaken discharge of another's obligations was the second category of case raised at the start of this section. Two scenarios can be distinguished. The first is the mistaken payment of another's debt. There are cases in German and South African law where payment of another's debt is unjustified enrichment. This is *Rückgriffskondiktion* in Germany[131] or the extended *negotiorum gestio* action in South Africa. Historically in the extended *negotiorum gestio* action of Roman-Dutch law, Voet suggested that even where the person (A) administering the other's (B's) affairs had no intention to benefit the latter but only himself, he had a claim up to the value of B's enrichment.[132] In South Africa it is possible to discharge another's debt without their consent if there are no vital reasons why the debtor must discharge it himself. In *Odendaal v Van Oudtshoorn*, the plaintiff bought a restaurant from the defendant, but the suppliers insisted on the latter's

[128] ibid [21].

[129] See Bant and Edelman (n 79) 182–83, arguing that unjust enrichment should lie; Tang, 'An Unjust Enrichment Claim for the Mistaken Improver of Land' (n 115) 26.

[130] [1979] 2 NZLR 111; *Cobbe v Yeoman's Row Management Ltd* [2008] UKHL 55, [2008] 1 WLR 1752 also involved a failure of consideration, revolving around failure to pay for work in obtaining planning permission [42]–[44] (Lord Scott); S Scott, 'Mistaken Improvers and a Recognisable Law of Unjust Enrichment' in C Rickett and R Grantham (eds), *Structure and Justification in Private Law: Essays for Peter Birks* (Oxford, Hart Publishing, 2008) 251–52, 261.

[131] G Dannemann, *The German Law of Unjustified Enrichment and Restitution: A Comparative Introduction* (Oxford, OUP, 2009) 118–19.

[132] *Commentarias ad Pandectas* 3.5.5, discussed by Visser (n 66) 569–70.

debts being cleared before resuming supplies.[133] The plaintiff paid and recovered from the defendant. The case requires that the right to recoup is not unlimited and raises the question whether the payer acted reasonably. Likewise in Scotland the rule is that – with safeguards – a stranger may discharge another's debt.[134] It may even be possible to discharge the debt against the debtor's expressed wishes.[135] In *Odendaal* itself there was no mistake, there was only a calculated decision on the part of the plaintiff to pay the defendant's debt to obtain a benefit for himself. English law, were it to accept that a third-party intervener can discharge another's debt, would need to separate claims where the payer is mistaken from claims where the payer pays for some other reason – and decide separately if it wants to accept the latter. This in fact provides another example of the impact of historical contingency. It is easier to extend *negotiorum gestio* to the *Odendaal* scenario than to extend English law, based as it is on mistake. Care will have to be taken with any extension. On its face, allowing relief outside the mistake context could protect an opportunistic or busybody claimant.

In England, however, despite criticism of the rule,[136] it is not generally possible to discharge another's debt without their consent. This means the debtor is not enriched (because he still owes the money) and so no claim against him lies. The claim is against the payee who is enriched by the receipt of the money. Whether a bank paying a customer's debt can recover from the customer or the payee is therefore generally determined by to whom the bank was performing, and this in turn is decided by whether the instruction to pay was valid or invalid. If invalid, the debt is not discharged because it is not generally possible for an unconnected third-party to discharge another's debt. If the intervener pays the debt voluntarily – ie, without any mistake or other legal liability to pay – it is not discharged.[137] The courts have given inconsistent answers to whether an unauthorised intervener can discharge a debt via a mistaken payment. In *Crantrave Ltd v Lloyds Bank*,[138] the Court of Appeal, however, said the payment would not of itself discharge the liability and this seems decisive.

The common law does accept liability in some cases of discharge of another's liability. A payment to a creditor which fails to discharge a debt can simply be reversed as against the creditor. Where the obligation is to provide services, however, that cannot be reversed *in specie*. The services can only be paid for. Take the decision of *County of Carleton v City of Ottawa*[139] which would be a case of

[133] *Odendaal v Van Oudtshoorn* 1968 (3) SA 433.

[134] *Caledonia North Sea Ltd v London Bridge Engineering Ltd* 2000 SLT 1123.

[135] *Standard Bank Financial Services Ltd v Taylam (Property) Ltd* 1979 (2) SA 383; *Bankton's Institutes* I.24.2.

[136] AS Burrows, *The Law of Restitution*, 3rd edn (Oxford, OUP, 2011) 464; C Mitchell and S Watterson (eds), *Subrogation: Law and Practice* (Oxford, OUP, 2007) para 2.05.

[137] *Electricity Supply Nominees Ltd v Thorn EMI Retail Ltd* (1991) 63 P&CR 143.

[138] *Crantrave Ltd v Lloyds Bank* [2000] EWCA Civ 127, [2000] QB 917; *Croxen v Gas and Electricity Markets Authority* [2022] EWHC 2826 (Ch), [214]–[219] (Zacaroli J).

[139] *County of Carleton v City of Ottawa* (1966) 52 DLR (2d) 220.

the extended action in *negotiorum gestio* in South Africa. The case involved the county making financial outlays believing that in doing so it was meeting its statutory obligations and therefore acting in its own interests. The local authority boundary lines were moved, but the county continued to provide financial and other support to Norah Baker, paying for her to stay in a care home. Neither authority appreciated that the boundary changes meant that the city should have taken on such responsibility and the latter was ultimately ordered to pay the county's expenses. The county paid expenses that the city was legally obliged to meet. The mistake the county made was as to its legal obligations to the individual in question – not to the City of Ottawa. It was not a performance claim as the county had no intention of performing services for the city's benefit; the nature of its error precluded that. Nonetheless, the city obtained a benefit through the discharge of its liability to Baker.

iii. Conclusion

Are these examples of the same cause of action? South African law has a different logic here, so we cannot simply say that because all these cases fall into the extended *negotiorum gestio* action that they are the same cause of action in English law as well. The mistaken discharge of liability cases might be subsumed to the common liability cases discussed in chapter six on the basis that they turn on the principle that that principal debtor should pay. However, there is one important difference. In the common liability cases, change of position should not be available; however, had the City of Ottawa spent money it would have spent on Norah Baker elsewhere the defence should have been (in principle) available.[140] The application of different defences is evidence that different causes of action are in play. In both mistaken discharge and improvement cases the mistake is that the actions are on the claimant's own behalf. In each, the attribution rules are basically causal. There is no chance of free acceptance, so in each the enrichment must be legally or factually necessary, or otherwise incontrovertible, and the only question thereafter is one of valuation. They seem to be the same cause of action, but distinct from the common liability cases.

II. Duress, Undue Influence and Unconscionable Bargains

In duress, undue influence and unconscionable bargains the defendant needs to do something. While we treat these as being three distinct doctrines, they are usually

[140] See *Surrey CC v NHS Lincolnshire Clinical Commissioning Group* [2020] EWHC 3550, [2021] QB 896 on the availability of change of position although there was no mistake on the facts.

treated as a unit for expositional purposes and suggestions have been made that they be unified doctrinally.[141] We see here that while duress and undue influence have a common origin in different forms of external influence on the claimant's decision making, unconscionable bargains doctrine is more concerned with the defendant's wrongdoing than the effect on the claimant's autonomy. Birks' original distinction, which has seemed to fall out of use, was between claimant-sided unjust factors like mistake and defendant-sided unjust factors such as duress. Mistake does not require the defendant to do anything and hence was claimant-sided or plaintiff-sided. We saw the justification for reliance on mistake in chapter three. Many of the cases discussed in this section – and indeed earlier in this chapter – are rescission cases. While we return to rescission in more detail in chapter seven, we need to justify their inclusion here. We can do so by pointing out the correlation between reasons for restitution and for rescission and that separating the two areas risks obscuring this important normative similarity;[142] the correlation, as we saw in chapter three, also exists in South African law.

In duress and undue influence, the defendant must inveigle his way inside the claimant's decision-making process in one way or another. In so doing, he must place the claimant in a position where he is 'in the grip of a norm'.[143] Essentially, 'acting in the grip of a norm' means the claimant does not act in accordance with his own guiding higher-level norms. In neither duress nor undue influence is there appropriate recognition of the higher-level governing norms of the claimant or any appropriate decision as to whether the reasons for action are justifying reasons by those norms. There seems an important connection here in that mistaken payments are also based on the failure of the claimant to act in accordance with his governing norms,[144] but the difference has several important consequences. One, to which we return in examining defences, is that the defence of change of position should not apply because the defendant needs to do something which leads us to believe he is not in good faith or acting reasonably (unless it is presumed undue influence).[145] The core reason for a duress or undue influence claim is based on the defect in the claimant's consent, although other factors creep in. Lack of consent does not explain the bar on relief if a practical alternative were available. The reason for this lies in security of contract and the protection of the institution of contract. A more pluralistic account explains rescission. It explains why the contract is voidable rather than void by licensing

[141] eg, M Moore, 'Why Does Lord Denning's Lead Balloon Intrigue Us Still? The Prospects of a Finding a Unifying Basis for Duress, Undue Influence and Unconscionability' (2018) 134 *LQR* 257.

[142] E Bant, *The Change of Position Defence* (Oxford, Hart Publishing, 2009) 90–93.

[143] D Sheehan, 'Defendant-Sided Unjust Factors' (2016) 36 *Legal Studies* 415, 429–30.

[144] D Sheehan, 'Mistake, Failure of Consideration and the Planning Theory of Intention' (2015) 28 *Canadian Journal of Law & Jurisprudence* 155.

[145] Sheehan, 'Defendant-Sided Unjust Factors' (n 143) 436–37.

a more flexible remedial approach.[146] The law is normatively pluralistic, and lack of consent alone under-determines the remedy.

Duress, undue influence and unconscionable bargains cases do not arise outside the performance context. A performance requires, as we saw in chapter two, that the claimant deliberately (intentionally) enters a transaction with the defendant which transfers a benefit to the latter. In these cases, the claimant does enter a transaction intentionally. The party benefited is always benefited intentionally. While the 'intention with which' the claimant acted has been unduly affected so that there is no true agential governance, there is agential direction,[147] and an intention that the defendant be benefited. There is no equivalent to the *Greenwood v Bennett* case where the intention was to benefit oneself.

A. Duress

There are three types of duress: duress to the person, where threats are made against the claimant or members of his family; duress to goods, where the threat is to damage property; and economic duress.[148] The crux of duress lies in one party making a threat[149] inducing another with no practical alternative to manifest contractual assent.[150] The essential structural feature is that there is both a proposal prong and a choice prong.

The first question therefore is about the illegitimacy of the pressure. This is not the same as unlawfulness; blackmail, which will be duress, involves a threat to do something that is lawful, but exploitation of knowledge of criminal activity is illegitimate.[151] Illegitimate and unconscionable conduct appear to be interchangeable terms here,[152] although given the separate doctrine of unconscionable bargains this is unfortunate and risks clouding the waters. Illegitimacy is quite difficult to prove where the conduct is legal, however. As Goff and Jones suggest, a definitive statement of what counts as illegitimate will be difficult,[153] and such pressure will rarely be found.[154] It was not found in *AG* v *R*.[155] The soldier signed a

[146] M Chen-Wishart, 'The Nature of Vitiating Factors in Contract Law' in G Klass, G Letsas and P Saprai (eds), *Philosophical Foundations of Contract Law* (Oxford, OUP, 2014).

[147] Sheehan, 'Defendant-Sided Unjust Factors' (n 143) 431.

[148] ibid 423.

[149] But it need not be a threat; see *Borelli v Ting* [2010] UKPC 21.

[150] *Universe Tankships Ltd v Monrovia* [1986] AC 366 (HL) 400.

[151] *Pakistan International Airline Co Ltd v Time Travel (UK) Ltd* [2021] UKSC 40, [2021] 3 WLR 727, [5]–[9] (Lord Hodge).

[152] ibid [21].

[153] *Goff & Jones* (n 11) para 10.55.

[154] *Pakistan International Airline Co v Time Travel (UK) Ltd* [2021] UKSC 40, [2021] 3 WLR 727, [30] (Lord Hodge).

[155] *AG v R* [2003] UKPC 22, [2003] 1 EMLR 24; A Phang and H Tijo, 'Drawing Lines in the Sand: Duress, Undue Influence and Unconscionability Revisited' [2003] *Restitution Law Review* 110.

confidentiality agreement under threat of being returned to unit (RTU in military jargon). For a serving SAS member, as he was, this was usually considered to be a punishment. The Privy Council held the threat was a legitimate one as the Ministry of Defence had perfectly proper concerns. The Ministry could reasonably take the view that one unwilling to sign the contract was unfit for the SAS and so the threat of RTU was justified in the circumstances. There was no duress. This suggests that there should be no reasonable connection between the pressure applied and the demand made.[156] Controversy also rages about threats to break a contract and whether we protect the old or the new bargain. However, for conduct in these circumstances to be illegitimate it must lead to an impairment of the claimant's consent and must involve some reprehensible conduct by the defendant. Hard-nosed exercise of monopoly power is not enough.[157]

Outside blackmail threats to do things which are completely lawful are normally insufficient. Lord Hodge, speaking for the majority in *Pakistan International Airline Co v Time Travel (UK) Ltd*[158] gave two examples of lawful act duress – *Borelli v Ting*[159] and *The Cenk K*.[160] On the basis of those decisions he required morally reprehensible conduct on the defendant's behalf in forcing the claimant to waive an otherwise good claim, rendering enforcement unconscionable. *Borelli* is particularly important. James Ting had used forged and false evidence to prevent the liquidators investigating his conduct of Akai Holdings' affairs. Ting then (illegitimately) threatened to block a restructuring plan – via a scheme of arrangement – unless the liquidators settled with him for that illegal conduct. The fraud was clearly unlawful but was described in *The Cenk K* as past conduct not a threat of future conduct.[161] This analysis is questionable; if the fraud were material, it was not an example of lawful act duress. If it were lawful act duress, it would be better to focus purely on the threat to block a scheme by use of Ting's minority shareholding.[162] *Borelli* was the same type of case as Pakistan International Airline (*PIAC*) where the airline refused to pay commission owed, and as part of its response to the ensuing litigation by its agents to recover the commission negotiated new terms with significantly lower levels of commission for the ticketing agencies. It was different in one respect. The airline genuinely believed it was not liable and merely exercised legitimate monopoly supplier pressure on the agencies to climb down.[163] Resting

[156] *Electricity Generation Corpn v Woodside Energy Ltd* [2013] WASCA 36, [25] (McLure P); *Al Nehayan v Kent* [2018] EWHC 333 (Comm) [188] (Leggatt LJ).

[157] *AG v R* [2003] UKPC 22, [2003] 1 EMLR 24, [57].

[158] [2021] UKSC 40, [2021] 3 WLR 727.

[159] [2010] UKPC 21.

[160] *The Cenk K* [2012] EWHC 273, [2012] 2 All ER (Comm) 855.

[161] ibid [34].

[162] O Jackson, 'Unconscionability, Illegitimacy and Lawful Act Duress' [2021] *Journal of Business Law* 701, 703–04; W Day, 'Duress and Uncertainty' (2022) 138 *LQR* 194.

[163] [2021] UKSC 40, [2021] 3 WLR 727, [60] (Lord Hodge); [138] (Lord Burrows).

relief on an amorphous idea of unconscionability is, though, unfortunate.[164] It would be preferable to rest relief on a more tightly defined concept of bad faith, such as that of Lord Burrows. Lord Burrows suggests that it is a necessary condition of lawful act duress that

> the demand is made in bad faith in the particular sense that the threatening party does not genuinely believe that it is owed what it is claiming to be owed or does not genuinely believe that it has a defence to the claim being waived by the threatened party.[165]

Lord Burrows himself is not clear[166] what the difference is between the formulae, particularly given Lord Hodge's earlier references to bad faith.[167] Lord Hodge seems to see relevance in the combination of the validity of B's claim – of which A seeks a waiver – and the behaviour that A uses to obtain the waiver. It is, however, hard to see how the test can be confined to unconscionable means to obtain a waiver of a claim as opposed to some other end. It may be easier to confine bad faith. Lord Burrows also accepted the importance in *Borelli* and *The Cenk K* of the behaviour of the party alleged to have made the illegitimate threat.[168] In the end he said, and it is difficult to see much practical difference with Lord Hodge here:

> The lawful act economic threat is illegitimate where: first, the threatening party has deliberately created, or increased, the threatened party's vulnerability to the demand; and, secondly, the 'bad faith demand' requirement is satisfied (ie the threatening party does not genuinely believe that it has a defence, and there is no defence, to the claim being waived).[169]

The *PIAC* case is the last word from the UK Supreme Court on lawful act duress. Although other solutions, tests and approaches have been put forward,[170] it seems unlikely that the majority's unconscionability test will be reappraised judicially soon.[171]

B. Undue Influence

Traditionally we have divided undue influence cases into two separate categories: actual and presumed undue influence. After the seminal decision in *RBS v*

[164] Jackson (n 162) 705–06; H Cooney and H Sanderson, 'Illegitimate Pressure in the Law of Duress' [2022] *Lloyd's Maritime & Commercial Law Quarterly* 496, 506–07.
[165] [2021] UKSC 40, [2021] 3 WLR 727, [102].
[166] ibid [133].
[167] ibid [56]–[59].
[168] ibid [104].
[169] ibid [112]; *D&C Builders v Rees* [1969] 2 QB 617; *Goff & Jones* (n 11) para 10.57; Burrows (n 136) 273.
[170] eg, Cooney and Sanderson (n 164); a version of their range of factors approach was rejected by Lord Burrows in *Pakistan International Airline Co v Time Travel (UK) Ltd* [2021] UKSC 40, [2021] 3 WLR 727, [195].
[171] See J Morgan, 'The Thin End of the Wedge: Morality, Contract Law and Lawful Act Duress' [2022] *CLJ* 17.

Etridge (No 2),[172] both types of undue influence can be seen as being based on the same idea of abuse of deferential trust. The ability of the claimant to decide for himself should be substantially affected by the impact of the defendant's wishes and action.[173]

Actual undue influence is proven entirely by evidence. In the context of presumed undue influence,[174] the law allows it to be proven in part with the help of presumptions. Actual undue influence therefore requires the complainant to prove that the defendant unduly exercised his influence. Lindley LJ in *Allcard* v *Skinner* talked of 'unfair and improper conduct … coercion … cheating, and generally, though not always, some personal advantage obtained'.[175] The law, however, adopts a protective attitude so that if the claimant proves that he reposed trust and confidence in the other party,[176] and that the transaction must be not readily explicable by the parties' relationship, a presumption arises that the influence was exercised and exercised unduly.[177] The 'not readily explicable' criterion replaces the former criterion that the transaction be of manifest disadvantage to the claimant, a criterion which had already been removed prior to *Etridge* in actual undue influence cases.[178] It is explained as raising a presumption that the influence was exercised; it would be absurd if every gift by a child to a parent were deemed suspect unless proven otherwise.[179] However, even substantively fair transactions should be able to be rescinded for undue influence if it emerges from the scope of the party's influence.[180] Typically, however, as Lord Nicholls said, presumed undue influence cases occur when one party puts trust in another to look after his interests and the latter in fact prefers his own interests,[181] which will usually lead to an unfair outcome. Some cases additionally allow the claimant to take advantage of another presumption, namely that if a relationship of a certain type (eg, parent and non-adult child) the relationship is one of influence. Consequently, if a parent–child relation is proven, all that needs to be proven additionally is the 'not readily explicable' criterion.

Acceptance or knowledge by the defendant is relevant where there is no factually or legally necessary benefit to the defendant. These cases are more obviously performance-based. *RBS v Etridge (No 2)* is an example. A unduly influences B in entering into a relationship with C (typically a bank) and the decision was concerned with the circumstances in which C should be deemed to have

[172] *RBS v Etridge (No 2)* [2001] UKHL 44, [2002] 1 AC 773.
[173] *Thorne v Kennedy* [2017] HCA 49, [32] (Kiefel CJ et al).
[174] *Goff & Jones* (n 11) para 11.06.
[175] *Allcard v Skinner* (1887) 36 Ch D 154 (CA) 181.
[176] ibid 798.
[177] ibid 796.
[178] *CIBC v Pitt* [1994] 1 AC 200.
[179] [2001] UKHL 44, [2002] 2 AC 773, 798–800.
[180] R Bigwood, *Exploitative Contracts* (Oxford, OUP, 2003) 455.
[181] *RBS v Etridge (no 2)* [2001] UKHL 44, [2002] 2 AC 773, 795.

sufficient notice to be liable. That knowledge – as in mixed systems – is needed to implicate the defendant.[182] The House of Lords provided detailed guidance to the bank in these cases. The bank is put on enquiry where the wife (B) (or other partner) is standing surety for the debts of A and not for their joint debts or those of a company jointly owned.[183] Lord Nicholls suggested that the most the bank could be expected to do was to take reasonable steps to bring home to the wife the effects and seriousness of the transaction she entered into, but given that the bank will not wish to engage in a private meeting with the wife themselves a solicitor is normally engaged.[184] He then provided some guidance as to what the solicitor should explain when he meets with the wife,[185] which the other members of the House effectively endorse. The wife (B) is entering into a transaction with C. She is doing so intentionally although the intention with which she does so may be affected in a way which vitiates the transaction. If she seeks to exit from the transaction – or recover assets transferred – C needs to be affected by A's undue influence in order to preserve the importance of C's autonomy, but also from a policy perspective to ensure that banks are not deterred from lending.[186]

C. Unconscionable Bargains

The unconscionable bargains doctrine has a different focus. It is used significantly more frequently in Australia, but the effect of *Kakavas v Crown Melbourne Pty Ltd*[187] is to narrow the doctrine. Kakavas was a gambling addict and high roller who repeatedly visited the defendant casino and argued that the casino dealt with him unconscionably by preying on that addiction. The High Court of Australia elucidated the major components of the Australian unconscionable dealing doctrine. The High Court required a special disadvantage and decided that a predilection for gambling alone was not such a disadvantage that a casino would be disentitled from taking advantage of, at least in the absence of other factors, perhaps obvious intoxication.[188] The Court also required proof of a predatory state of mind, which entails knowledge of the weakness on the claimant's part, and unconscientious exploitation of that weakness. Mere inadvertence or heedlessness is insufficient.[189] In England, the advantage-taking must be such as to have been

[182] In South Africa see *Malilang v MV Houda Pearl* 1986 (2) SA 714.
[183] [2001] UKHL 44, [2002] 2 AC 773, 804 (Lord Nicholls).
[184] ibid 805–06.
[185] ibid 807–08.
[186] ibid 800–01.
[187] *Kakavas v Crown Melbourne Pty Ltd* [2013] HCA 25, (2013) 87 ALJR 708; *Thorne v Kennedy* [2017] HCA 49, [37]–[40] (Kiefel CJ et al); [109]–[115] (Gordon J).
[188] [2013] HCA 25, (2013) 87 ALJR 708, [30], [135].
[189] ibid [161].

morally reprehensible, the claimant must have been at a serious disadvantage, and the resulting transaction must be hard and oppressive. This is narrow in its terms and tracks in significant respects the Australian formulation.[190]

The doctrine is rationalisable in terms of wrongdoing[191] in that it depends on the fault of the defendant and a breach of duty. It can be excluded from unjust enrichment. Some cases, however, track presumed undue influence in one important respect. In *Earl of Aylesford v Morris*, the 22-year-old heir took out a loan at a 60 per cent interest rate.[192] The heir's vulnerability and need for the money was a weakness which the moneylender had exploited with the extortionately high interest rate. Once that vulnerability and the substantive unfairness were proven, the burden of proof switched to the moneylender to prove that there was no exploitation.[193] In presumed undue influence cases the criterion that the transaction be 'not readily explicable'[194] also triggers the presumption and the defendant's need to prove there was no undue influence.

III. Conclusion

This chapter has tried to classify the causes of action in unjust enrichment that rely on some flaw in the claimant's decision-making process. Normally such claims are performance claims in the sense explained in chapter two. However, some claims relying on the claimant having improved chattels or land belonging to the defendant, mistakenly believing the asset to be his or that he was otherwise carrying on his own business or where the claimant discharged some obligation of the defendant, again believing himself to be carrying out his own business, are not. These non-performance claims have different rules about attribution – who is the correct claimant, and how is the enrichment of the defendant at his expense? That means they are different causes of action and mistake cuts across the performance/non-performance divide.

[190] D Capper, 'The Unconscionable Bargain in the Common Law World' (2010) 126 *LQR* 403, 408–10; *Multiservice Bookbinding v Marden* [1979] Ch 84; *Alec Lobb Garages Ltd v Total Oil (GB) Ltd* [1983] 1 WLR 87; for a comparison of the jurisdictions, see YK Liew and D Yu, 'The Unconscionable Bargains Doctrine in England and Australia: Cousins or Siblings?' (2021) 45 *Melbourne University Law Review* 206.

[191] *Tanwar Enterprises Pty Ltd v Cauchi* (2003) 217 CLR 315; *Bridgwater v Leahy* (1998) 194 CLR 457; J Edelman, *Gain-Based Damages* (Oxford, Hart Publishing, 2002) 60–62.

[192] *Earl of Aylesford v Morris* (1873) 8 Ch App 484.

[193] Burrows (n 136) 302.

[194] *RBS v Etridge (No 2)* [2001] UKHL 44, [2002] 2 AC 773, 793.

5

Intent-Based Restitution II: Failure and Absence of Basis

Introduction

Failure of consideration – or basis – is an intent-based unjust factor. It is based on the failure of a condition of a collective intention.[1] A collective intention arises in circumstances where the two parties' individual intentions mesh as part of a joint plan to do X. My intention that we do X must be communicated to you and likewise your intention so we both know the other accepts the plan to do X.[2] If the basis for my intention fails (ie, you do not do your part, or are prevented from doing so or another condition is unfulfilled), the collective intention collapses.[3] I no longer intend to do my part in the plan which in turn removes the basis for your intention. This type of claim only arises as a performance claim. Free acceptance should not be recognised as a separate ground of restitution.[4] Free acceptance is said to apply where the defendant had an opportunity to reject the benefit, knowing of the claimant's expectation of payment for his actions, but failed to do so.[5] In such cases, there is no need for a request by the defendant, but he understands that the basis of the transfer or services is that they would be paid for, and it fits the failure of basis rubric. As a performance claim, the cause of action will not change depending on the type of benefit – be that money, goods or services. As an illustration of this, in *Barnes v Eastenders Cash & Carry plc*,[6] the Supreme Court said that a receiver invalidly appointed under the Proceeds of Crime Act 2002 could recover for services rendered in failure of basis. This would amount to a restitutionary quantum meruit.

[1] D Sheehan, 'Mistake, Failure of Consideration and the Planning Theory of Intention' (2015) 28 *Canadian Journal of Law & Jurisprudence* 155.

[2] ibid 171–75.

[3] ibid 176–78.

[4] E Bant and J Edelman, *Unjust Enrichment*, 2nd edn (Oxford, Hart Publishing, 2016) 325–28, but see *Weatherby v Banham* (1832) 5 Car & P 227, 172 ER 950.

[5] In England see, rejecting free acceptance as an unjust factor, *Barton v Morris* [2023] UKSC 3, [230] (Lord Burrows); in Australia see, *Andrew Shelton & Co Pty Ltd v Alpha Healthcare Pty Ltd* [2002] VSC 248; *Abb Power Generation Ltd v Chapple* [2001] WASCA 414, (2002) 25 WAR 158; *Steele v Tardiani* (1946) 72 CLR 386; *Liebe v Molloy* (1906) 4 CLR 347.

[6] *Barnes v Eastenders Cash & Carry plc* [2014] UKSC 26, [2015] AC 1.

It is important to keep restitutionary quantum meruit analytically separate from contractual quantum meruit which is assessed differently, has different requirements and is based on a different cause of action.[7] In *Energy Venture Partners Ltd v Malibu Oil & Gas*,[8] Gloster LJ sitting as a trial judge said that it was accepted that there was an important distinction between a contractual right to a quantum meruit where the court decided what the reasonable sum payable was, and a restitutionary right where the court had regard to the value of benefit to the defendant of the services received, ie, what a reasonable person would pay for the benefit in question.[9] A non-contractual quantum meruit then is an action in debt to pay reasonable remuneration for an executed consideration.[10]

The method of calculating such a non-contractual quantum meruit is laid out in *Benedetti v Sawiris*.[11] Benedetti had made an agreement (the Acquisition Agreement) with Sawiris (and his associated companies) whereby they would jointly acquire Wind, a telecommunications company, from the Italian energy firm, Enel, with the aid of outside investors. The method by which the acquisition was to take place changed considerably. The services that Benedetti provided were not those contracted for. As Arden LJ put it in the Court of Appeal, the agreement simply ran out.[12] The test was expressed in different ways. Lord Clarke alighted on the 'price a reasonable person in the defendant's position would have had to pay'.[13] He then went on to discuss whether and when that might be adjusted; in principle he accepted that subjective devaluation is possible to protect the defendant's autonomy.[14] This allows the defendant to say that he would not have paid the market value and should only be liable for what he would have paid. Subjective devaluation can be defeated by the claimant proving that the benefit was legally or factually necessary or otherwise incontrovertible.[15] Because incontrovertible benefit obviates the need to show that the defendant freely accepted or requested the benefit,[16] it will affect the choice of cause of action. Where it is present mistake will be possible, although if there is a request as well failure of basis may be an alternative. Lord Clarke also rejected subjective revaluation.[17] That was not needed to protect the defendant's freedom of choice.

[7] *Barton v Morris* [2023] UKSC 3, [204] (Lord Burrows); GJ Virgo and W Day, 'Risks on the Contract/Unjust Enrichment Borderline' (2020) 138 *LQR* 349, 350.

[8] *Energy Venture Partners Ltd v Malibu Oil & Gas* [2013] EWHC 2118.

[9] ibid [281]–[282].

[10] *Mann v Paterson Construction (Pty) Ltd* [2019] HCA 32, (2019) 267 CLR 560, [73] (Gageler J).

[11] *Benedetti v Sawiris* [2013] UKSC 50, [2014] AC 938.

[12] [2010] EWCA Civ 1427, [3].

[13] [2013] UKSC 50, [2014] AC 938, 957.

[14] ibid 959–60.

[15] *Proctor & Gamble Philippine Manufacturing Co Ltd v Peter Cremer GmbH* [1988] 3 All ER 843; factually similar is *Gadsden Pty Ltd v Strider 1 Ltd (The AES Express)* (1990) 20 NSWLR 57.

[16] [2013] UKSC 50, [2014] AC 938, 960 (Lord Clarke).

[17] ibid 961.

Lord Reed preferred a different approach, acknowledging the question of which approach was appropriate did not need to be decided because Sawiris had freely accepted the services.[18] He described enrichment as, 'What a reasonable person in the position of the defendant would have agreed to pay'.[19] On its face there is little (if any) difference between these positions. Lord Reed did refer, however, to a distinction therefore between the 'ordinary market value' and the 'objective value of the benefit'.[20] The former is the price which would have been agreed in the market in the absence of some unusual characteristic of the purchaser; the latter is the value of the benefit to the reasonable person in the position of the defendant.[21] While Lord Reed eschewed talk of subjective devaluation, his Lordship did refer to the question of whether imposing liability was consistent with the defendant's autonomy and freedom of choice, the very consideration he accepted that 'subjective devaluation' is intended to address.[22] There is one possible difference between Lord Clarke and Lord Reed: that is where a service is provided and the defendant accepts that it has received value, albeit less than market value, whether this lesser subjective figure of the defendant's should be accepted. Even here, Lord Reed accepted a court could make an award below market value to preserve the defendant's freedom of choice,[23] for example, if accepted at half price. The defendant's idiosyncratic valuation of the services will not be accepted though. The important point therefore is that the claimant recovers the market value of the services provided, modified, if needed, to respect the defendant's autonomy, and not any marketable residuum. This, as we have said before, is the value of the performance rendered.

A failure of basis may arise in the context of a failed contract – terminated, frustrated, or rescinded – or outside that context where the contract is void or was wrongly anticipated. The first part of this chapter examines the requirement of total failure. The second examines restitution within valid contracts: for example, cases of frustration, or termination for breach. The third section examines the issue of performance in anticipation of a contract that never arises. It is an important question which we address as to whether failure of basis is one cause of action or several (and whether it is contractual, restitutionary or both). The fourth section examines absence of consideration or basis and whether the performance claims that English law recognises should be seen as based purely on absence of basis. The answer is no; unjust factors remain of analytical and normative importance in the English performance claims.

[18] ibid 988 (Lord Reed).
[19] ibid 982.
[20] ibid 987.
[21] G Virgo, 'Evaluating Enrichment' [2013] *CLJ* 508, 509.
[22] [2013] UKSC 50, [2014] AC 938, 987–88.
[23] ibid 960 (Lord Clarke) and 987, 992–93 (Lord Reed).

I. Total Failure of Basis

There are, importantly, two senses of 'basis' here. The first sense of basis is that used in civilian performance claims: is there an obligation justifying the transfer? The basic model is that if there is a contract, that contract must be removed somehow. If it is not removed, the basis (ie, the obligation) remains; it justifies any enrichment which occurs as a result of contractual performance. If a contract provides that payment is only due on the completion of a specified task and this is not done or only partially done, it is not open to the party to sidestep contract and claim in unjust enrichment.[24] We saw this rule in the context of mistake claims as well. If there is a valid basis for the payment it cannot be recovered. The rule can result in fine questions of contractual interpretation as to whether a question is covered by the express or implied contract terms. In *Barton v Gwyn-Jones*,[25] the Court of Appeal held that there was a gap in the contract.[26] A contractual right to be paid £1.2 million existed if Barton introduced a purchaser for the land and the purchase price were greater than £6.5 million. The land was sold for £500,000 less, but the Court of Appeal held the contract had not impliedly removed any non-contractual rights to be paid. This result was overturned by the majority on appeal to the Supreme Court,[27] holding that a term that remuneration is to be paid in certain circumstances necessarily excludes any right to be paid if those circumstances did not arise. While the conclusion by Lady Rose speaking for the majority seems correct, Lord Leggatt and Lord Burrows disagreed, holding that the express terms did not in fact bar the Court from finding an implied contractual term for reasonable remuneration,[28] which itself then excluded an unjust enrichment claim,[29] although had there been no implied term Lord Burrows would have made an award in unjust enrichment.[30]

There is either a valid obligation or not. There is no such thing as partial nullity or partial voidability. Apportionment is possible, however, in the sense that some clauses can be valid and others invalid. In *Roxborough v Rothman Pall Mall of Australia*, the state government of New South Wales charged an unconstitutional excise duty on cigarettes which was passed on to buyers.[31] The buyers sought recovery of the itemised 'licence fee' from the sellers when the invalidity came to light and succeeded. The rest of the contract was, however, valid. In *Stevenson v Snow*, a ship sailed from London to Portsmouth but failed to make the next leg of

[24] *MacDonald Dickens & Macklin v Costello* [2011] EWCA Civ 930, [2012] QB 244; *Mann v Paterson Construction (Pty) Ltd* [2019] HCA 32, (2019) 267 CLR 560.

[25] *Barton v Gwyn-Jones* [2019] EWCA Civ 1999, [2020] 2 All ER (Comm) 652.

[26] ibid [33]; see also on unjust enrichment's role as a gap-filler, *Coshott v Lenin* [2007] NSWCA 153.

[27] [2023] UKSC 3, [96] (Lady Rose).

[28] ibid [188] (Lord Leggatt); [241] (Lord Burrows).

[29] ibid [194] (Lord Leggatt); [226] (Lord Burrows).

[30] ibid [241].

[31] *Roxborough v Rothman Pall Mall of Australia* [2000] HCA 68; (2001) 208 CLR 506.

the journey to Canada.[32] The cost of insurance could be divided so that the part of the premium devoted to the transatlantic voyage was recoverable. What matters is whether apportionment can be carried out without undue difficulty.[33] An apportioned contract in this sense does not therefore need to be invalidated or removed in its entirety. Unapportioned contracts will.[34]

Authority for the second sense of 'basis' is found in *Fibrosa Spolka Ackzjyna v Fairbairn Lawson*,[35] which clarified that failure of consideration in the restitutionary sense was failure of the defendant's counter-performance. It could also be the failure of a contingent condition which may be unrelated to D's counter-performance. In either case, the reason the value of the claimant's performance is recoverable is that the condition on which it was paid has failed. To allow the defendant to retain it would be to make the performance unconditional when it was not. What that condition might be is, as we see, a matter of construction. Set-offs can still be made, although care needs to be taken. In *Baltic Shipping Ltd v Dillon (The Mikhail Lermontov)*, Mrs Dillon went on a cruise, but the cruise ship sank part way through the cruise.[36] The contract was not apportioned in the sense that nowhere in the contract was it stated that the price of the cruise was per night or per day. She sought the return of her money. In fact, she had had a part refund already and was refused the full refund. This was on the basis she had had 10 days of the cruise. It is important that she had to show she received nothing because she had already had a part refund for the days she had not had. If she had received the full refund, she would have had to give credit for the 10 days already enjoyed. Or would she? Stevens argues the contract was not apportioned so she had not paid separately for each day, but for the full cruise. On that basis, she had not got what she paid for.[37] In *School Facility Management Ltd v Christ the King College*, the College had entered a contract which turned out to be ultra vires to supply, build and hire a temporary building for sixth-form teaching.[38] Properly understood, they had entered a finance lease which counted as borrowing. The College had no power to borrow without the Secretary of State's consent, which had not been sought. The College defaulted on hire payments and the claimants (SFM) purported to terminate the contract for breach and sought the balance of the hire payments for the whole period of occupation. The College claimed the contract was void, hence could not be terminated, and claimed the payments already made under the contract, conceding the need for counter-restitution relating to their use

[32] *Stevenson v Snow* (1761) 1 Black W 315, 96 ER 176.

[33] *Goss v Chilcott* [1996] AC 788 (HL) 798 (Lord Goff); *Giedo van der Garde BV v Force India Formula One Team Ltd* [2010] EWCA Civ 2373 [299]–[300]; *David Securities Pty Ltd v Commonwealth Bank of Australia* (1992) 175 CLR 353.

[34] T Baloch, *Unjust Enrichment and Contract* (Oxford, Hart Publishing, 2009) 152.

[35] *Fibrosa Spolka Ackzjyna v Fairbairn Lawson* [1943] AC 32 (HL) 77; *Stocznia Gdanska v Latvian Shipping Co* [1998] 1 WLR 574 (HL) 588 (Lord Goff).

[36] *Baltic Shipping Ltd v Dillon (The Mikhail Lermontov)* (1993) 176 CLR 344.

[37] R Stevens, *The Laws of Restitution* (Oxford, OUP, 2023) 119–20.

[38] *School Facility Management Ltd v Christ the King College* [2021] EWCA Civ 1053.

of the building. It is a matter of equitable transaction set-off. Popplewell LJ said, 'The benefits for which the claimant must give credit are those which are sufficiently closely connected with the benefits provided to the defendant that justice requires him to do so'.[39] This is best explained under the 'two-claims'[40] theory, by which the claim for the recovery of payments made by the school triggered a counter-claim in failure of basis by SFM. Another approach is to decide if any of the benefit received by the claimant can be disregarded.[41] Hence, it is not whether the claimant received a benefit, but whether he received any part of the performance objectively bargained for.[42]

The total failure of basis requirement is in effect a dead letter; counter-restitution can be given of benefits provided to the claimant where the defendant's compliance with an order to make restitution entails the failure of the basis on which those benefits were transferred to the claimant. However, no case has ever explicitly rid the law of the need for total failure. The rule continues a shadow existence, forever subject to 'scrutiny someday – but not today'.[43]

The question of what was objectively bargained for, however, requires us to identify what the basis or essential purpose of a transfer was.[44] In *Rowland v Divall*[45] the claimant made use of a car which he had purportedly bought. The question was whether, once it became clear he had received no good title, the use he had had meant there was no total failure. Use of the car was not the essential purpose of the contract, however. Ownership was. The corollary of this when we turn to termination of contracts for breach is that such collateral benefits need not be contractually due. What was contractually due to the claimant was legal title. In *Ebrahimi Dawood Ltd v Heath*, the claimant was able to recover 80 per cent of the purchase price when he rejected that proportion of the goods supplied as non-conforming.[46] This pro rata approach is not limited to cases where an express price per item is listed. Apportionment is also possible in services cases and the payer is entitled to restitution of the sum paid for which no basis was provided.[47]

[39] ibid [83], Stevens, *The Laws of Restitution* (n 37) 383–85; see also *Geldof Metaalconstructie NV v Simon Carves* [2010] EWCA Civ 667, [2010] 4 All ER 847; D Sheehan, *The Principles of Personal Property Law*, 2nd edn (Oxford, Hart Publishing, 2017) 294–95.

[40] E Bant, *The Change of Position Defence* (Oxford, Hart Publishing, 2009) 94–102; T Pilkington and D Winterton, 'Void Contracts, Counter-Restitution and Change of Position' (2022) 138 *LQR* 21; the two-claims theory has been adopted in South Africa; see *Yarona Healthcare Network (Pty) Ltd v Medshield* 2018 (1) SA 513, 530–31; see ch 8 for discussion of the effect of a change of position by, for example, the claimant.

[41] *Giedo van der Garde BV v Force India Formula One Team Ltd* [2010] EWCA Civ 2373, [268].

[42] ibid [270]–[272]; *Rover International v Cannon Film Sales* [1989] 1 WLR 912; *David Securities v Commonwealth Bank of Australia* (1992) 175 CLR 353 (HCA) 382; *Fostiff v Campbell Cash & Carry Ltd* (2005) 218 ALR 166; *HEB Enterprises Ltd v Richards* [2023] UKPC 7.

[43] C Mitchell and P Mitchell, 'Recurring Issues in Failure of Basis' [2020] *Lloyd's Maritime & Commercial Law Quarterly* 498, 515.

[44] *Giedo van der Garde v Force India Formula One Team* [2010] EWCA Civ 2373, [285].

[45] *Rowland v Divall* [1923] 2 KB 500; *Barber v NWS Bank plc* [1996] 1 All ER 906, but contrast *Hunt v Silk* (1804) 5 East 449, 102 ER 1142.

[46] *Ebrahimi Dawood Ltd v Heath* [1961] 2 Lloyds Rep 561.

[47] *Giedo van der Garde BV v Force India Formula One Team Ltd* [2010] EWCA Civ 2373, [323]; *DO Ferguson v Sohl* (1992) 62 BLR 95; *Baltic Shipping v Dillon* (1993) 111 ALR 289.

In *Giedo van der Garde BV v Force India Formula One Team Ltd*, therefore, the Court of Appeal held that it was possible to apportion between kilometres provided – ie, that the team were allowed to drive – and not provided. It also held that the sponsorship money was collateral and not part of the essential bargain,[48] although other rights provided were held to be essential and barred restitution.[49]

The basis of the transfer – ie, what is expected in return and on which the transfer is conditional – must be worked out objectively. This, in turn, illuminates which benefits are collateral. In *Benzline Auto Pte Ltd v Supercars Lorinser Pte Ltd*, Benzline held the master dealership in Singapore for Lorinser cars but did not want to deal directly with the public.[50] They entered negotiations with the defendants for them to become sub-dealers. Negotiations broke down, but only after Supercars had paid S$300,000 to Benzline which was paid on to Daimler as a deposit for 100 cars. Prakash JA put the question: 'what was the payment for?'[51] It was to enable Benzline (who did not want to pay the deposit) to do so and avoid future delay.[52] Further, it was on the basis that Benzline would offer the dealership to Supercars on substantially the terms of the draft agreement. 'That is what an objective observer would conclude from the whole course of conduct'.[53] If therefore A voices his understanding of a transfer and B apparently assents (even if B had private doubts), the basis can be taken as agreed.[54] Goff and Jones suggest this is similar to the approach in contractual construction and that this is an advantage because there will be only one body of principles about interpretation.[55] In *Simpson Marine Pte Ltd v Jiaravanon*, Jiaravanon wished to buy a yacht.[56] He paid Simpson a deposit of €1 million to secure two yachts (yachts 1 and 2) for a fixed period. Yacht 1 had been sold but Jiaravanon and Simpson agreed the money be used to secure yachts 2 and 3. In the end Jiaravanon bought yet another yacht – yacht 4. The Singapore Court of Appeal held that the basis of the payment had to be construed objectively and jointly understood by the parties and said the process of identifying the basis was very similar to that of interpreting a contract.[57] On the facts, the basis did not fail as it was not an agreed basis of the payment that Jiaravanon would buy one of the two yachts (2 or 3). Likewise, in *Benzline* the basis did not fail because Benzline was happy to move forward with the deal.[58]

[48] [2010] EWCA Civ 2373, [327]–[330].
[49] ibid [369].
[50] *Benzline Auto Pte Ltd v Supercars Lorinser Pte Ltd* [2018] SGCA 2, [2018] 1 SLR 239.
[51] ibid [23].
[52] ibid [65].
[53] ibid [68].
[54] C Mitchell, P Mitchell and S Watterson (eds), *Goff & Jones: The Law of Unjust Enrichment*, 10th edn (London, Sweet & Maxwell, 2022) para 13.02.
[55] ibid para 13.04.
[56] *Simpson Marine Pte Ltd v Jiaravanon* [2019] SGHCA 7, [2019] 2 Lloyds Rep 196.
[57] ibid [49] (Andrew Phang JA).
[58] The 'ready and willing' formula in *Thomas v Brown* (1876) 1 QBD 714.

II. Failure of Basis in Valid Contracts

As we have seen, the basic model is that the contract needs to be removed in some way if unapportioned. It is only by removing the contract that the claimant's performance can be reversed.[59] Put differently, if a valid contract requires the payment of money or the provision of services to the defendant, it would undermine contract to allow the claimant to recover it back. The high water-mark of this view came in a case called *Chandler v Webster*.[60] That was a frustration case but decided that there could be no failure of basis because the contract was initially valid and therefore valid consideration had been given. The decision was reversed in *Fibrosa Spolka Ackzjyna v Fairbairn Lawson*.[61] The latter decision involved the payment by a Polish company of advances for the delivery of machinery. That delivery became illegal after the German invasion of Poland and subsequent declaration of war. The House of Lords decided in failure of consideration cases consideration referred to contractual performance not the consideration needed for a valid contract.[62] Consequently, because the contractual counter-performance was not forthcoming, restitution of the money was possible.

We divide this section into four subsections. We first look at the rules regarding the statutory claim – cause of action – under the Law Reform (Frustrated Contracts) Act 1943. The second subsection examines the rules relating to termination for breach. The third looks at subsisting and unenforceable contracts. Finally, we ask whether these are contract claims or not.

A. Frustrated Contracts

Frustration relates to supervening impossibility; it discharges the relevant obligations and allows for recovery of the value of the parties' performance. In England, the law on the latter point is now found in the Law Reform (Frustrated Contracts) Act 1943. Prior to the Act, a claimant was unable to recover money transferred if he had received a non-returnable benefit such as services in counter-performance. The suspicion that allowing counter-restitution of the value of such services might amount to the part-performance of a discharged contract still exists, but for reasons we examine below is not a serious concern. The Act has attracted little litigation. There are two significant cases – *BP v Hunt (No 2)*[63] and

[59] W Swain, 'Cutter v Powell and the Pleading of Claims in Unjust Enrichment' [2003] *Restitution Law Review* 46.
[60] *Chandler v Webster* [1904] 1 KB 493.
[61] [1943] AC 32 (HL).
[62] ibid 48.
[63] *BP v Hunt (No 2)* [1979] 1 WLR 783.

ICM/Fair Warning v Gamerco.[64] On its face the Act does not seem very restitutionary. Section 1 provides:

> (2) All sums paid or payable to any party in pursuance of the contract before the time when the parties were so discharged (in this Act referred to as 'the time of discharge') shall, in the case of sums so paid, be recoverable from him as money received by him for the use of the party by whom the sums were paid, and, in the case of sums so payable, cease to be so payable:
>
> Provided that, if the party to whom the sums were so paid or payable incurred expenses before the time of discharge in, or for the purpose of, the performance of the contract, the court may, if it considers it just to do so having regard to all the circumstances of the case, allow him to retain or, as the case may be, recover the whole or any part of the sums so paid or payable, not being an amount in excess of the expenses so incurred.
>
> (3) Where any party to the contract has, by reason of anything done by any other party thereto in, or for the purpose of, the performance of the contract, obtained a valuable benefit (other than a payment of money to which the last foregoing subsection applies) before the time of discharge, there shall be recoverable from him by the said other party such sum (if any), not exceeding the value of the said benefit to the party obtaining it, as the court considers just, having regard to all the circumstances of the case and, in particular, –
>
> (a) the amount of any expenses incurred before the time of discharge by the benefited party in, or for the purpose of, the performance of the contract, including any sums paid or payable by him to any other party in pursuance of the contract and retained or recoverable by that party under the last foregoing subsection, and
> (b) the effect, in relation to the said benefit, of the circumstances giving rise to the frustration of the contract.

Section 1(2) therefore covers money claims and section 1(3) covers non-money claims. Section 1(2) allows the claimant to recover the full amount prepaid, irrespective of whether the condition under which he paid remains unfulfilled[65] and even if this allows him to escape a bad bargain, subject to the defendant's ability to set off his expenses.[66] This (and the same rule regarding recovery of non-money benefits) is at odds with the position in termination for breach cases. The claimant in such cases can only recover a payment if the condition on which it was made was unfulfilled, but even if the condition for a given payment had already been met the 1943 Act allows for a complete unwinding subject to the proviso. In *BP v Hunt (No 2)* Lord Goff rationalised this proviso as an application of the change of position defence. Having received the money – or anticipating receiving the money – the defendant changes his position by incurring expenses.[67] The

[64] *ICM/Fair Warning v Gamerco* [1995] 1 WLR 1226.
[65] *Goff & Jones* (n 54) para 15.13; Stevens, *The Laws of Restitution* (n 37) 140.
[66] AS Burrows, *The Law of Restitution*, 3rd edn (Oxford, OUP, 2011) 363; Stevens, *The Laws of Restitution* (n 37) 140–42, noting that some of the more ridiculous possibilities this opens up are barred by section 2(4).
[67] [1979] 1 WLR 783, 800.

proviso, as Burrows (now Lord Burrows) argues, goes beyond the effect of change of position in that the expenses are recoverable even if no payment was made.[68] In *ICM/Fair Warning v Gamerco*, Garland J implicitly rejected the change of position rationale and simply suggested the proviso allowed for what was just,[69] and said that there was on the facts no question of any change of position by the plaintiff.[70] The claimant concert promoters had paid the defendants – the corporate identity of Guns N' Roses – $412,500. The defendants incurred some expenses ($50,000) as opposed to the $450,000 incurred by the claimants. Garland J made no deduction. This amounts to limited loss apportionment, which is precisely what Robert Goff J said the Act was not intended to allow.[71]

Section 1(3) is much more difficult. While there is reference to the benefit obtained by the parties, the defendant is only obliged to repay a 'just sum' and the subsection splits the idea of performance and benefit in a way at odds with the general approach taken in this book. In other words, the claim is not for the value of the services but the enrichment consequent on that. That is problematic from the perspective of a performance claim. In all other such claims the relief is based on the value of the performance alone. There are three stages to the enquiry. The benefit must be identified, valued and a just sum assessed.[72] Section 1(3)(a) Goff J also analysed as a partial change of position defence.[73] In deciding the just sum he said that the court should adopt the same frame of analysis as in calculating a quantum meruit.[74] Burrows has argued that Goff J made an important wrong turn in that he makes a distinction between the services and their end product.[75] In general terms this is correct;[76] in unjust enrichment we are concerned with the value of the performance rather than trying to divide the services from their result. Goff J held, however, that references in section 1(3)(b) to 'benefit' could only refer to the end product since a frustrating event cannot affect the services themselves.[77] He was clear that this was in the context of the wording of the statute and said that apart from this he would have been happy to see the services themselves as enriching.[78] What matters is that the services were provided intentionally at the other party's request or acceptance. That performance, which as we saw in chapter two counts as the defendant's enrichment irrespective of a marketable residuum, can then be valued. In terms of valuing the performance for the purposes of quantum of relief, it is the (adjusted) objective market value that is critical. Burrows, however, confuses the issue by talking about the receipt of services. This is a red

[68] Burrows, *The Law of Restitution* (n 66) 364.
[69] [1995] 1 WLR 1226, 1237.
[70] ibid 1236.
[71] *BP v Hunt (No 2)* [1979] 1 WLR 783, 799.
[72] ibid 801–05.
[73] ibid 804.
[74] ibid 805.
[75] Burrows, *The Law of Restitution* (n 66) 370; see Stevens, *The Laws of Restitution* (n 37) 143–46.
[76] *Goff & Jones* (n 54) para 5.41.
[77] *BP v Hunt (No 2)* [1979] 1 WLR 783, 802.
[78] ibid 801–02.

herring. One does not receive services. Services are performed, or not.[79] The value of the services rendered should then be the pro rata contract price.[80] That can then be reduced by any expenses incurred as a result of section 1(3)(b).

Despite efforts to incorporate aspects of the law of unjust enrichment within the statute, the Act aims, albeit without saying so explicitly, to engage in an exercise of loss allocation. The statute, as it stands, does not, however, succeed in this and Virgo has argued that a reformed statutory regime is needed protecting both the restitutionary and reliance interest and allowing for some allocation of loss.[81] Burrows has not been so keen, taking the position that loss-splitting contradicts the traditional individualistic bent of English contract law and the tradition that a party responsible for the risk of loss is preparing to perform a contract.[82]

A common law unjust enrichment action could satisfactorily remedy the situation of a frustrated contract, allowing for restitution and counter-restitution of performances rendered. This is the position in South Africa where the claim exists in the *condictio sine causa specialis* in its guise as the *condictio ob causam finitam*.[83] It is also the position in Scotland where – anomalously – the action is the *condictio causa data causa non secuta*.[84] Both actions work reasonably well. Whatever the issues may be with the Act, however, there is no desire to reform or abolish it. There are important points of difference with common law performance claims. The Act apportions losses. The proviso to section 1(2) and section 1(3)(a) go further than change of position allows. These factors lead Goff and Jones to conclude it is a hybrid statutory claim which should not be brought into scope.[85] This seems right. Once we begin to apportion losses – and this is also the case for any pre-contractual cases that involve redistribution – we find a significant normative dissimilarity. In essence, the justification for apportioning losses must be normatively distinct from any justification for reversing performances and returning to the status quo ante, precisely because the apportionment of losses is not designed to put the parties *in statu quo ante*. Put in terms of our discussion from chapter one, this is not the **function** of unjust enrichment and does not provide an answer to our question: how is restitution of gains made justified in the absence of a wrong?

B. Contracts Terminated for Breach

Restitution after termination of a contract for breach is prospective and so there is no relief (outside contract) for the provision of performances which have been

[79] *Stocznia Gdanska v Latvian Shipping Co* [1998] 1 WLR 574 (HL) 588 (Lord Goff).

[80] *Goff & Jones* (n 54) para 15.44; *Atwal v Rochester* [2010] EWHC 2338.

[81] GJ Virgo, *The Principles of the Law of Restitution*, 3rd edn (Oxford, OUP, 2015) 365–67.

[82] Burrows, *The Law of Restitution* (n 66) 366.

[83] D Visser, *Unjustified Enrichment* (Durban, Juta, 2008) 486–87; *Kudu Granite Operations (Pty) Ltd v Caterna Ltd* 2003 (5) SA 193 (SCA).

[84] *Cantiere san Rocco SA v Clyde Shipbuilding Co Ltd* [1924] AC 226.

[85] *Goff & Jones* (n 54) paras 15.06–15.10.

earned by the party providing them – ie, for which counter-performance has been made or is contractually due. Unjust enrichment liability can only lie to reverse a performance where there has been no contractually due counter-performance.[86] This is a significant consequence of the contractual rules on the mutual dependency and conditionality of performances under a bilateral contract.[87]

In terms of elucidating the actual rules, there are two cross-cutting category divisions. The first is between the innocent party claiming restitution or the breaching party doing so. The second is between restitution of money and benefits in kind. Can a prepayment be recovered whether by an innocent party or the contract-breaker? *Giles v Edwards* is an example of the first case: the innocent claimant.[88] The claimants had contracted to buy wood from the defendant and prepaid the contract price. They only received a fraction of the wood ordered (and presumably rejected it as short delivery). They recovered the full price paid. There has been discussion of whether this action should allow the claimant to escape a bad bargain. This does not happen often, but the American case of *Bush v Canfield* is often cited.[89] There the price of flour dropped, and the seller oddly failed to deliver the flour to the buyer – despite the buyer paying $3,000 over the odds. The buyer terminated and sought the $5,000 prepayment back. He succeeded, and rightly so. The action is not about fulfilling the parties' expectations but returning them to the status quo ante. In recommending that partial failure should ground relief in these cases, the Law Commission proposed that the work done by the party in breach should be valued in terms of its benefit to the other party with a pro rata contract price cap.[90] Where the party seeking restitution is the contract-breaker, authority is found in *Dies v British & International Mining and Finance Corpn*.[91] The claimant contracted for a quantity of rifles and ammunition. He made a prepayment but failed to take delivery and sought to recover the prepayment. He succeeded, although Stable J thought the right to recover was contractual,[92] and subject to a set-off for any claim in damages. If damages exceeded the £100,000 prepayment, nothing would therefore be payable.[93] Nor would anything have been repayable if it had been a deposit – which are agreed to be irrecoverable.

There are few cases regarding benefits in kind, but in the context of the innocent claimant *De Bernardy v Harding* illustrates the law.[94] The defendant let seats

[86] *Hurst v Bryk* [2002] 1 AC 195; *Johnson v Agnew* [1980] AC 367.

[87] P Butler, 'Advance Contractual Payments: Enforcement and Restitution for Failure of Basis' in C Rickett and R Grantham (eds), *Structure and Justification in Private Law: Essays for Peter Birks* (Oxford, Hart Publishing, 2008) 234.

[88] *Giles v Edwards* (1797) 7 TR 181, 101 ER 920.

[89] *Bush v Canfield* (1818) 2 Conn 485; *Wilkinson v Lloyd* (1845) 7 QB 27, 115 ER 398.

[90] Law Commission, *Report on Pecuniary Restitution on Breach of Contract* (Law Comm No 121 1983) paras 3.6–3.11.

[91] *Dies v British & International Mining and Finance Corpn* [1939] 1 KB 724.

[92] ibid 744; See Burrows, *The Law of Restitution* (n 66) 354–55.

[93] ibid 747.

[94] *De Bernardy v Harding* (1853) 8 Exch 822, 155 ER 1586.

to see the Duke of Wellington's funeral procession. The claimant had advertised abroad and made accommodation arrangements for overseas visitors and sent applicants for tickets to the defendant in accordance with a contract with the defendant, which the latter repudiated. Alderson B rightly allowed the claimant to sue in quantum meruit. In *Planché v Colburn*, the author sought to recover in a quantum meruit for work done in writing part of an uncompleted (and now due to the defendant's breach, never to be delivered manuscript).[95] The case has proven difficult, but on a performance analysis makes sense. The judgments of the case are only consistent with the quantum meruit count,[96] but it is thought a difficult case because of the lack of marketable residuum.[97] Virgo combines reliance and restitution by suggesting that because the defendant made a representation that he would accept the book which the claimant relied on to his detriment, the former is estopped from denying that he has had a benefit.[98] This is all unnecessary. The work once done could not be undone. *Planché* can be explained therefore as the value of the work done – an apportionable segment of the full contractual performance, the basis for which had failed. The lack of any marketable residuum is irrelevant. In *Gillett v Mawman*,[99] which would be treated as frustration today, the claimant sought reimbursement for his work in an action for work and labour. The work – printing a translated book – was nearly done when fire consumed the premises and destroyed everything. Although the claimant lost because of the customs of the printing trade, a general rule was affirmed that a workman is entitled to be paid when the work is destroyed through no fault of his own. The key is that performance was rendered.

There is some dispute as to whether the claimant should be allowed to escape a bad bargain. The classic American case of *Boomer v Muir* allowed the recovery of $257,000 rather than a pro rata $20,000 under the contract.[100] In *Lodder v Slowey*,[101] the appellants agreed with the respondent for the latter to complete certain work. They then delegated the supervision of the contract to the local authority (the corporation). The latter then improperly prevented the respondents from doing the work and the innocent respondents were allowed to sue in quantum meruit. The Privy Council approved the view that there is no contract

[95] *Planché v Colburn* (1831) 8 Bing 14, 131 ER 315.

[96] Baloch (n 34) 137.

[97] C Mitchell and C Mitchell, 'Planché v Colburn' in C Mitchell and P Mitchell (eds), *Landmark Cases in the Law of Restitution* (Oxford, Hart Publishing, 2006) 91–92; *Goff & Jones* (n 54) para 5.43; see also *Gill v Garrett* [2020] NSWSC 795, [436]–[462] (Slattery J) where pure care-giving services were accepted as being enriching in principle, although on the facts enrichment was not made out.

[98] Virgo, *The Principles of the Law of Restitution* (n 81) 68–69.

[99] *Gillett v Mawman* (1808) 1 Taunt 137, 127 ER 784; see also *Menetone v Athawes* (1764) 3 Burr 1594, 97 ER 998; *Bull v Sibbs* (1799) 8 TR 327, 101 ER 1415 where B was liable for rent despite C being in occupation and benefiting. Baloch (n 34) 137–39.

[100] *Boomer v Muir* 24 P 2d 570 (1933).

[101] *Lodder v Slowey* [1904] AC 442; cases to like effect include *Iezzi Constructions Pty Ltd v Watkins Pacific (Qld) Pty Ltd* [1995] 2 Qd R 350; *Renard Constructions Ltd v Ministry for Public Works* (1992) 26 NSWLR 234; *Sopov v Kane (No 2)* [2009] VSCA 141; *O'Brien v Buffalo Narrows Airways Ltd* (1998) 171 Sask R 217.

ceiling. This has been extremely controversial, and the case has been described as 'devoid of legal reasoning'.[102] By contrast with *Lodder*, in *Taylor v Motability Finance Ltd*, the judge said restitution in excess of his contractual entitlement should not be possible.[103] Otherwise, he would be able to recover more than his contractual entitlement.[104] Burrows argues that not to allow the escape from a bad bargain would be inconsistent with the position allowed in the context of payments of money.[105] He does, however, take the view that there is a valuation ceiling not a contract ceiling. If the objective value of the services is greater than the contract price, the contract price is evidence that he would not have paid more than that.[106] The end result is much the same because it is (or should be) the value of the performance that is recovered, not anything else and certainly not any alleged realised gain.

This is the result of the decision of the High Court of Australia in *Mann v Paterson Construction (Pty) Ltd* where restitution was capped at the contract price or that part of the contract price attributable to the work done.[107] The Manns had employed Paterson to build two houses and payment was to be made at given stages of the work. The Manns made several requests for additional work to which Paterson agreed and charged an agreed extra price for. Paterson claimed the Manns owed A$49,000 for extra work. The Manns said the work was defective. In the end the Manns were found in breach of contract for preventing Paterson completing the work and the contract was terminated following the Manns' repudiation of it. Paterson argued that they were enriched by A$945,000 by work they had not paid for. To the extent that the work reflected completed contractual stages, Paterson was limited to either damages or to an action in debt for sums contractually due. Contractual entitlement accrued when the work was done and therefore no unjust enrichment claim could arise.[108] Some work comprised part of an uncompleted stage. In such cases no contractual right to payment accrued. The High Court was split over recovery in this context. The minority saw no room for unjust enrichment.[109] The plurality – Nettle, Gordon and Edelman JJ – held that an unjust enrichment claim in failure of basis was possible and further that the relief was (prima facie) capped by the pro rata contract price. Gageler J held that overlapping remedies were not a problem, citing concurrent tort and contract actions.[110]

[102] *Mann v Paterson Construction (Pty) Ltd* [2019] HCA 32, (2019) 267 CLR 560, [69] (Gageler J); on the question more generally see SA Smith, 'Concurrent Liability in Contract and Unjust Enrichment: The Fundamental Breach Requirement' (1999) 115 *LQR* 245.

[103] *Taylor v Motability Finance Ltd* [2004] EWHC 2619.

[104] ibid [25].

[105] Burrows, *The Law of Restitution* (n 66) 348–49.

[106] ibid 350.

[107] *Mann v Paterson Construction (Pty) Ltd* [2019] HCA 32, (2019) 267 CLR 560.

[108] ibid [19], [27] (Kiefel CJ et al); [62] (Gageler J); *Cadogan Petroleum Holdings v Global Process Systems LLC* [2013] EWHC 214; *Quirkco Investments Ltd v Aspray Transport Ltd* [2011] EWHC 3060, [63]; *PCE Investors v Cancer Research UK* [2012] EWHC 884, [39]–[55]; see Butler (n 87) 235 on the acquisition of unconditional rights to payment on the performance of a divisible part of the contractual performance.

[109] [2019] HCA 32, (2019) 267 CLR 560, [20].

[110] ibid [84].

He held that the amount recoverable on a non-contractual quantum meruit as remuneration for services under an enforceable contract cannot exceed the portion of the contract price attributable to the services.[111] As the plurality put it, where a contract is terminated for breach it is not inconsistent to assess restitution by reference to the contract price, which reflects the parties' agreed allocation of risk.[112]

Sometimes pro rata assessment is impossible. In *Barton v Gwyn-Jones*,[113] the contract provided for remuneration of £1.2 million for Barton if he introduced a purchaser for the relevant land to Gwyn-Jones and the sale price were at least £6.5 million. While the Supreme Court overturned the decision that Barton was entitled to any remuneration, Asplin LJ, in the Court of Appeal, had held the circumstances of the right to £1.2 million were so peculiar that it could not be used as a benchmark for any pro rata assessment of quantum meruit.[114] The award must be assessed separately from any consideration of the contractual award. While the circumstances are not identical, the plurality in *Mann* suggested that there may be cases where confining the claimant to the contract valuation is unconscionable, but failed to explain when that might be.[115] A similar suggestion was made in *Sopov v Kane (No 2)*.[116] The Victoria Court of Appeal stated that the contract price is relevant as evidence of the value of the services,[117] but that a valuation in excess of the contract price was possible.[118] However, the contract price really is the best evidence of value to the parties and should – as Gageler J said in *Mann* – always be respected.

Mann involved an innocent claimant. *Sumpter v Hedges*[119] and *Bolton v Mahadeva*[120] involved claims by the contract-breaker. The contracts, or more properly the obligations, were entire; payment was conditional on full performance.[121] A party in breach cannot claim the value of services unless he has an accrued contractual entitlement to be paid.[122] In *Sumpter* itself the builder contracted to build two buildings but in fact left the job unfinished. The fee for the work was £565 and the value of the work done £333. The builder was denied the claim for the value of work done. The entire obligations rule (which is a rule of contract law

[111] ibid [101]–[102].
[112] ibid [205].
[113] [2019] EWCA Civ 1999.
[114] ibid [50] (Asplin LJ).
[115] [2019] HCA 32, (2019) 267 CLR 560 [216]; F Wilmot-Smith, 'Contract and Unjust Enrichment in the High Court of Australia' (2020) 136 *LQR* 196, 199.
[116] [2009] VSCA 141.
[117] ibid [21]–[24].
[118] ibid [26]; for discussion, see D Winterton and T Pilkington, '*Mann v Paterson Constructions (Pty) Ltd*: The Intersection of Debt, Damages and Quantum Meruit' (2020) 44 *Melbourne University Law Review* 679, 715–21.
[119] *Sumpter v Hedges* [1898] 1 WB 673.
[120] *Bolton v Mahadeva* [1972] 1 WLR 1009.
[121] B McFarlane and R Stevens, 'In Defence of *Sumpter v Hedges*' (2002) 118 *LQR* 569, 577; this is often put in terms of lump sum contracts. See also *Cutter v Powell* (1795) 6 TR 320, 101 ER 573.
[122] McFarlane and Stevens (n 121) 569; see *Boston Deep Sea Fishing and Ice Co v Ansell* (1888) 39 Ch D 339 (CA) 364–65 (Bowen LJ).

not unjust enrichment) can operate harshly where the builder commits a trifling omission.[123] In *Mahadeva* therefore an exception was mooted that if the plaintiff had substantially performed, he was still able to insist on being paid, although on the facts Bolton's installation of the heating system was so defective that there was no substantial performance. In *Hoenig v Isaacs* as well it was held that minor breaches do not preclude the claimant from claiming substantial performance was made.[124] The question in all these cases is whether the contract-breaker has earned his contractual entitlement to be paid. Two points can be made. The first is that not all obligations are entire. Some will be divisible,[125] but this will be a matter of contractual construction and contractual entitlement to payment. The second is that even if the obligation is entire, unjust enrichment may be possible. In *Mann v Paterson Construction (Pty) Ltd* the obligations were entire, but the Manns set out to prevent the company from doing the work.

C. Subsisting and Unenforceable Contracts

i. *Subsisting Contracts*

With unapportioned contracts we need to remove the whole contract before we can give restitution, but apportioned contracts do not need to fall in their entirety. In *Stevenson v Snow*, the court decided that the voyage being insured was divisible and therefore the premium for the section of the voyage that was not completed was recoverable.[126] Likewise with short delivery or instalment deliveries – if the claimant pays on the first of the month for deliveries at the end of the month and the defendant seller misses one month but then begins correct delivery – it would be better to recover the money for one instalment than to have to terminate the whole contract.[127] These cases would be historically for the action for money had and received, but *indebitatus assumpsit* was also available historically in cases where the sum fixed for services was agreed.[128] In *Roxborough v Rothmans Pall Mall of Australia*[129] unconstitutional excise duties had been levied on the import of cigarettes from Victoria into New South Wales. Wholesalers included the tax in their pricing and retailers then passed it on to consumers. Leaving the questions of passing on to one side, once the duties were declared illegal and ultra vires the state

[123] Butler (n 87) 233, but for criticism of the substantial performance exception see Law Commission (n 90) para 2.17.

[124] *Hoenig v Isaacs* [1952] 2 All ER 176.

[125] *Oliver v Lakeside Property Trust Pty Ltd* [2005] NSWSC 1040, [77]–[78]; on the definition of divisible obligations see Butler (n 87) 232.

[126] *Stevenson v Snow* (1761) 3 Burr 1237, 97 ER 808.

[127] A Tettenborn, 'Restitution within Subsisting Contracts: A Little Scepticism' [2002] *Restitution Law Review* 1.

[128] Baloch (n 34) 130.

[129] (2001) 208 CLR 516.

government retailers claimed the tax back. They succeeded on the basis that the tax was severable from the rest of the price and had only been paid on the basis of the duty's legality. In other words, despite the validity of the contract term providing for the payment of the tax, that requirement to pay could only be on the basis that the tax was due.

ii. Unenforceable Contracts

The difficulty with restitution in this context is that it should not be indirect enforcement. In *Pavey & Matthews Pty Ltd v Paul*[130] a building contract was unenforceable as being oral and not written. A quantum meruit claim was nonetheless permitted. Mason and Wilson JJ argued that once the true basis of the action were established, the execution of work and its acceptance by the defendant, it is hard to see the quantum meruit as indirect enforcement of the contract.[131] What seemed to be critical is the addition of the defendant's acceptance, because if all the claimant needed to prove was that he had done the work and not been paid the contract price, that might have appeared as indirect enforcement. Mason and Wilson JJ further commented that the contract was enforceable against the builder, although not by him and this could not be on the basis that he could or would not be paid.[132] Brennan J was rather more explicit. He explored the policy behind the unenforceability of the contract and argued that the policy behind the provision was the protection of the building owner, so it was clear what work was to be done and for what price. However, he argued that the effect was to preclude the builder from maintaining an action under an unwritten contract whether he has executed it or not.[133] The question then ultimately turns on whether the policy behind the unenforceability is defeated or stymied by a non-contractual quantum meruit. This is the same test as should be applied to decide whether the illegality of a contract precludes an unjust enrichment claim and we return to this in chapter eight. In *Pavey & Matthews* the statutory policy did not preclude relief. If the policy were to preclude the builder from attempting to raise additional charges that were un-bargained for, that policy is not pursued by refusing all remuneration.[134] In terms of calculating quantum, Gageler J said in *Mann v Paterson Contruction (Pty) Ltd* that the contract price was evidence of the value of the services.[135] In this he echoed Deane J in *Pavey & Matthews v Paul*, who said that in a claim for reasonable remuneration the unenforceable agreement could be evidence of appropriate compensation.[136]

[130] *Pavey & Matthews Pty Ltd v Paul* (1987) 162 CLR 221; in Canada, see *Deglman v Guaranty Trust Corpn* [1954] SCR 725.
[131] (1987) 162 CLR 221, 227.
[132] ibid 228–29.
[133] ibid 242–44.
[134] ibid 263 (Deane J).
[135] [2019] HCA 32, (2019) 267 CLR 560 [100].
[136] (1987) 162 CLR 221, 257; *Horton v Jones (No 2)* (1934) 34 SR (NSW) 368.

D. Claims in Contract or Unjust Enrichment?

Setting the scene, two points are important. First, it is worth stressing again that based on the classificatory methodology taken in this book there is no reason why these claims cannot be both. Chapter one established that in answering a legal question we can draw on principles from across the law and chapter three showed how contract principles are required to make sense of unjust enrichment. Unjust enrichment is inescapably **normatively pluralistic**.

Second, from a comparative perspective there is no common civilian approach. In German law when performance was rendered there was an obligation, and it was discharged. This explains why the *condictio ob rem*, which is sometimes seen as the equivalent of failure of basis, can only apply outside the contractual context in German law.[137] Mixed jurisdictions have a much less strict view of what counts as a causa or basis and therefore too much reliance on the strict logic of German law will lead us astray in understanding those jurisdictions. In Scotland, *Connelly v Simpson* involved a sale of shares.[138] The shares were paid for but never transferred before the voluntary liquidation of the company. It was a termination (or reduction) of the contract for breach case. Lord McCluskey said that there was no right to elect between contractual and unjustified enrichment remedies,[139] and Lord Sutherland expressly said that the payment was in consideration for a personal right to demand the shares, which they had received.[140] *Connelly v Simpson* has its difficulties, however. It suggested not only that the *condictio causa data causa non secuta* was not available, but restitution was not available in any guise; the remedy was damages. In *PEC Printers v Forth Printers*, however, a typesetting firm completed part of the work for a printers' firm, but then said they could not finish it on time.[141] The printers rescinded the contract and hired a typesetter to work in-house. The subcontractors sued for the work they had done. A quantum meruit was granted based on an implied contract. The sheriff said obiter, however, that there might be a recompense claim for work done. The traditional South African rule is that the return of money or returnable benefits is contractual, but restitution of non-returnables such as services is based on unjustified enrichment.[142] From a Birksian perspective this looks odd because services and money are axiomatically treated as being merely different forms of enrichment.[143] It is also odd if we are returning the value of the party's performance. The contradictions are

[137] §812(I)(2); T Krebs, *Restitution at the Crossroads* (London, Cavendish, 2001) 144.

[138] *Connelly v Simpson* 1994 SLT 1096.

[139] ibid 1101.

[140] ibid 1110.

[141] *PEC Printers v Forth Printers* 1980 SLT (Sh Ct) 118.

[142] S Miller, 'Unjustified Enrichment and Failed Contracts' in R Zimmermann, D Visser and K Reid (eds), *Mixed Legal Systems in Comparative Perspective* (Oxford, OUP, 2004) 441.

[143] Virgo, *The Principles of the Law of Restitution* (n 81) 62.

partly historical in origin,[144] but create coordination problems between the two sets of rules;[145] where the results are different this will lead to attempts to 'squeeze' the case in one category or the other.[146]

There are two main points to make. First, in all these cases failure of basis has the same analytic and normative structure. There has been a performance rendered by the claimant to the defendant; the claimant acted to pay, or transfer chattels or perform services and did so intentionally. The basis on which he did so failed. That is precisely the same as happens in non-contractual cases where no contract ever materialised and where a contract is terminated for breach and analogies can be drawn between those cases just as they are between pre-contractual cases and frustration.[147] Given that the performance rationale applies in both contractual and non-contractual cases, we might conclude that the cause of action lies outside contract. Some authors will reply that the fact all failure of basis claims involve some type of agreement means they are all contractual in a broad sense.[148] We cannot pursue this here, although we rejected Jaffey's arguments to this effect in chapter three. Taking a comparative perspective, the same analysis has been offered in South Africa; the performance was on the assumption of proper counter-performance by the defendant which does not occur. That would fall under the *condictio causa data causa non secuta* and this is the solution preferred by Hutton, who argues that these are unjustified enrichment claims in South Africa.[149] The case for saying these are unjust enrichment claims is particularly clear if we look past the fact that the rules on restitution are contextually contractual to their underlying function, which in this context is the unwinding of an intentional performance.[150]

A second point is that the policy questions are the same in the wide variety of contexts for the operation of failure of basis. This tends to militate in favour of there being one cause of action, and to treat some cases as unjust enrichment and others as contract, obscures this. One question is who should bear the risk of the loss or destruction of a transferred chattel.[151] Take the case where the purchaser is the innocent party and the asset is destroyed or lost without his being at fault, the availability of change of position to the purchaser renders the contract-breaker an insurer for the innocent party, because the purchaser can recover the price, but

[144] S Meier, 'Unwinding Failed Contracts: New European Developments' [2017] *Edinburgh Law Review* 1, 8–9.

[145] ibid 11–12.

[146] ibid 19.

[147] *Jennings & Chapman v Woodman, Matthews & Co* [1952] 2 TLR 409.

[148] See, eg, P Jaffey, 'Unjust Enrichment and Contract' (2014) 77 *MLR* 983.

[149] S Hutton 'Restitution after Breach of Contract: Rethinking the Conventional Jurisprudence' [1997] *Acta Juridica* 201, 215.

[150] D Visser, 'Rethinking Unjustified Enrichment: A Perspective on the Competition between Contractual and Enrichment Remedies' [1992] *Acta Juridica* 203, 225–29.

[151] Meier, 'Unwinding Failed Contracts (n 144) 22–23, or as in *Gillett v Mawman* (1808) 1 Taunt 137, 127 ER 784 one to be transferred.

the seller cannot recover the asset or its value. If the aggrieved party is the seller and the purchaser is the wrongdoer, the aggrieved party can repackage the claim in damages, but this is impossible if the claimant is the purchaser.[152] Miller argues this might subvert contractual risk allocation. One reply is that change of position need not be a feature of every unjust enrichment claim. It probably does not apply in cases of duress (because of the defendant's bad faith or unreasonableness) and there are differing views as to its applicability in failure of basis, one argument being that the recipient of money or goods always knew that receipt was conditional and would have to be reciprocated and so cannot plead that they believed otherwise.[153] This seems to work for loans cases,[154] but probably does not work in all cases.[155] We return to this in chapter eight. However, in the absence of clearly delineated sets of failure of basis cases, some of which are susceptible to change of position and some not, the defence's availability says little about there being multiple causes of action. Returning to our damaged chattel, it may be that we decide that the fact of the seller being a wrongdoer justifies his being an insurer, but if we decide otherwise this simply means change of position is not available in such cases. Questions of who should take the risk of the destruction equally need answering in frustration cases, and in apportioned subsisting contracts. The lesson is that we miss illuminating comparisons between the cases if we corral failed contract cases into a different category outside unjust enrichment, notwithstanding the contractual context. Further, historically these claims were seen as non-contractual in the sense that they were not based on consent or express promise.[156]

III. Failure of Basis as Failure of a Contract to Materialise

A and B negotiate for a contract; while negotiations are ongoing and both parties believe that they will be concluded successfully, B requests that A begin work. A does so, but negotiations break down and no contract is concluded. If money is paid there is often no issue. In *Chillingworth v Esche*[157] one party paid a deposit pursuant to an agreement to buy land 'subject to contract'. The purchasers then refused to sign the contract but could recover the deposit. If services are rendered the situation appears more complex. This is not least because both parties may have suffered loss through reliance on the other or acquired a gain through (partial) reciprocal performance. As Barker puts it, 'The scene is littered with unallocated

[152] Miller (n 142) 448–49.
[153] R Stevens, 'The Unjust Enrichment Disaster' (2018) 134 *LQR* 574, 587.
[154] *Goss v Chilcott* [1996] AC 788.
[155] Burrows, *The Law of Restitution* (n 66) 545–46.
[156] Baloch (n 34) ch 1.
[157] *Chillingworth v Esche* [1924] 1 Ch 97; *Goff & Jones* (n 54) para 14.02.

gains and losses and the law is left, brush in hand, to clean up the mess'.[158] Those losses may be caused by some fault of the defendant in which case the matter might be relatively straightforward, but sometimes, just as in frustration cases, there is no fault on either side and parallels are drawn between the pre-contractual and post-contractual cases. There are several possibilities. One is that there is a contract. Other plausible models are estoppel, unjust enrichment, or a model concentrating on loss. A rough consensus seems to have emerged that – in an example of our third model – there should be liability for reliance losses where the defendant has led the claimant to believe a contract will be concluded and the latter reasonably relies.[159] A fifth, redistributive, model which encompasses both gains and losses[160] is also possible and quantum meruit has been used to disguise such judicial redistribution.[161] These cases are not unjust enrichment cases. As observed earlier, a redistributive or loss-based model requires a different normative justification as it is not simply designed to reverse the enrichment inherent in a performance rendered.

One example highlighting the uncertain boundary between gain and loss is *Countrywide Communications v ICL Pathway Ltd*.[162] Nicholas Strauss QC held first that there was no binding contract. A consortium had been established to bid for a computer project and a bid vehicle, ICL Pathway Ltd, formed. Countrywide was later replaced as PR consultant to the consortium. Strauss QC acknowledged an informal understanding that if the bid succeeded Countrywide would be appointed. He did, however, list several factors a court would consider in deciding whether to award a quantum meruit. Was the work normally done for free? Did the defendant obtain a benefit and why did the contract fail to materialise?[163] He characterised the benefit to the defendant as saved expense – the cost of obtaining the desired and requested PR work elsewhere.[164] Strauss QC went on that he had found it almost impossible to deduce a general principle from the cases due to the difficulty in attempting to categorise what is really a loss as an enrichment.[165] This is, however, an important distinction and courts need to clearly recognise when gains are in play and when losses as the latter are not unjust enrichment cases.

In *RTS Flexible Systems v Mölkerei Alois Müller GmBH*,[166] it was said that where a contract is being negotiated subject to contract and work begins prior

[158] K Barker, 'Coping with Failure: Reappraising Pre-Contractual Remuneration' (2003) 19 *Journal of Contract Law* 105, 106.

[159] B McFarlane, 'The Protection of Pre-Contractual Reliance: A Way Forward' (2010) 10 *Oxford University Commonwealth Law Journal* 95; A Hutchinson, 'Liability for Breaking off Contractual Negotiations' (2012) 129 *South African Law Journal* 164.

[160] See Barker (n 158) 107–19 for these models.

[161] ibid 117; *Jennings & Chapman v Woodman Matthews & Co* [1952] 2 TLR 409.

[162] *Countrywide Communications v ICL Pathway Ltd* [2000] CLC 324.

[163] ibid 349.

[164] ibid 351.

[165] ibid 349; *MSM Consulting Ltd v Republic of Tanzania* [2009] EWHC 121, [171]; *ERDC v University of Brunel* [2006] EWHC 687; *Clarke & Sons Ltd v ACT Construction Ltd* [2002] EWCA Civ 972.

[166] *RTS Flexible Systems v Mölkerei Alois Müller GmBH* [2010] UKSC 14, [2010] 1 WLR 753.

to the formal contract there will only unusually be a collateral contract already present.[167] Just as in failure of basis, in deciding whether a contract is formed, the question is what (if anything) the parties have objectively agreed. What differs between the unjust enrichment and contract cases is mainly the specificity of what is agreed. Where there is a contract, it defines the rights and obligations of the parties. It is only where there is no contract or it has been disposed of that unjust enrichment bites.[168] The implication, however, is that if a contract is properly implied in fact it should be so, but courts should not strain to find a contract.[169] If no fiction is involved contract is the primary analysis.[170] An example where a contract was found is *Brewer Street Investments Ltd v Barclays Woollen Co Ltd*.[171] Dietrich, for instance, argues that these cases are all contractual; there are no separate unjust enrichment cases,[172] and the similarity between the actions was affirmed in *Whittle Movers Ltd v Hollywood Express Ltd*.[173] It was said that there was little difference between a contract entitling the provider to reasonable remuneration and a restitutionary remedy based on unjust enrichment.[174] Despite this, Edelman (now Edelman J of the High Court of Australia) describes the objection that these cases are contractual as 'simple, elegant and wrong'.[175] It is precisely because the parties have not agreed a contract that the claim arises and the same point can be made about the German *condictio ob rem* which operates in this fact scenario. There might be too much uncertainty about the bargain, or it might be unenforceable. It is fictional to say they agreed a price 'to be determined by a court'.

Unjust enrichment liability arises where A does work and both A and B understand a contract will arise and this does not occur.[176] Havelock has considered the importance of establishing an enrichment.[177] If we can successfully establish that the work was requested and accepted on the basis that a contract would eventuate, the services – whether preparatory or not – will count as performance. It is the value of the performance that must be paid, not an extant enrichment to be returned. Havelock is in the end correct to insist that both parties must objectively expect a contract to be concluded and must know and rely on the fact that the other expects this and the very services expected are performed.[178] Indeed this test, slightly modified, can also be used where there is a contract, but it 'runs out' as in *Benedetti v Sawiris*.[179] It will be clear that unjust enrichment reasoning has a

[167] ibid 772.
[168] R Havelock, 'A Taxonomic Approach to Quantum Meruit' (2016) 132 *LQR* 470, 477.
[169] *Benourad v Compass Group Ltd* [2010] EWHC 1182.
[170] Havelock, 'A Taxonomic Approach to Quantum Meruit' (n 168) 486.
[171] *Brewer Street Investments Ltd v Barclays Woollen Co Ltd* [1954] 1 QB 428.
[172] See J Dietrich, 'Classifying Pre-Contractual Liability: A Comparative Analysis' (2001) 21 *Legal Studies* 153, 164.
[173] *Whittle Movers Ltd v Hollywood Express Ltd* [2009] EWCA Civ 1189, [2009] 2 CLC 771.
[174] ibid 782–83.
[175] J Edelman, 'Liability in Unjust Enrichment when a Contract Fails to Materialise' in AS Burrows and E Peel (eds), *Contract Formation and Parties* (Oxford, OUP, 2010) 178–79.
[176] Havelock, 'A Taxonomic Approach to Quantum Meruit' (n 168) 493.
[177] R Havelock, 'Anticipated Contracts that do not Arise' [2011] *Restitution Law Review* 72, 78–84.
[178] ibid 86.
[179] *Benedetti v Sawiris* [2013] UKSC 50, [2013] 3 WLR 351.

relatively narrow role here, as a gap-filler where the understanding is too imprecise for a contract or where it is clear no price was agreed. In such cases where we can identify an objectively understood common acceptance that requested or accepted work would be paid for (at an unspecified rate) or that a contract would come to fruition, the failure of that common intention gives rise to a claim in unjust enrichment for the value of that performance. Sometimes there might be a mistake as to the existence of the contract which might justify relief,[180] although in most cases the action will be based on failure of basis.

This is obscured by the language in the case law. Sometimes the question is put in terms of risk – did A take the risk of the contract not being concluded? Most commentators seem to agree that it should be objective risk;[181] the question thus becomes whether the reasonable observer would say that the party had taken the risk. Sometimes, as in *Regalian Properties v LDDC*[182] the question is framed in terms of the party's freedom to withdraw from the negotiations at any time. If so, all expenses incurred are at the party's own risk and irrecoverable. This is potentially conclusory. Why does the claimant take the risk in some cases but not others?[183] Edelman contrasts *Regalian* with *Sabemo Pty Ltd v North Sydney MC*[184] where it was decided Sabemo did not take the risk of the unilateral withdrawal of the Council from negotiations, although it is not clear from the facts what triggers this different conclusion. Sheppard J in *Sabemo* did, however, make the point that the Council made the decision for reasons that had nothing to do with the claimant. This is unsatisfactory as a distinction because a party might take the risk of the counter-party taking decisions on any basis at all[185] whether that reason is connected to the claimant or not.

Let us take another example. Unfortunately, it merely muddies the waters further and therefore helps illustrate the inutility of risk-taking reasoning. *Cobbe v Yeoman's Row Management Ltd* is largely concerned with a proprietary estoppel claim, which was rejected.[186] For present purposes what is important is Lord Scott's dictum that where an agreement is reached under which an individual provides services in return for a legal but unenforceable promise which is not carried out, there is a restitutionary remedy.[187] Lord Scott saw it as uncontroversial that there should be a quantum meruit because Yeoman's Row had requested and accepted the services. In essence, Cobbe was a property developer who entered a joint venture with Yeoman's

[180] *Easat Antennas v Racal* [2000] 6 WLUK 537 may be an example of this. See [72] the claimant 'would not have agreed to incur the costs concerned without recharge to the defendant had it not believed they would have been recovered under the promised sub-contract' (Hart J) and [38]–[49] for details of why the contract was too uncertain to be enforceable.

[181] J Goodwin, 'Failure of Basis in the Contractual Context' [2013] *Restitution Law Review* 24; PS Davies, 'Risk in Unjust Enrichment' [2012] *Restitution Law Review* 57.

[182] *Regalian Properties v LDDC* [1995] 1 WLR 282; *Stephen Donald Architects Ltd v King* [2003] EWHC 1867.

[183] Edelman (n 175) 159, 160–61.

[184] *Sabemo Pty Ltd v North Sydney MC* [1977] 2 NSWLR 880.

[185] ibid 902–03.

[186] *Cobbe v Yeoman's Row Management Ltd* [2008] UKHL 55, [2008] 1 WLR 1752.

[187] ibid [43].

Row. The latter would acquire vacant possession of some town houses; Cobbe would obtain planning permission, buy them from the defendant and develop them. Cobbe engaged architects, obtained planning permission and Yeoman's Row demanded new terms. The contract was oral and therefore unenforceable under the Law of Property (Miscellaneous Provisions) Act 1989. The proprietary estoppel claim was rejected as the oral agreement was subject to contract. The purchaser's interest in the property is then dependent on the other party's behaviour.[188] Cobbe's belief that Yeoman's Row would honour the agreement was speculative; he knew it was unenforceable.[189] There was therefore no possible mistake claim. It was also accepted that there was a need for further negotiation as to terms. Cobbe, however, would therefore receive payment at the rate appropriate for an experienced developer doing the work of obtaining planning permission (as opposed to the difference in value between the land with and without such permission) and this would reflect the company's unjust enrichment.[190] As Edelman points out, it is unclear from Lord Scott's speech why Cobbe took the risk for the purpose of denying an estoppel, but did not take the risk for the purpose of a failure of basis claim.[191] Risk-taking reasoning is circular therefore – we decide A has taken a risk because B has no liability. B has no liability because A took the risk. Risk-taking as an idea does not explain the cases.[192] The terms of the request, however, make it clear what risk the claimant was taking. For Edelman – bringing us back to our earlier discussions – we need to keep an eye on the objective basis for the work being done; if the work was within the scope of the request then the claimant was entitled to payment, because that was the understanding.[193]

IV. Failure of Basis in Void Contracts

A. The Workings of Failure of Basis

In principle this is straightforward. The workings can best be illustrated through the swaps cases. In the 1990s, a set of restitution cases were litigated arising out of the decision in *Hazell v Hammersmith LBC*[194] that so-called interest rate swaps agreements entered by local authorities were – despite prior widespread legal advice to the contrary – void. Essentially, these agreements involved one side pretending to lend a notional sum to their counterparty at a fixed rate of interest and the counterparty

[188] ibid [25].
[189] ibid [27].
[190] ibid [42]; see on risk also *Stephen Donald Architects Ltd v King* [2003] EWHC 1867; *Whittle Movers Ltd v Hollywood Express Ltd* [2009] EWCA Civ 1189, [2009] 2 CLC 771.
[191] Edelman (n 175) 161.
[192] F Wilmot-Smith, 'Replacing Risk-Taking Reasoning' (2011) 127 *LQR* 610.
[193] *Nu Line Construction Group Pty Ltd v Fowler* [2014] NSWCA 51; *MSM Consulting Ltd v Republic of Tanzania* [2009] EWHC 121, [171]; *Angelopoulos v Sabatino (No 2)* (1995) 65 SASR 1; *Vedatech Ltd v Crystal Decisions Ltd* [2002] EWHC 818; *William Lacey (Hounslow) Ltd v Davis* [1957] 2 All ER 712.
[194] *Hazell v Hammersmith LBC* [1992] 1 AC 1.

pretending to lend the same amount at a floating rate. Each gambled that interest rates would move their way and so make a profit. Swaps were characterised as open swaps – where at the time *Hazell* was decided, payments by the parties were still to be made – and closed swaps where there were no such payments to be made. Open swaps could be unwound as the losing party could point to the fact that no more payments to it would be made to justify the basis on which its own payments had been made having failed. Where there was a closed swap, this claim was impossible.

The importance of barring a claim where the parties have in fact received what they wanted can also be seen in *Simposh v Sharma*.[195] The defendant entered into negotiations with the claimant for the sale of a building. An agreement was reached whereby the defendant would not offer the building for sale until the redevelopment works were completed and would then offer it first to the claimant. The defendant did this, took the property off the market, finished the development and offered it to the claimant, who decided not to buy and requested £53,400 be repaid – the sum paid for the defendant to delay any sale. The agreement was void under section 2 of the Law of Property (Miscellaneous Provisions) Act 1989 as being an unwritten agreement purporting to create or sell an option to purchase land. The Court of Appeal decided that the claimant's expectations had been fulfilled and there was no failure of basis.[196] This was approved by the Singapore Court of Appeal in *Benzline v Lorinser Supercars*. If the claimant receives what he expected there is no failure of basis. This does not usually matter as in the absence of a natural obligation a mistake claim will lie. A natural obligation should be recognised in English law, and bar a mistake claim, where the reason for the obligation's nullity neither shows a reason to protect the claimant (eg, mistake, ultra vires) or some substantive defect of which the law disapproves (eg, illegality).[197] This explains why the fact the swaps were closed swaps does not bar recovery; the swaps contracts were ultra vires the local authority, which indicates the claimant (or their taxpayers?) does need protecting even if it gets everything it wanted. Informality of the contract does not indicate the claimant needs such protection. There was a natural obligation on this view in *Simposh*. To call this inappropriate curing of a void obligation or resurrection of the part-performance doctrine[198] is to make the same error corrected in *Fibrosa*.

The rule that full performance barred relief in contracts ultra vires and void therefore came under pressure as litigants attempted to find ways to recover without challenging the rule that payments under a mistake of law were irrecoverable.[199] It found its form in the idea of what was originally referred to as 'absence of

[195] *Simposh v Sharma* [2011] EWCA Civ 1383, [2013] Ch 23.

[196] ibid [55]; see also *Tootal Clothing Ltd v Guinea Properties Ltd* (1992) 64 P&CR 452; Stevens, *The Laws of Restitution* (n 37) 97–98.

[197] D Sheehan, 'Natural Obligations in English Law' [2004] *Lloyd's Maritime & Commercial Law Quarterly* 172.

[198] Tang Hang Wu, 'Natural Obligations and the Common Law of Unjust Enrichment' (2006) 6 *Oxford University Commonwealth Law Journal* 133, 149.

[199] *Bilbie v Lumley* (1802) 4 East 469, 102 ER 448.

consideration', but here largely referred to as 'absence of basis'. Ultimately, the mistake of law bar was challenged successfully in *Kleinwort Benson v Lincoln City Council*.[200]

B. Absence of Basis

i. The History of Absence of Basis

Absence of consideration or basis cropped up first in Hobhouse J's judgment in *Westdeutsche Landesbank Girozentrale v Islington LBC*.[201] The facts were that the parties had engaged in a swaps transaction. That was wholly void from the outset as ultra vires the local authority, and Hobhouse J said that the purpose of the payments failed as a result. Failure of consideration presupposed that there had been at some stage a valid contract, partially performed by one party. Since this contract was void, the proper term, his Lordship said, was absence of consideration.[202] Absence of consideration would ground relief, whatever the reason for the avoidance of the contract, be it that the parties were mistaken, or that the contract was ultra vires. Hobhouse J therefore held that in both the closed and open swaps the cause of action was absence of consideration,[203] and this allowed litigants to sidestep the mistake of law bar. After the mistake of law bar's removal, and despite some flirtation by Lord Walker in *Deutsche Morgan Grenfell v IRC*[204] with absence of basis, the unjust factors model has been reaffirmed.[205]

In *Guinness Mahon v Kensington v Chelsea RLBC*, the bank was the losing party in a closed swap and claimed relief on the grounds of failure of basis.[206] It succeeded. Morritt LJ said that the consideration had failed totally because the bank had bargained for a legally enforceable right to the money,[207] which the nullity of the contract meant did not exist. It was the fact the contract was void that constituted the total failure of basis. In saying this Morritt LJ reformulated the law's understanding of what we bargain for. On one level we might legitimately say that we bargain for two things – counter-performance and the right to enforce it. We might doubt this, however, as an empirical matter. Most people when asked would say a sale contract involved bargaining for the goods, not a legal right that the goods be delivered. The Court of Appeal though believed itself bound by its

[200] *Kleinwort Benson v Lincoln City Council* [1999] 2 AC 349 (HL).
[201] *Westdeutsche Landesbank Girozentrale v Islington LBC* [1994] 4 All ER 890.
[202] ibid 929–30.
[203] ibid 930.
[204] *Deutsche Morgan Grenfell v IRC* [2006] UKHL 49.
[205] *Samsoondar v Capital Insurance Ltd* [2020] UKPC 33.
[206] *Guinness Mahon v Kensington v Chelsea RLBC* [1999] QB 215 (CA).
[207] ibid 227; S Meier, 'Restitution after Executed Void Contracts' in PBH Birks and FD Rose (eds), *Lessons of the Swaps Litigation* (London, Mansfield Press, 2000) 209–10.

decision in *Westdeutsche Landesbank Girozentrale v Islington LBC*, which had likewise held that restitution was justified by the lack of a binding contract and of an enforceable right to the money.[208] Absence of basis was never affirmed in the House of Lords in *Westdeutsche Landesbank Girozentrale v Islington LBC*,[209] as the council involved in the closed swap did not appeal,[210] but Hobhouse J's and the Court of Appeal's reasoning appears flawed. Much of the reasoning is based on a series of cases under the Grants of Life Annuities Act 1777,[211] which provided that the borrower (grantor) could treat an annuity as void if not registered in Chancery within 20 days. As Swadling has observed, however, there are annuity cases that prove relief was not based on nullity alone, but on failure of basis. *Davis v Bryan*[212] therefore provides an example of a case where relief was denied because the testator had received everything he bargained for and his representative failed in his claim. The reasoning is also in essence 'upside down' *Chandler v Webster*.[213] The contract was frustrated because the coronation procession was cancelled and there was no longer anything to watch. However, the fact of the initial validity of the contract meant there was no failure of basis. In both *Westdeutsche* and *Guinness Mahon* the fallacy is to think consideration means the same thing in unjust enrichment and contract.

ii. Absence of Basis in Principle

It may still be right to say that English law recognises a right to restitution in performance claim purely because of the nullity of the obligation under which the putative performance was carried out. Hobhouse J talked in terms of absence of consideration and the sufficiency of the nullity of a contract; the principle, however, if it is English law, goes wider than just void contracts. It covers all types of putative performance. There are a number of features of English law that point towards an absence of basis analysis in performance claims.

We have already seen that the absence of a basis is in fact part of the cause of action. To say that there was a valid obligation – to assert the 'defence' of good consideration – is to assert that part of the cause of action that the claimant must prove is missing. It is a denial. A second feature is that it is important in English

[208] [1994] 1 WLR 938 (CA) 946 (Dillon LJ); 953 (Leggatt LJ). Other cases resting on absence of basis are *South Tyneside MBC v Svenska Intl* [1995] 1 All ER 545 (CA) 556; *Kleinwort Benson v Birmingham CC* [1997] QB 380 (CA) 387.

[209] But see [1996] AC 669 (HL) 710–11 (Lord Browne-Wilkinson).

[210] PBH Birks, 'Mistakes of Law' [2000] *Current Legal Problems* 205, 232.

[211] See, eg, *Hicks v Hicks* (1802) 2 East 16; *Holbrook v Sharpney* (1812) 19 Ves Jun 131, 34 ER 467.

[212] *Davis v Bryan* (1827) 6 B&C 651 108 ER 591; WJ Swadling, 'Restitution for No Consideration' [1994] *Restitution Law Review* 73, 77–78; PBH Birks, 'No Consideration: Restitution after Void Contracts' (1993) 23 *University of Western Australia Law Review* 195, 214–16. For an alternative analysis of the cases, see B Kremer, 'Recovering Money Paid under Void Contracts: Absence of Consideration and Failure of Consideration' (2001) 17 *Journal of Contract Law* 37.

[213] [1904] Ch 493; Swadling (n 212) 78–79.

law to work out who is performing to whom. It is this that lies behind the workings of mistaken payments by banks where the proper defendant depends on whether there was a valid mandate for the payment – ie, on whose behalf was the payment made and which obligation does the bank purport to be discharging? A third feature is that, despite appearances, it is not true that all causal mistakes count in English law. Meier and Zimmermann suggest that giving relief for all errors is too broad; restrictions are needed and only absence of basis analysis can allow for that.[214] They suggest that it would be unreasonable to allow the claimant relief where he has merely mistaken his tax liability or discovered that the recipient of the money is an enemy of a relative of his.[215] However, where he meant to give £100 but actually gave £1,000 relief would be reasonable. English law, they argue, ought to distinguish between the two cases. Meier therefore suggests a distinction between mistakes in forming the intention and executing it. Only mistakes affecting the formation of the intention to transfer the value as a gift or in pursuance of an obligation should attract relief. Only they affect the legal ground. The mistake must be purpose oriented;[216] it must affect the purpose that the party had in mind before making the gift or payment. She suggests that this is in keeping with the old requirement of a liability mistake, because liability mistakes too were purpose oriented.[217] We saw in chapter two and chapter four that English law does not allow any old mistake to count, although the distinctions English law in fact draws are not quite the same as those Meier argues for. The fourth feature is the lack of spent mistake doctrine. The fact that such a doctrine exists in South Africa, as evidenced in *Legator McKenna v Shea*,[218] is critical to Scott's argument that unjust factors are vital and that South Africa does not know a pure absence of basis system. In *Legator* the court decided that it was a condition of relief under the *condictio indebiti* that any expected counter-performance not have been forthcoming; even if there is an excusable mistake as to liability if the claimant got the expected counter-performance there is no cause of action. The absence of this doctrine points us to absence of basis as being sufficient because, in England, despite counter-performance, restitution is still available. Mistake, therefore, allowed relief in the closed swaps cases. Consequently, the argument goes, English law concentrates on the nullity of the obligation rather than its performance and this is an argument strengthened on the view that there was no real mistake in *Kleinwort Benson v Lincoln City Council*. The case would thus rest on retrospective nullity, not retrospective mistake.

[214] S Meier and R Zimmermann, 'Judicial Development of the Law, *Error Juris*, and the Law of Unjustified Enrichment: A View from Germany' (1999) 115 *LQR* 556, 562–63.

[215] ibid 562–63. Meier, 'Restitution after Executed Void Contracts' (n 207) 212.

[216] § 812-I (2) BGB; B Dickson, 'The Law of Restitution in the Federal Republic of Germany: A Comparison with English Law' (1987) 36 *ICLQ* 751, 775.

[217] See T Krebs, 'A German Contribution to English Enrichment Law' [1999] *Restitution Law Review* 271, 274, discussing Meier's doctoral thesis in German, S Meier, *Irrtum und Zweckfehlung; Das System der Unjust-Gründe bei rechtgrundlosen Leistungen im englischen Recht* (Tübingen, JCB Mohr, 1999).

[218] *Legator McKenna v Shea* 2010 (1) SA 35.

Nonetheless four counter-arguments may be put. First, Meier believes that the unjust factors used to justify restitution do no more than mirror those used to justify the vitiation of the contract, or other legal ground.[219] Zimmermann has independently commented on this as a weakness of English law.[220] This turns out not to be quite right. Not all reasons for invalidity are reasons for restitution. Incapacity is not.[221] There is therefore no simple mirror, so that a contract void for reason x will always give ground for restitution for reason x. None of the swaps cases were argued on the ground that recovery was available on the basis of the authorities' incapacity. Nor is incapacity sufficient in minors' contracts cases. In *Steinberg v Scala (Leeds) Ltd*, for example, an infant bought shares in a company and later wanted to remove her name from the register and receive her money back.[222] She had not attended any company meetings or received any dividends. Lord Sterndale MR said that she could not recover if she did not prove a total failure of basis.[223] At no point was there a suggestion that the minority in and of itself generates a claim.

Second, unjust factors make it easier to make connections between performance and non-performance claims in English law and provide a normative glue justifying treating them together. We saw in chapter four the importance of mistake in justifying claims such as *Greenwood v Bennett*[224] and *County of Carleton v City of Ottawa*.[225] From the perspective of the argument of this book that a developmental taxonomy charting a historically contingent path is dependent on incremental analogical change this is important, and indeed reflected in the common law method of judicial law-making. According to Scott and Visser, the common law judge will draw the principle on which she relies to adjudicate the case in favour of one party narrowly.[226] This precludes the possibility inherent in the conservatism of the methodology of the principle being used to expansively redefine liability, although it does not preclude incremental change and development based on the presence of a significant family resemblance, such as mistake. The absence of basis analysis is simply at odds with this conservatism.[227] Just as importantly, the common law judge tends to reach for the most obvious and easily justifiable concrete positive reason for relief.[228] Mistake counts as such. Absence of basis does not and the history of the doctrine, which emerged in its modern form as a result of litigants'

[219] Meier, 'Restitution after Executed Void Contracts' (n 207) 211.

[220] R Zimmermann, 'Unjustified Enrichment: The Modern Civilian Approach' (1995) 15 *OJLS* 403, 416.

[221] E O'Dell, 'Incapacity' in PBH Birks and FD Rose (eds), *Lessons of the Swaps Litigation* (London, Mansfield Press, 2000).

[222] *Steinberg v Scala (Leeds) Ltd* [1923] 2 Ch 452 (CA).

[223] ibid 458; 461 (Warrington LJ); 464 (Younger LJ); and *Pearce v Brain* [1929] 2 KB 310.

[224] *Greenwood v Bennett* [1973] QB 195.

[225] *County of Carleton v City of Ottawa* (1966) 52 DLR (2d) 220.

[226] H Scott and D Visser, 'The Impact of Legal Culture on the Law of Unjustified Enrichment: The Role of Reasons' in E Bant and M Harding (eds), *Exploring Private Law* (Cambridge, CUP, 2010).

[227] ibid 164–65.

[228] ibid 164.

reluctance to challenge *Bilbie v Lumley*,[229] but which has now largely disappeared from judicial note, is evidence of this.

Third, recognition of an absence of basis regime would require a significant reformulation of English law.[230] It would require us to reformulate our understandings of consideration to little obvious gain and Birks' attempts to do this lead to problems in (say) the analysis of terminability of contracts for breach. In essence, in order to square the availability of restitution and damages, Birks needed to make of terminability a strange type of halfway house – invalid enough for restitution but not invalid enough to avoid liability in damages.[231] English property law also cuts across the system in ways we examine in chapter seven.[232] The difficulties in coherently making a switch to a German-style system can be illustrated by the difficulties of Canadian law, which McInnes argues is committed to such a switch. He argues for example, and by his own admission in the teeth of the case law, that if contract damages are available the contract is a juristic reason barring relief in unjust enrichment.[233] Such – and other – contortions to make the Canadian formula of absence of juristic reason slot into a civil law system should be cautionary.[234]

Last, we might note that the German approach works, precisely because of its codified law and the automatic triggering effect of the word '*nichtig*'. But the automation can break down.[235] One problem, requiring the use of unjust factors, lies in the case where the claimant pays money, knowing it is not owed in order to prevent the cut-off of supplies by the defendant. Scott suggests the only sensible explanation for recovery is compulsion,[236] and proof of compulsion (or mistake etc) within the *condictio indebiti* is required for relief in South African law.[237] Otherwise, we are forced to say that the money is paid to discharge the non-existent debt (even though that flies in the face of the evidence). Compulsion is also important for another, related, reason. There is a defence in German law that the payer knew that the

[229] (1802) 4 East 469, 102 ER 448.

[230] G Dannemann, 'Unjust Enrichment as Absence of Basis: Can English Law Cope?' in AS Burrows and A Rodger (eds), *Mapping the Law* (Oxford, OUP, 2006).

[231] PBH Birks, *Unjust Enrichment*, 2nd edn (Oxford, Clarendon, Press, 2005) ch 5; for critique, see D Sheehan, 'Unjust Factors or Restitution of Transfers Sine Causa' [2008] *Oxford University Comparative Law Forum* 1.

[232] See also D Sheehan, 'Resulting Trusts, Sine Causa and the Structure of Proprietary Restitution' (2011) 11 *Oxford University Commonwealth Law Journal* 1.

[233] M McInnes, 'Contracts Discharged for Breach and Unjust Enrichment: A Matter of Principle' (2022) 52 *Advocates' Quarterly* 481, 504–06.

[234] D Sheehan, 'Unjust Factors, Absence of Juristic Reason and the Development of Canadian Unjust(ified) Enrichment Law' (2016) 49 *University of British Columbia Law Review* 619.

[235] H Scott, 'Restitution of Extra-Contractual Transfers: Limits on the Absence of Legal Ground Analysis' [2006] *Restitution Law Review* 93, 97–98.

[236] ibid 103.

[237] *Union Government v Gowar* [1915] AD 426. Du Plessis discusses the different roles of duress in civil law condictiones in J du Plessis, 'Duress and Related Forms of Pressure: A Comparative Perspective' in C Mitchell and WJ Swadling (eds), *The Restatement Third: Restitution and Unjust Enrichment* (Oxford, Hart Publishing, 2013).

payment was not due.[238] This cannot apply in cases of physical duress,[239] and ought not to do so in the economic duress cases, although there is no sure basis for the defence's disapplication in the Civil Code. The point is that you want it back **because** you knew it was not due but were forced into paying anyway. All this feeds into a recognition that there are no systems that are pure unjust factors or pure absence of basis. All systems recognise that if there is a valid obligation under which the transfer is made, that there can be no relief.[240] Equally there are no systems that are pure absence of basis.[241] Despite a belief in some quarters that these are simply incompatible explanations,[242] every system is mixed to some degree; in the end English law and the civilian systems seem to meet half way.

V. Conclusion

There are differences between the situations described in this chapter, and we should not be surprised by this. However, if a failure of basis is failure of the collective intention to do x, this justifies restitution in all cases of failure of basis whether (say) the claimant's performance was based on a valid, but terminated, contract or where there is no valid contract. The statutory frustration action is a separate cause of action, although there are significant difficulties with it as discussed in section II.A. Equally, failure of basis in the failed anticipated contract cases might amount to a separate cause of action to the extent it concerns itself with losses as well. To the extent to which these actions do concern losses we should not consider them part of the law of unjust enrichment. Loss does not form part of the value of the rendered performance of which restitution is ordered. While we are constrained by the 1943 Act in quantifying relief in frustration, it remains open to us to be clear that it is gain in the form of the value of the performance rendered which is recovered in pre-contractual cases.

Absence of basis is not a viable description of the English law of performance claims. The next chapter shows how some cases – we use necessity as an example – which have been included in unjust enrichment by prominent authors do not fit the performance framework and need to be excluded from our subject matter. Other controversial cases such as restitution of overpaid tax can be included.

[238] § 814 BGB.

[239] B Markesinis, W Lorenz and G Dannemann, *An Introduction to the German Law of Obligations: Contract and Unjustified Enrichment* (Oxford, OUP, 1997) 736; MünchKomm § 814, no 3, no 9; AS Burrows, 'Absence of Basis: The New Birksian Scheme' in AS Burrows and A Rodger (eds), *Mapping the Law* (Oxford, OUP, 2006) 39 has another example where the defence may not run – the open swap where the bank paid knowing the contract was void.

[240] P Gallo, 'Unjust Enrichment: A Comparative Analysis' (1992) 40 *American Journal of Comparative Law* 431, 432.

[241] LD Smith, 'Demystifying Juristic Reasons' (2007) 45 *Canadian Business Law Journal* 281, 291.

[242] See, eg, Stevens, *The Laws of Restitution* (n 37) 104.

6

Policy-Motivated Unjust Factors?

Introduction

This chapter examines two possible policy-motivated unjust factors. Alongside the intent-based factors and failure of consideration, factors such as necessity, legal compulsion, moral compulsion, undue tax and the policy against accumulation have been raised. Degeling has explained that such unjust factors may be unstable and the list of possible policies never ending.[1] She suggests any instability is minimised by the insistence on the core unjust enrichment principles.[2] This rather begs the question of what those core principles might be and we see that, once properly understood, those principles bar some of these alleged policy-motivated unjust factors from unjust enrichment. In this chapter we examine the *Woolwich* claim and necessity, the former of which should be included in unjust enrichment and the latter of which should not. The important question to be answered in both cases is whether or not they can be described in terms of a performance claim, and the reasoning for saying that the former claim is, and the latter case is not a defective performance can usefully be contrasted to show the analytical power of the idea.

I. Restitution of Undue Taxes

There are a variety of statutory grounds for relief and means of recovering overpaid tax. It is beyond the scope of this book to cover them in detail, but they are unsatisfactorily inconsistent with each other in that some, such as section 33 of the Taxes Management Act 1970,[3] are exclusive in their operation and some are not. This section concentrates on the common law. That action is not exclusive. Pre-*Woolwich* actions remain, such as where money is demanded 'under colour of office'.[4] There may be also a mistake of law in many cases. The section is divided

[1] S Degeling, 'Understanding Policy-Motivated Unjust Factors' in R Grantham and C Rickett (eds), *Structure and Justification in Private Law: Essays for Peter Birks* (Oxford, Hart Publishing, 2008) 269.

[2] ibid 289–90.

[3] Law Commission, *Restitution: Mistakes of Law and Ultra Vires Exactions by Public Authorities* (Law Comm No 227, 1994) recommended its repeal at para 9.25.

[4] ibid paras 6.13–6.15.

into two. First, we ask how the common law action works and the scope of the principle that underpins it asking, for instance. what sort of defendants are subject to the action and what defences are available. Second, we ask whether the *Woolwich* action is a public law action, or an unjust enrichment action and indeed whether it matters.

A. Scope of the Principle

i. *The Cause of Action*

In *Woolwich BS v IRC* itself the claimant building society made a payment to the IRC of a disputed tax debt.[5] They paid believing that it was not owing and protested as much. There was therefore no argument of mistake to be run. Essentially, perhaps in part to preserve their reputation, they chose to pay now and argue later. The House of Lords held that if an ultra vires tax was demanded it must be repaid.[6] The building society had already successfully sought to strike down the secondary legislation, the Income Tax (Building Societies) Regulations 1986, under which the tax was demanded.[7] That invalidity therefore triggered the liability to repay. In practice if this action lies there is very little room for mistake, although arguments that a mistake action should be barred as a matter of principle seem to be misguided.[8] The main advantage of a mistake claim would be access to the deferred start point of limitation under section 32(1)(c) of the Limitation Act 1980. That advantage has been removed by a combination of section 320 of the Finance Act 2004 and section 107 of the Finance Act 2007.[9]

The quantum of relief under *Woolwich* is the difference between the amount paid under the invalid demand or statutory instrument and the amount which could otherwise have been lawfully charged. The public authority is not allowed to say that had it realised the invalidity it would have taken other steps to raise the money.[10] The principle is the flipside of *Auckland Harbour*

[5] *Woolwich BS v IRC* [1993] AC 70 (HL).

[6] R Williams, *Unjust Enrichment and Public Law* (Oxford, Hart Publishing, 2010) 37; on the need for a judicial review see also *Jones v Powys LHB* [2008] EWHC 2562 (Admin); *Hemming v Westminster City Council* [2012] EWHC 1260 (Admin).

[7] In *R v IRC ep Woolwich BS* [1990] 1 WLR 1400; the immediate response was s 53 Finance Act 1991 which retrospectively validated those regulations against all other claimants, and which itself triggered litigation in the European Court of Human Rights in *National Provincial BS v UK* (1998) 25 EHRR 127.

[8] D Sheehan, 'Mistaken Overpayments of Tax' in S Elliott et al (eds), *Restitution of Overpaid Tax* (Oxford, Hart Publishing, 2013); *Deutsche Morgan Grenfell v IRC* [2006] UKHL 49, [2007] 1 AC 558, [18] (Lord Hoffmann).

[9] Currently – although this becomes less important, presumably, over time after Brexit – those sections are disapplied in cases involving EU law: Sheehan, 'Mistaken Overpayments of Tax' (n 8) 57. See also *Jazztel plc v HMRC* [2022] EWCA Civ 232.

[10] *Vodafone v Office for Communications* [2020] EWCA Civ 183; *Waikato Regional Airport Ltd v AG New Zealand* [2003] UKPC 50, [2004] 1 NZLR 1; *Littlewoods v HMRC (No 2)* [2014] EWHC 868, [2014] STC 1761.

Board v R[11] which stated that the Crown can recover any payment made out of the 'Consolidated Fund' without authority, although in practice there are statutory safeguards to protect recipients of, for example, overpaid social security benefits.[12]

One obvious further scenario where it applies is the misapplication of a valid statutory instrument. If the exaction is ultra vires, the principle applies whether that is due to the statutory instrument being ultra vires, a misunderstanding of the scope of an intra vires instrument, or just a mistake as to what the facts were.[13] Another question is whether a demand by the public authority is required. In principle there seems little reason why it should be.[14] Despite this, Henderson J suggested in *Test Claimants in the FII Group Litigation v HMRC* that *Woolwich* did require a demand by the HMRC.[15] The decision in *FII* involved the question whether the claimants, who were all members of the BAT group of companies, could reclaim additional tax paid on overseas income which would have been tax free if earned in the UK and whether they could recover Advance Corporation Tax (ACT), which they had not been able to choose to offset against mainstream UK corporation tax, because all or most of their profits came from sources taxed overseas rather than in the UK. These companies claimed that ACT in effect became an unlawful secondary or double tax which penalised companies who invested abroad. As ACT is not subject to an assessment or demand by the Revenue, if Henderson J were correct only a mistake claim would have been available. The Court of Appeal, however, rejected Henderson J's contention that an unlawful demand was required for a *Woolwich* claim to lie;[16] the claim lay whenever the tax payments were not due whether a formal demand was made or not; this has been affirmed by the Supreme Court decision in *FII*.[17] Of course this still means the tax must have been *not* due. The critical point is that the policy behind the claim is the public law one of legality and that taxes cannot be levied without authority.[18]

There is a question as to which bodies or types of payment the principle applies to. An officer of central or local government exercising a power to require payment of some licence fee or tax is covered. However, conceivably any public service provider whose ability to charge derives from public law could be covered.[19]

[11] *Auckland Harbour Board v R* [1924] AC 318.

[12] eg, Social Security Administration Act 1992, s 71.

[13] *British Steel plc v Customs and Excise Commissioners* [1997] 2 All ER 366.

[14] AS Burrows, *The Law of Restitution*, 3rd edn (Oxford, OUP, 2011) 507–08.

[15] *Test Claimants in the FII Group Litigation v HMRC* [2008] EWHC 2893, [2009] STC 254, [260]; see also *NEC Semi-Conductors v HMRC* [2006] EWCA Civ 25, [2006] STC 606.

[16] [2010] EWCA Civ 103, [2010] STC 1251, [152]–[174]. On mistake see [170].

[17] See, eg, [2012] UKSC 19, [2012] 2 WLR 1149, [71]–[84] (Lord Walker), [171]–[174] (Lord Sumption), [221] (Lord Reed); the Law Commission initially commented this ought to be so Law Comm (n 3) para 6.42.

[18] C Mitchell, P Mitchell and S Watterson (eds), *Goff & Jones: The Law of Unjust Enrichment*, 10th edn (London, Sweet & Maxwell, 2022) para 22.20.

[19] ibid para 22.22.

Cases of ultra vires contracts with public authorities are out of scope. Burrows (now Lord Burrows) argues the question turns on whether the payment is subject to judicial review;[20] the Law Commission took the view that what matters was that the recipient of the money was acting outside its statutory authority. Cases such as *South of Scotland Electricity Board v British Oxygen Ltd*,[21] which involved a nationalised state industry – not subject to judicial review – levying discriminatory charges, would then be covered. The wider view seems appropriate as the evil in question is the receipt of money purportedly paid under statutory compulsion, as opposed to under the normal private law regime, which covers ultra vires contracts.

ii. Defences

Just as there are questions about the scope of the cause of action, there are questions around the scope of applicable defences. An obvious question concerns the applicability of restitutionary defences such as change of position, but there are also specific statutory defences such as the general practice defence[22] and that the claimant would be unjustly enriched by repayment.[23] The question has been clouded by EU law. The EU law principle of effectiveness bars the availability of defences other than the European-recognised one of passing on where taxes are reclaimed as having been charged contrary to EU law.[24]

One poor justification for barring the change of position defence domestically is that proffered by Henderson J in the *FII Group Litigation*.[25] He suggested that the state was a wrongdoer. One of the limitations to the defence raised in its initial formulation in *Lipkin Gorman v Karpnale Ltd* was that the defendant not be a wrongdoer.[26] The first point is that this may no longer be defensible as a strict bar after the decision of *Cavenagh Investments Pty Ltd v Kaushik* where change of position was allowed for an innocent trespasser.[27] We look at this is greater detail in chapter eight. The second, that it is a necessary condition (although not sufficient) for the state to be seen as a wrongdoer, is that the action would require an unlawful demand. Requiring a demand renders simple invalidity of the tax insufficient for relief,[28] but this is not English law. The fact the tax was not due (for whatever reason whether invalidity or otherwise) is by itself

[20] Burrows (n 14) 508.

[21] *South of Scotland Electricity Board v British Oxygen Ltd* [1959] 1 WLR 587.

[22] Taxes Management Act 1970, s 33.

[23] VAT Act 1994, s 80.

[24] *Test Claimants in the FII Litigation v HMRC* [2008] EWHC 2893, [2009] STC 254, [304], [339]–[340]; [2010] EWCA Civ 103, [2010] STC 1251, [191].

[25] [2008] EWHC 2893, [2009] STC 254.

[26] *Lipkin Gorman v Karpnale Ltd* [1991] 2 AC 548 (HL).

[27] *Cavenagh Investments Pte Ltd v Kaushik Rajiv* [2013] SGHC 45.

[28] *Murphy v AG* [1982] IR 241; N Connolly, 'Overpaid Taxes and Constitutional Redress in Ireland' in S Elliott et al (eds), *Restitution of Overpaid Tax* (Oxford, Hart Publishing, 2013).

sufficient to ground relief in English law and this is inconsistent with the state's being treated always as a wrongdoer.

Henderson J, however, had another bite at the cherry in terms of justifying the disapplication of change of position in a subsequent *FII* decision,[29] where he rested it on stultification. The availability of the defence would stultify the point of the *Woolwich* action, and, although Henderson J backed away from this conclusion in *FII*, it should also bar the mistake claim. This is mirrored in the reasoning behind the non-availability of the defence in German law.[30] Change of position would allow the state to retain moneys that it should not be allowed to retain, whether the claim is pleaded as *Woolwich* or mistake. As stated later in this chapter, to allow the state to retain money (for any reason) exacted in contravention of those rules is to (effectively) deny the rules.

A stultification justification will apply generally to all instances of the *Woolwich* claim. It is not obvious that the final proposed rationale applies generally. The defence is said not to be apt to claims against the state. Where the government spends on its normal programmes, it does not change its position in reliance on the receipt because if it were unable to spend this money, it would have spent money from different sources (raised by different taxes or borrowing) instead.[31] That may not be a given in that the state might be able to show it would have made cuts instead, but generally this will be almost impossible to demonstrate given that spending commitments are often multi-year in nature. The fact that the defence, developed for claims between private individuals, turns on expenditure in reliance on receipt and that the state rarely spends in reliance on receipt makes the defence inapplicable in its terms,[32] but if the action applies to local government or nationalised industries charging statutorily authorised fees, the practical argument that they never change their position in reliance becomes shaky. The stultification argument appears the best of the three canvassed arguments.

If any defence is needed it must be a policy-motivated one[33] and maybe one legislatively mandated. Such defences remain controversial in this context, however. Three are worth discussing – fiscal chaos, passing on and settled understanding of the law. *Air Canada v British Columbia* discussed the first two defences.[34]

[29] *Test Claimants in the FII Litigation v HMRC (No 2)* [2014] EWHC 4302 (Ch); [2015] STC 1471, [315]; E Bant, 'Change of Position as a Defence to Restitution of Unlawfully Exacted Tax' [2012] *Lloyd's Maritime & Commercial Law Quarterly* 122, 140–41.

[30] S Nanchahal, '"But We've Spent the Money": Defending Overpaid Tax Claims under English and German Law' [2020] *Oxford University Comparative Law Forum* 1.

[31] G Virgo, 'The Law of Taxation is No Island – Overpaid Taxes and the Law of Restitution' [1993] *British Tax Review* 443, 459–60; PBH Birks, 'Restitution from the Executive: A Tercentenary Footnote to the Bill of Rights' in PD Finn (ed), *Essays on Restitution* (Sydney, Law Book Co, 1990) 201; Williams, *Unjust Enrichment and Public Law* (n 6) 142–45.

[32] But see, Law Comm (n 3) para 10.6 suggesting the defence should be available, but without endorsing a version in the proposed statutory scheme, para 11.

[33] N Cleary, 'Property, Proportionality and the Change of Position Defence' in S Elliott et al (eds), *Restitution of Overpaid Tax* (Oxford, Hart, 2013) 127.

[34] *Air Canada v British Columbia* [1989] 1 SCR 1161.

Payments were made to the British Columbia Revenue under a taxing statute, later held to be ultra vires the province. The sums involved were huge, and the airline had passed on the burden of the tax to the passengers. The airlines sought to recover the money on the basis of a mistake as to their legal liability to pay. LaForest J expressly removed the mistake of law bar;[35] however, he placed several limitations on the right to recover,[36] including a defence of fiscal chaos. LaForest J justified the separate defence of fiscal chaos as protecting the Treasury.[37] It might, for instance, be obliged to reimpose the tax to pay for the refunds and extra administrative burdens. Fiscal chaos has found little favour in the courts and commentary. Although the Law Commission was concerned in its report to protect public bodies from 'administrative inconvenience and waste of repaying then reimposing tax',[38] it ultimately decided not to recommend a statutory version of the fiscal chaos defence.[39] In Canada, fiscal chaos was abolished by *Kingstreet Investments Pty v New Brunswick Department of Finance*[40] and fiscal chaos has never been part of English law. In essence, the justification for this is that the state's inconvenience is beside the point. The defence carries with it a risk of undermining the policy in favour of restitution, which is usually put as one of legality – the state should only receive and accept legally owed monies. An outcome such that the more egregious the illegality the more likely the state is to be allowed to keep the money hardly supports that policy.

The defence of passing on finds statutory form in defences of 'unjust enrichment'.[41] In *Air Canada*, LaForest J held the defence of passing on applied as a matter of Canadian law where the loss suffered by the plaintiff has been recouped from third parties and held its requirements had been satisfied on the facts.[42] However, the defence has not been introduced into the common law of unjust enrichment in England and was abolished by *Kingstreet* in Canada. The decision in *Kleinwort Benson v Birmingham CC* is key,[43] as seen in chapter eight. The bank and local authority had entered into void interest rate swap agreements; the bank also entered protective hedging transactions. When the bank therefore claimed its money back because of the nullity of the contract and the consequent failure of consideration, the local authority countered that it had lost nothing

[35] ibid 1201.

[36] ibid 1202–08.

[37] ibid 1204–07.

[38] Law Comm (n 3) para 10.5.

[39] ibid para 11.6.

[40] *Kingstreet Investments Pty v New Brunswick Department of Finance* [2007] SCC 1, [2007] 1 SCR 3, [21].

[41] See, eg, VAT Act 1994, s 80(3).

[42] [1989] 1 SCR 1161, 1202–03.

[43] *Kleinwort Benson v Birmingham* CC [1997] QB 380; *Westdeutsche Landesbank Girozentrale v Islington LBC* [1994] 4 All ER 890. For Australia, see *Commissioner of State Revenue v Royal Insurance Australia Ltd* (1994) 182 CLR 51; *Roxborough v Rothman's Pall Mall of Australia* (2001) 208 CLR 516 (HCA); *Mason v New South Wales* (1959) 102 CLR 108; and *Hilliard v Westpac Banking Corporation* [2009] VSCA 211, [83]–[84].

because of the hedge transactions. Saville LJ argued that mitigation was irrelevant, and that 'at the expense of' referred to immediate expense.[44]

The Law Commission discussed a form of a settled understanding of the law defence. The idea is that overpayments of tax should not be recoverable if the taxpayer paid in accordance with a settled view of the law that the payment was due, and later judicial decisions have departed from that view.[45] The suggested defence, despite a general practice defence forming part of section 33 of the Taxes Management Act 1970, does not form part of the general English law on recovery of ultra vires taxation – and rightly so as it seems to run directly contrary to the principle of legality standing behind the action; the Law Commission itself argued the defence be disapplied the defence in cases of the ultra vires nature of subordinate legislation creating the tax charge,[46] but should have simply accepted it should not apply to the *Woolwich* claim at all. The Commission did, however, take the view that the settled understanding defence should apply to mistake claims against public bodies as well as payments by mistake of law between private parties. This has not been the position taken by English law since *Kleinwort Benson v Lincoln City Council*,[47] which, as is generally known, allows for so-called retrospective mistakes whereby a party acting under a commonly understood view of the law is still said to have been mistaken when later authority overturns that common understanding or prior judicial authority.

B. Public Law? Does it Matter?

The reader might well expect, given the general argument of this book in chapters one to three, that the argument will be that the action is a hybrid. All causes of action are hybrids to some degree – not because there is no such thing as an area of law, but because there are always criss-crossing principles that straddle different areas. This is no different. The first subsection outlines the reasoning of the Supreme Court of Canada in concluding that it is a public law action. The second looks at Williams' view that it is a hybrid. The third examines the interactions of unjust enrichment and public law.

i. Kingstreet: *A Public Law Action*

In *Kingstreet Investments v New Brunswick Dept of Finance* the Supreme Court of Canada was clear that an action to recover payments made pursuant to ultra

[44] [1997] QB 380, 394-395; *Roxborough v Rothman's Pall Mall of Australia* (2002) 208 CLR 513, 528–30 (Gleeson CJ); 541 (Gummow J); *Commissioner of State Revenue v Royal Insurance Australia* (1994) 126 ALR 1.

[45] Law Comm (n 3) para 10.20.

[46] ibid para 10.30.

[47] *Kleinwort Benson v Lincoln City Council* [1999] 2 AC 349 (HL); See defending the lack of a settled understanding of the law defence; Sheehan, 'Mistaken Overpayments of Tax' (n 8) 62–68; D Sheehan, 'What is a Mistake?' (2000) 20 *Legal Studies* 538.

vires tax demands was different from the normal private law action and should be treated as a purely public law phenomenon.[48] The facts of the case were that the taxpayers had been operating a number of licensed nightclubs and paid a user charge on purchase of their alcohol supplies. They challenged the validity of this charge and succeeded in having it declared an unconstitutional indirect tax. However, in lower courts they had difficulty in recovering the full amount, in part due to the application of the passing on defence; the taxpayers had recouped the cost of the charge from their customers. The Supreme Court held that restitution was generally available to recover ultra vires taxation. This was – paralleling the reasoning in *Woolwich*[49] – to uphold important constitutional principles such as the rule of law and that no tax be levied without valid authority from the legislature; these constitutional principles placed the principle firmly in the province of public law.[50]

Bastarache J also considered whether the principle might fall within the private law of unjust enrichment and provided several further reasons to distinguish the case from *Garland v Consumer Gas*.[51] Bastarache J argued that questions of benefit (to the state) and loss (to the taxpayer) are inapposite[52] and that the two-stage test described in *Garland* focused on different concerns from those in play in the overpaid tax cases. In essence, the unjust enrichment analysis makes the application of the key constitutional ideas more difficult. He said the *Garland* approach was complex and argued that the putative juristic reasons raised to explain the enrichment had to be considered in the light of public policy and the reasonable expectations of the parties.[53] Those proper policy considerations should be those that have traditionally informed the development of unjust enrichment law; considerations relating to preservation of the 'public purse' did not fall into the public policy issues category in unjust enrichment, a category, he argued, that was more appropriately directed at 'broad principles of fairness'.[54]

The third point is that for Bastarache J restitution is a tool of corrective justice understood in its Aristotelian sense.[55] His Honour did not expand on this, but from the tenor of the decision we can infer that he did not think the separate constitutional restitutionary principle is a tool of corrective justice. It is worth exploring whether this is right. Walpole has shown that the Weinribian view of corrective justice which combines Aristotelian corrective justice with Kantian

[48] See R Williams, 'Recovery of Ultra Vires Taxes: A Wholly Public Approach?' [2007] *Restitution Law Review* 130; J McCamus, 'Restitutionary Liability of Public Authorities in Canada' in R Grantham and C Rickett (eds), *Structure and Justification in Private Law* (Oxford, Hart Publishing, 2008) 310–18. McCamus takes the view at 313 that the public law approach also applies to demands pursuant to a misinterpretation of intra vires legislation. But see *Elder Advocates of Alberta v Alberta* 2011 SCC 24.

[49] As alluded to at 2007 SCC 1, [2007] 1 SCR 3, [15]–[18] (Bastarache J).

[50] ibid [31].

[51] *Garland v Consumer Gas* 2004 SCC 25.

[52] 2007 SCC 1, [2007] 1 SCR 3, [35].

[53] ibid [36].

[54] ibid [38].

[55] ibid [32].

right does not fit the *Woolwich* principle. This is because even though there is an intentional transaction by which A pays B (the state) and the reason for restitution is defendant-sided, it does not create correlativity of reason between defendant and claimant.[56] Walpole does, however, suggest that if we allow non-Kantian norms into corrective justice, we can accommodate *Woolwich* within corrective justice.[57] More generally, the idea of mutual respect for the independence of the self which is inherent in Weinrib's Kantian explanation of private law claims is too thin. It leads Weinrib to an unnecessarily strict position on bilaterality and a requirement that the defendant must always accept the enrichment proffered by the claimant as having been non-donative. In chapter three we therefore rejected the Weinribian framework of corrective justice. A different framework for corrective justice becomes not just possible but necessary. The driving force behind relief in the context of overpaid public law imposts is not Kantian; it is based on constitutional policy and Walpole acknowledges that this means a corrective justice framework including *Woolwich* and *Kingstreet* would have 'pluralist substantive content'.[58] Two points are worth making. The first is that this is in line with the theme of this book that any area of law, including unjust enrichment, can tolerate some normative pluralism in the reason for relief. The second point, however, is that a distributive justice argument is also possible. If the state represents the collective, there is no reason vis-a-vis other members of the collective why this individual should shoulder the full risk of the invalidity of the collective's rule rather than spreading that risk around. Which we prefer (corrective or distributive justice) may turn on whether we see the state as merely representing the collective in which case a distributive justice argument is preferable or as having some 'life' of its own separate from the collective. In this context it is worth pointing out that on the wide view of the scope of the action, nationalised industries, which cannot be sensibly seen as merely representing the collective, are included along with central government which more clearly can be seen in that way. Since the wide view is better reflected in the positive law, the corrective justice view seems preferable.

ii. Hybrid Action: Rebecca Williams' View

Williams suggests that by seeing public law as the reason for restitution the law gains full access to the crucial event, thus allowing a truly hybrid approach,[59] neither fully public nor private. What she means by this is that it is impossible to explain *Woolwich* neatly using only illegality, incapacity, transactional inequality or any of the other private law bases canvassed by Lord Browne-Wilkinson in

[56] S Walpole, 'Justifying the *Woolwich* Principle: An Exploration of the Normative Boundaries of Unjust Enrichment and Corrective Justice' [2018] *Restitution Law Review* 42, 55.

[57] ibid 56–58.

[58] ibid 57.

[59] Williams, *Unjust Enrichment and Public Law* (n 6) 73.

the case.[60] All are relevant. It is a hybrid action because Williams also accepts that from a public law perspective it is hard to see why the remedy must be return of the money; the claimant's expense and relevant defences must then be worked out in the usual private law manner.[61]

There is one major difference between Williams' position and my own. She argues for a hierarchy of reasons so that if the *Woolwich* principle is engaged the claim for mistaken payment ought to be barred;[62] it is wrong, however, for the law to remove a perfectly good cause of action and force a claimant into a more complex enquiry – which they may well eschew for precisely that reason. Her example is a company which pays a tax on redheaded employees, believing it has red-haired employees. In fact, it does not. There are two problems. First, they are mistaken as to the applicability of the regulations in their own terms, but also the regulations are silly and void. It is not for the law to force the company to prove the nullity of the regulations if a simple mistake claim 'We thought we had redheads, but we don't' will succeed.

iii. Public Law as Distinct from Private Unjust Enrichment?

The question whether the action is one in public law or the private law of unjustified enrichment also raises its head in civil law jurisdictions. German law does not consider this to be unjustified enrichment at all. However, much of this insistence is procedural in nature given the long existence of separate courts to deal with administrative and public law matters.[63] Substantively, as we have noted, it has been conceded that these actions can be seen as based on absence of basis,[64] but despite this similarity no defence of disenrichment of the state applies because to allow the defence is to permit the state to retain and benefit from money it had no statutory right to retain. England does not have this tradition of total separation. Outside the procedure for judicial review public bodies are seen as subject to the same law as everyone else.[65] We saw in chapter one that all areas of law are **normatively pluralistic** to some degree and this section aims to illustrate how this normative pluralism works and the way in which unjust enrichment is a category cutting across private and public law.

Allan has argued that the law applicable in any given case is always determined by a reflective engagement with basic principles. That generates a moral unity to public law.[66] The moral unity that Allan points to is the moral unity of respect for

[60] [1993] AC 70 (HL) 196–200.

[61] Williams, *Unjust Enrichment and Public Law* (n 6) 37–38.

[62] Sheehan, 'Mistaken Overpayments of Tax' (n 8) 51–52.

[63] B Haecker, 'Public Law Restitutionary Claims: The German Perspective' in S Elliott et al (eds) *Restitution of Overpaid Tax* (Oxford, Hart Publishing, 2013).

[64] A Sanders, 'Absence of Basis: A German Perspective' in S Elliott et al (eds), *Restitution of Overpaid Tax* (Oxford, Hart Publishing, 2013) 214–15.

[65] See Crown Proceedings Act 1942, s 1.

[66] T Allan, 'The Moral Unity of Public Law' (2017) 67 *University of Toronto Law Journal* 1, 2.

human rights and human flourishing and the need to control state power to that regard. From the perspective of the argument of this book there are two points that should be made. First, that moral unity is not bought at the expense of public law's integration with other sectors of the law. Quite the contrary, Allan argues that a legal proposition is correct when it 'is consistent with the best available integration of our political values'.[67] This is Dworkinian in its feel and Allan has explicitly defended a view of law similar but not identical to Dworkin.[68] Allan argues for a fusion of legality and legitimacy as a concomitant of the requirement for a reasoned justification for all coercive state action. This in turn is required by our acceptance of fundamental rights, the need for political equality between citizens, and the need for a connected and coherent approach to all questions of the exercise of governmental power.[69] That requirement that we be fairly treated as equals – which is one of Dworkin's key constraints in his account of the common law's methodology – demands a coherent moral vision, which protects our fundamental rights but also integrates them into our traditional common law method.[70] Allan's point is that all the different branches of public law can be united under this banner of fair treatment as equals. However, it also illustrates in concrete terms that the traditional common law method is used throughout the law, both public and private. The implication is that there are connections outside public law into private law and vice versa. This suggests precisely the type of cross-cutting interlinkages that we might expect from a Dworkinian view. We saw in chapter one that Dworkin does accept the existence of what he calls 'local priority', but his entire theory is based on the ability of Hercules to draw from principles and values across the law.[71] Public law therefore, while it may have a coherent unity of its own and indeed forms an accepted and traditional compartment of law that contributes to our being able – as citizens – to make sense of the law, cannot be an island unto itself. There are good reasons to accept this conclusion. Our values are the values our society holds dear. That society is the society that creates our law, both public and private. It would be odd if different sets of values informed the two branches.

The second point is that the same sort of question can come up in both areas. A private actor may generate an expectation in another party that X is true or that Y will be done. Should the other party act to their detriment in reliance, an estoppel may arise to protect that expectation, but there appears to be a public law doctrine very similar in character. Williams describes the development of this doctrine as simply reinventing a private law wheel.[72] Oliver[73] has also drawn

[67] ibid 6.

[68] ibid 9–14; T Allan 'Law as a Branch of Morality: The Unity of Principle and Practice (2020) 65 *American Journal of Jurisprudence* 1.

[69] Allan, 'Law as a Branch of Morality (n 68) 28–29.

[70] ibid 30.

[71] R Dworkin, *Law's Empire* (Cambridge, MA, Harvard University Press, 1986).

[72] R Williams, 'The Multiple Doctrines of Legitimate Expectations' (2016) 132 *LQR* 639, 646–47.

[73] D Oliver, 'Common Values in Public and Private Law and the Public/Private Divide' [1997] *PL* 630; J Beatson, 'Finessing Substantive Public Law Principles into Private Law Relations' [1997] *Acta Juridica* 1.

attention to some of these common values in arguing that the common law has a supervisory jurisdiction whereby it compels decisions by private law actors to be rational and fair. Equity, too, has a supervisory jurisdiction and similarities can be found between grounds for attacking the discretionary decisions of a trustee or fiduciary and those of a public body, although, as Conaglen points out, a nuanced appreciation of the context is needed to understand both the similarities and differences between the actions.[74] It is of course true that public law is different from private law in the sense that there are discrete public law remedies that are not available to private law litigants.[75] Equally, it may be appropriate to restrain a public body from acting – or making decisions – in circumstances where no private law right is at issue, and where no wrong is committed. There is after all no general doctrine whereby an ultra vires act sounds in damages unless a private law wrong is committed.[76] Historically, there were procedural differences and considerable dispute as to whether a given issue needed to be heard under one procedure rather than another.[77] However, these differences should not obscure the similarities and the practical examples of how the Dworkin/Allan fusion of public and private play out. The similarities allow for a constant interchange of ideas, comparison of the rationales behind doctrines in a way that permits private law and public law to develop together.

Public law deals with our interactions as subjects of the state, and private law is the law governing our interpersonal relationships. Public law deals with our rights against the state and private law our rights against each other. Public law is concerned with our collective goals and private with the construction of our interpersonal relations. However, public law cannot be entirely separate from private law in the sense understood by Weinrib that private law is bilateral, linking the claimant to the defendant and public law omnilateral, linking everyone to everyone else, giving each a distinct dimension.[78] Private law's sole function for Weinrib is to be 'private law', but the reciprocal freedom that we all enjoy from each other can only be fully secured via an omnilateral public ordering. As one might imagine, Weinrib's argument has a formal character; public right requires that rights be public, known to all and make a systematic union of norms.[79] Private and public law are, however, for Weinrib separate. Private law takes the form of principles elaborating reciprocal freedoms as against each other. Public and constitutional law enshrine rights and freedoms inherent in human dignity to maintain the conditions for the exercise of reciprocal freedom. Recognising the distinctiveness of private and public law is not, however, an exercise in separation. It is

[74] M Conaglen, 'Public–Private Intersection: Comparing Fiduciary Conflict Doctrine and Bias' [2008] *PL* 58.

[75] Williams, *Unjust Enrichment and Public Law* (n 6) 11.

[76] ibid 17.

[77] *O'Reilly v Mackman* [1983] 2 AC 237.

[78] E Weinrib, 'Private Law and Public Right' (2011) 61 *University of Toronto Law Journal* 191, 196.

[79] ibid 198; see also, E Weinrib, *Reciprocal Freedom: Private Law and Public Right* (Oxford, OUP, 2022) ch 4, 207–09.

impossible not to take the substantive values we hold dear into account in both public and private law. There is therefore no strict division of labour between the two areas because public law considerations, and collective goals inevitably affect in a substantive way our interpersonal and horizontal interactions.[80] Both private and public law need to recognise this. Private law therefore needs to take both collective and individual goals into account. We can resist the 'reductionist understanding' of private law as exhausted by the collectivist considerations while at the same time rejecting the formalist approach epitomised by Weinrib. We can see a *via media*. Just as something can be both unjust enrichment and contract, depending on the significant similarities one picks out for different purposes, so a claim can, depending on the resemblances one picks out and contrary to both the assumption of Bastarache J in *Kingstreet* and the position taken by Williams, be both unjust enrichment and public law. This just reflects normative overlaps in action.

It is public law because it involves our interactions with the state, but it is unjust enrichment law because of the significant normative similarities with other performance claims as understood in chapter two. When I pay to discharge a non-existent debt to the state, I enter an intentional transaction to do so. Like any other intentional transfer or rendering of services, that is a performance rendered to the state. If that payment is mistaken it seems identical to any other mistaken payments. Even in the *Woolwich* type case where I pay knowing it is an invalid demand, I do not – just as in *Nurdin & Peacock v DB Ramsden & Co*[81] – intend to make a gift to the state. If one of the **functions** of unjust enrichment is to reverse defective enrichments, whether conferred by performance or in some other way, the *Woolwich* claim fulfils that function. Ultimately, the reason I therefore recover a mistaken payment from the state is the same as the reason I recover my mistakenly overpaid grocery bills.[82] But even if, as in *Woolwich v IRC* itself the payer knew the payment was not due, the state has a duty to return it. While the state legality rationale preferred here appears one derived from public law rather than private law, this merely demonstrates the **normative pluralism** of unjust enrichment and in particular the normative pluralism of performance claims. Performance claims overlap with both private law and public law, bringing us full circle to the view that this is a hybrid claim, drawing on principles from public law, but also the general private law of unjust enrichment.

II. Necessity

Necessity becomes relevant in different scenarios. It can demonstrate that the defendant is enriched, or it can serve as the reason posited for relief – the

[80] H Dagan and B Zipursky, 'The Distinction between Private Law and Public Law' in H Dagan and B Zipursky (eds), *Research Handbook on Private Law Theory* (Cheltenham, Edward Elgar, 2020) 12–15.
[81] *Nurdin & Peacock v DB Ramsden & Co* [1999] 1 WLR 1249.
[82] Sheehan, 'Mistaken Overpayments of Tax' (n 8) 49.

alleged unjust factor. The first case therefore includes such cases as where I make necessary repairs to your car, believing it my own. That type of case and others like it were considered in chapter four. We concentrate in this section on the second case where necessity is the claimed unjust factor. We saw in chapter two that English law knows not merely a set of performance claims, but also some non-performance claims, primarily the intermediary claims and improvement claims. The necessity claims can be subdivided. Birks referred to an unjust factor of legal compulsion[83] where the claimant (C) is compelled by law to pay B thus benefiting the defendant (D). A voluntary payment will not lead to the discharge of D's debt to B, as we saw in chapter four, but one under legal compulsion will.[84] Separately, Birks referred to moral compulsion[85] where A is morally obliged to act for the benefit of B. I have argued that these cases can be gathered together, and a wider principle generalised from them.[86] That is the principle of *negotiorum gestio*, which is not classified as unjustified enrichment in civil law systems and Birks also later excluded it.[87]

The typical scenario where necessity finds its expression in legal compulsion is where A owes B £100. C has maybe guaranteed the debt and therefore owes B £100 (if A fails to pay). C is secondarily liable. C pays B. C seeks to reclaim from A. Under such circumstances C, as surety for A, is entitled to subrogation[88] as against A to support any contribution claims,[89] whether at common law or under the Civil Liability (Contribution) Act 1978.[90] The first point is that C is performing a valid obligation (and one owed to A as well as B). As such it is hard to see it as a performance claim. It is equally hard to see it as falling into the non-performance claims mentioned in chapter two. It is not an intermediary claim, nor is there a mistake that C is undertaking his own business when he is not. Whether such discharge cases are unjust enrichment cases was considered in *Croxen v Gas and Electricity Markets Authority*.[91] The decision involved a Supplier of Last Report (B Ltd) being appointed by Ofgem to supply energy to customers of a failed energy company (A Ltd). When B Ltd honours customers' credit balances and pays them over does that discharge A Ltd's debt and allow B to recover in unjust enrichment from A? Zacaroli J argued that A Ltd had essentially agreed to B Ltd's honouring the credit balances; indeed, to object would be inconsistent with their own energy supply licence conditions. Further, they knew that B Ltd expected to be

[83] PBH Birks, *An Introduction to the Law of Restitution*, rev edn (Oxford, Clarendon Press, 1989) 185–93.

[84] *Ibrahim v Barclays Bank plc* [2012] EWCA Civ 640, [2013] Ch 400, [40-48] (Lewisham LJ).

[85] Birks, *An Introduction to the Law of Restitution* (n 83) 193–202.

[86] D Sheehan, '*Negotiorum Gestio*: A Civilian Concept in the Common Law' (2006) 55 *ICLQ* 253; see against such a general category in English law, R Stevens, *The Laws of Restitution* (Oxford, OUP, 2023) ch 10.

[87] PBH Birks, *Unjust Enrichment*, 2nd edn (Oxford, OUP, 2005) 24.

[88] Mercantile Law Amendment Act 1856, s 5.

[89] C Mitchell and S Watterson (eds), *Subrogation: Law and Practice* (Oxford, OUP, 2007) para 6.16.

[90] ibid para 6.06 on the underlying unity of subrogation, contribution and reimbursement.

[91] *Croxen v Gas and Electricity Markets Authority* [2022] EWHC 2826 (Ch).

reimbursed (at least to the extent possible) by A with the remainder recovered via a Last Resort Supplier Payment.[92] However, he went on to say that B Ltd was essentially compelled by the regulator to honour these balances and this justified restitution within an unjust enrichment claim.[93] His decision is therefore ambiguous between two different explanations of the claim. This is important because if B Ltd is paying to perform an obligation to A Ltd and fails to be reimbursed, there is a failure of basis which will count as a performance claim. If B Ltd is compelled to pay based on a regulatory requirement, B would be discharging its own valid obligation which should bar unjust enrichment. The real explanation for recovery is that A Ltd is **primarily** liable and remains so.[94] The person who ought to have paid must pay, and this seems the best explanation in civilian and mixed jurisdictions too. Whitty, for example, has made a very strong argument that these cases simply involve ordering the priority of debtors. Unjust(ified) enrichment is at best superfluous.[95] Burrows has suggested, however, that without an unjust enrichment analysis change of position would not be available.[96] The primary debtor often agrees to the debt. It seems inappropriate to allow him to escape that voluntarily assumed liability by change of position.[97] Unlike in the mistaken discharge of liability cases, discussed in chapter four, it is never credible for the defendant to say he thought it was a voluntary contribution by the other party. This is another pointer that a different principle is in play.

That principle is that the claimant must relieve the defendant of a liability properly the latter's to bear.[98] In *Moule v Garrett*,[99] the claimant was the tenant of premises and assigned the lease to B who assigned to the defendants. The landlord recovered damages from the claimant for breach of a repair covenant. The defendants were primarily liable as in possession and the claimants secondarily so by virtue of the original contract with the landlords. The claimants were able to recover the sum from the defendants, who had an obligation to indemnify the original lessee, irrespective of covenants with the intermediate tenant and assignor. The same analysis applies to *Exall v Partridge* where the claimant's (C's) carriage was detained by A on the defendant's (B's) land and the claimant paid

[92] ibid [155]–[161].

[93] ibid [172].

[94] *Duncan, Fox & Co v North and South Wales Bank* (1880) 6 App Cas 1; Stevens (n 86) 154.

[95] N Whitty, 'Rights of Relief, Subrogation and Unjustified Enrichment in Scots Law' [2019] *Acta Juridica* 493, 509. See also E West, 'The Interaction of Rights of Relief and Unjustified Enrichment in Scots Law' [2020] *Edinburgh Law Review* 202; S Meier, 'No Basis: A Comparative View' in AS Burrows and A Rodger (eds), *Mapping the Law* (Oxford, OUP, 2006) 360–61.

[96] Burrows (n 14) 438.

[97] M Hoyle, 'Splitting the Difference: Surrey CC v NHS Lincolnshire Clinical Commissioning Group and Contribution between Public Bodies' (2021) 137 *LQR* 537, 542, discussing *Surrey CC v NHS Lincolnshire Clinical Commissioning Group* [2020] EWHC 3550, [2021] QB 896.

[98] *Niru Battery Manufacturing Ltd v Milestone Trading Ltd (No 2)* [2004] EWCA Civ 487 {2004] 2 All ER (Comm) 289; Mitchell and Watterson (n 89) paras 6.16–6.31.

[99] *Moule v Garrett* (1872) LR 7 Exch 101; *Brook's Wharf and Bull Wharf Ltd v Goodman Bros* [1937] 1 KB 534.

for its release.[100] The carriage was legally detained by the payee (A) (or it would have been duress to goods) to enforce a debt owed by B. C then claimed repayment from B and succeeded. It was B's debt. In *Gebhardt v Saunders* the liability in question was to abate a nuisance.[101] The local authority served the notice at the relevant premises and not specifically and directly to the owner. It became clear that because of the nature of the problem, arising from structural issues with the building that the owner, not the tenant who had done the work, was liable. Day J put liability to pay for the work on the shoulders of the person 'who was primarily liable'[102] and allowed the tenant to recover in money had and received against the owner.

Cases exist in English law following the same pattern as *negotiorum gestio* and allowing relief in the same way that the civil law provides the intervener under the *actio negotiorum gestorum contraria*. There must be an intention to manage someone else's affairs by doing necessary acts with the intention of recovering expenses.[103] If the owner becomes aware of the intervener's actions and requests him to stop or the intervener knows that he is acting against the owners' express wishes, he must not continue. This is why as a general rule it must be impractical to communicate with the owner or principal.[104] A couple of examples will suffice for our purposes.[105] In *Great Northern Railway v Swaffield*,[106] the claimant sent a horse to a livery stable when the defendant failed to turn up to collect it at the station. The stable refused to release the horse until it had been paid for the necessary food and accommodation charges; the defendant refused to pay, but the claimant paid. The court held that the payments were necessary and therefore recoverable expenses. In *Re Rhodes*,[107] the family paid for a 'lunatic' to be kept in an asylum for several years. The court decided that where necessaries are supplied to a person unable to contract, an obligation to repay nonetheless arose. That obligation is justified by reference to a policy of encouraging necessary interventions.

One reason for thinking these are not unjust enrichment cases is that enrichment may not even be needed. First, it is hard to see how you would measure enrichment in medical intervention cases – how much is a few minutes' extra human life worth?[108] Second, in some cases where the intervention is unsuccessful

[100] *Exall v Partridge* (1799) 8 TR 308.
[101] *Gebhardt v Saunders* [1892] 2 QB 452.
[102] ibid 457.
[103] Sheehan, '*Negotiorum Gestio*' (n 86) 255–59.
[104] ibid 257.
[105] ibid 267–78; see J Kortman, *Altruism in Private Law* (Oxford, OUP, 2005) ch 11 for more examples.
[106] *Great Northern Railway v Swaffield* (1874) LR 9 Ex 132; *Chapman v Chapman* [1954] AC 429.
[107] *Re Rhodes* (1890) 44 Ch D 94; see also *Re Gibson* (1871) LR 7 Ch App 52, *Williams v Wentworth* (1842) 5 Beav 325, 49 ER 603.
[108] M McInnes, 'Enrichment Revisited' in J Neyers et al (eds), *Understanding Unjust Enrichment* (Oxford, Hart Publishing, 2004) 186–87; J Dawson, '*Negotiorum Gestio*: The Altruistic Intermeddler' (1961) 74 *Harvard Law Review* 1073, 1115–16; We value life under the Fatal Accidents Act 1976 for example, but refuse to value it in other areas, such as the 'wrongful life cases'. See *McKay v Essex AHA* [1982] QB 1166 (CA).

(and the patient dies), we may still wish to reimburse the intervener his expenses or loss to protect the incentive effects of the policy,[109] and this lack of any success requirement is equated in South African law to allowing relief even in the absence of any enrichment.[110] We could argue that the defendant's enrichment is the market value of the services (the performance) provided. What would a reasonable person in the position of the defendant have had to pay? Leaving to one side that in the context of medical services in the UK that could, arguably, be zero, it raises a separate question. If this is a performance claim, what is the defect in the otherwise valid transaction? There does not seem to be one. The claimant acts deliberately, fully aware of the facts and the law encourages him to do so for reasons that, as we also noted in chapter three, are significantly different in policy terms from duress or mistake. Civil law and mixed systems like South Africa in fact provide that *negotiorum gestio* is a valid causa.[111] Arguably this is also true in England. English law provides a necessity defence to a claim for an intentional tort.[112] The criminal law's recognition that conduct may be justified by its necessity leads to the conclusion that there is nothing wrong with acting that way and the conduct is lawful.[113] For Virgo, this is true by analogy in tort law.[114] Where the claimant therefore removes the defendant's horse for its own safety to a stables and pays relevant charges, he prima facie commits trespass to goods, but the necessity of his actions renders them lawful. The civil law naturally also provides a defence to any similar delictual liability, but the owner could sue in the *actio negotiorum gestorum directa* for losses caused negligently by the intervener. The effect of the defence of necessity not covering the tort of negligence is the same. Indeed Lord Browne-Wilkinson has expressed a principle, which has been applied in rescue cases and is very similar to that underlying the *actio directa*, saying in effect that by choosing to act the defendant creates a special relationship to which the law attaches a duty of care.[115] English law therefore has a set of actions which effectively produce the same outcome as the South African law. English law could usefully embrace this and conclude that these 'morally compelled' performances are also valid and made so to encourage necessary interventions. In other words, when the claimant removes the horse and pays for its upkeep, he is validly performing an obligation he has taken up vis-a-vis the horse's owner. His claim against the owner is not an unjust enrichment claim.

[109] H Dagan, *The Law and Ethics of Restitution* (Cambridge, CUP, 2004) 109.

[110] D Visser, *Unjustified Enrichment* (Durban, Juta, 2008) 568.

[111] ibid 565.

[112] Sheehan, '*Negotiorum Gestio*' (n 86) 278; for the defence of necessity in tort, see A Tettenborn (ed), *Clerk and Lindsell on Torts*, 23rd edn (London, Sweet & Maxwell, 2022) ch 3, section 6(a).

[113] PH Robinson, 'A Theory of Justification: Societal Harm as a Prerequisite for Criminal Liability' (1975) 23 *University of California Los Angeles Law Review* 266, 274.

[114] GJ Virgo, 'Justifying Necessity as a Defence in Tort Law' in A Dyson et al (eds), *Defences in Tort* (Oxford, Hart Publishing, 2017).

[115] *White v Jones* [1995] 2 AC 207 (HL) 273–74 (Lord Browne-Wilkinson); *Hedley Byrne & Co v Heller & Partners* [1964] AC 465 (HL) 495 (Lord Morris); *Barrett v MoD* [1995] 3 All ER 87; Kortman (n 105) 60–61.

III. Conclusion

We have examined two scenarios in this chapter. In the first part, we asked whether claims to recover wrongly paid tax could be seen as unjust enrichment. They can. We can see them as performance claims despite the different underlying justificatory rationale. In the second part, we asked the same question about those necessity claims that have been brought into unjust enrichment. Necessity is not, however, in any case an unjust factor. In cases of legal compulsion there is a much easier route to liability, and in the moral compulsion cases we would be better off accepting that, despite the lack of agreement, the claimant's actions were justified in the sense that they provide a valid basis for a transaction. The contrast between these scenarios therefore illustrates the analytical power of the performance claim idea.

7

Proprietary Claims

Introduction

Chapters four to six largely concerned the workings of personal claims to unjust enrichment. I say 'largely' because it was not possible to avoid discussions of rescission of contracts for duress and undue influence in explaining the conditions for relief under these unjust factors, or to avoid the discussion of rescission of voluntary instruments for mistake, which have proprietary implications. We did not, however, examine in detail the way in which the proprietary claim operates and differs from personal claims. That is the task of this chapter.

A proprietary unjust enrichment claim is in (almost) all cases to be explained as a power. The claimant has an equitable power to vest title to the asset back in himself. He has a power to obtain a vested right in the asset.[1] Very rarely will he have a common law power.[2] In none of these cases of proprietary claims (just as for the personal) can the defendant be said to have a duty to return the asset immediately on receipt.[3] Just as with personal claims the defendant need have no idea of the claim against him. The word 'almost' was bracketed though. This is because if automatic resulting trusts are seen as responding to unjust enrichment – and nothing much in practice turns on this – they will not be restitutionary powers in the same sense.[4]

Personal claims involve restitution of value. The defendant has typically received value (more accurately something of value be that money, chattels or services) from the claimant. In performance claims, the value of the performance rendered must be quantified irrespective of marketable residuum and in non-performance claims, the value (say) of the improvements must be quantified. It will not in many cases (improvements, services) be possible to return the enrichment *in specie*. However, if the claim rests on the transfer of a specific right, or sometimes, as we saw in chapter two with our discussion of subrogation, the

[1] A Lodder, *Enrichment in the Law of Unjust Enrichment and Restitution* (Oxford, Hart Publishing, 2012) 64.

[2] *Lipkin Gorman v Karpnale Ltd* [1991] 2 AC 548 (HL); D Sheehan, 'Proprietary Claims for Mistake and Ignorance: an Unseen Equivalence' [2002] *Restitution Law Review* 69; for a trust analysis of the case, see B MacFarlane, *The Structure of Property Law* (Oxford, Hart Publishing, 2008) 293–98.

[3] But see A Reilly, 'Is the Mere Equity to Rescind a Legal Power? Unpacking Hohfeld's Concept of Volitional Control' (2019) 39 *OJLS* 779.

[4] WJ Swadling, 'Unjust Enrichment, Value, Rights and Trusts' (2021) 137 *LQR* 56, 63.

discharge of a legal right, it can be reversed *in specie*. A claim to specific restitution of a right is a proprietary claim.[5] We do not therefore need to concern ourselves with the defendant's freedom of choice in quite the same way in proprietary restitution as we do in personal restitution.[6] Questions of whether it was requested or necessary are not relevant and value, while relevant to counter-restitution in rescission claims and to change of position, has no relevance to the order to make restitution itself.

Many proprietary claims follow a performance pattern, particularly the rescission claims in section III; at least some 'lending' subrogation claims do also. Others follow the pattern of an *actio de in rem verso*, such as the trustee misappropriation cases in section IV. While some non-performance claims (improvement claims) can, as we saw in chapter four, be fitted into an unjust factors mould, intermediary claims cannot so easily be slotted into the same pattern. They do, however, resemble the civil law *versio*-claim, which is placed in the unjustified enrichment category. There are clear differences between English and civil law in that the civil law does not recognise the *versio*-claim as proprietary and indeed many modern civil law or mixed systems simply do not recognise the *actio de in rem verso* at all; South African law therefore treats some of these scenarios inside the *condictio indebiti*. This chapter therefore examines the different scenarios in turn, beginning with void transfers where legal title remains with the 'transferor', resulting trust scenarios, rescission and trustee misappropriation cases.

I. Void Transfers

Legal title to tangibles can be transferred in one of three ways.[7] It can be transferred by contract, by deed or delivery. These three modes of conveyance interact. A contract may be void and be incapable of transferring title, but delivery of the asset may still transfer title.[8] In *Cundy v Lindsay*, for example, a fraudster called Blenkarn signed his name to resemble Blenkiron and Co.[9] The claimant sent him goods and was never paid; the fraudster sold the goods on to the defendant whom the claimant then sued. Lord Cairns said that the claimant knew nothing of the fraudster and intended to contract with the company. His mistake was in thinking that he was contracting with the company rather than the fraudster. The contract was therefore void and property did not pass to the fraudster and

[5] R Chambers, 'Two Kinds of Enrichment' in R Chambers, C Mitchell and J Penner (eds), *Philosophical Foundations of the Law of Unjust Enrichment* (Oxford, OUP, 2009).

[6] Lodder (n 1) 63.

[7] D Sheehan, *The Principles of Personal Property Law*, 2nd edn (Oxford, Hart Publishing, 2017) ch 2.

[8] *Singh v Ali* [1960] AC 167.

[9] *Cundy v Lindsay* (1878) 3 App Cas 459 (HL).

hence not to the third party either.[10] Factors vitiating intention can therefore, if sufficiently fundamental, vitiate both the contract and the passage of property by delivery. Similar observations might be made of the transfer of intangible assets. It is for example conceivable for a fundamental mistake to vitiate the on-chain transfer of a crypto-asset and similar rules should apply to such intangibles as to tangibles.[11]

In *Moffatt v Kazana*, the claimant had left a tin of money up a chimney and on selling the house moved out without taking the tin.[12] The buyer found the tin and the case revolved around whether title had passed to the purchaser of the house. It had not. The tin was not a fixture, and nobody seriously argued it was. Title did not therefore pass automatically to the buyer of the house, and although there was a physical transfer of possession the claimant's total ignorance that the tin was in the chimney prevented title passing. There is some dispute as to whether there is an action in unjust enrichment or not. Burrows (now Lord Burrows) has argued that it is an unjust enrichment claim.[13] There are difficulties with an unjust enrichment claim in this context, however. Swadling argues that the recipient is not enriched because the legal owner retains legal title.[14] That is dubious. The recipient has an original title through bare possession,[15] which definitely enriches the recipient, although it is not derivative of the owner's title. None of this really matters though. The only way that a defendant can avoid a claim in unjust enrichment is to say, 'I am not enriched because the property is yours'. From the defendant's perspective, this is a self-defeating argument.[16] In making this point, Stevens was in fact concerned to defend the availability of an unjust enrichment claim, making the point that any argument on the defendant's behalf that knocks it out in fact demonstrates the existence of another ground of claim, although he would now not express it in the same way. Given the ferocious nature of the tort of conversion as an alternative, most cases can be expected to be argued in conversion.[17]

[10] ibid 465–66.

[11] Law Commission, *Digital Assets: Final Report* (Law Com No 412, 2023) paras 5.46–5.47; there are few (if any) examples of void assignments of choses in action like debts.

[12] *Moffatt v Kazana* [1969] 2 QB 152.

[13] AS Burrows, *The Law of Restitution*, 3rd edn (Oxford, OUP, 2011) 403–09.

[14] WJ Swadling, 'Ignorance and Unjust Enrichment: The Problem of Title' (2008) 28 *OJLS* 627.

[15] *Costello v Chief Constable of Derbyshire* [2001] EWCA Civ 381, [2001] 1 WLR 1437; *R v Seed* [2021] EWCA Crim 1198, [2021] 1 WLR 6033.

[16] R Stevens, 'Three Enrichment Issues' in AS Burrows and A Rodger (eds), *Mapping the Law* (Oxford, OUP, 2006) 63–64; R Stevens, *The Laws of Restitution* (Oxford, OUP, 2023) 211 arguing now that what matters is the right to the thing not whether anyone was enriched.

[17] Its ferocity lies in how damages reflect the full loss caused to the claimant and the strictness of liability. *Douglas v Hello! (No 3)* [2007] UKHL 21, [2008] 1 AC 1, 90 (Baroness Hale); *Kuwait Airways v Iraqi Airways* [2002] UKHL 19, [2002] 2 AC 883 (HL) 1090 (Lord Nicholls).

II. Resulting Trusts

There are conventionally said to be two types of resulting trust,[18] which we take in turn.

1. Presumed resulting trusts.
2. Automatic resulting trusts.[19]

A. Presumed Resulting Trusts

In the absence of a contrary presumption, the presumption of resulting trust throws the onus of proof onto the transferor to show that the transfer was meant to transfer title outright.[20] It applies in cases where a transfer of money or other assets, but possibly not land,[21] has been made gratuitously.[22] It also applies in purchase cases where A's money is used to purchase assets, including land, in B's name. A contrary presumption – the presumption of advancement – is sometimes described as a presumption that a gift was intended. A provision to abolish it was enacted in 2010 although it has still not been – and probably never will be – brought into force.[23] The principle has been followed on multiple occasions, although very much more often than not negatively – a nod to the principle as the presumption is rebutted. Only very occasionally is the presumption dispositive and often those cases are criticised heavily.[24] There is an oft-examined debate between Swadling and Chambers as to the nature of the presumed resulting trust, although other views exist.[25]

[18] *Re Vandervell (No 2)* [1974] 1 All ER 47.

[19] WJ Swadling, 'Explaining Resulting Trusts' (2008) 124 *LQR* 72, 72–73; WJ Swadling, 'A New Role for Resulting Trusts?' (1996) 16 *Legal Studies* 110, 113.

[20] *Dyer v Dyer* (1788) 2 Cox Eq 92, 30 ER 42.

[21] Law of Property Act 1925, s 60(3); J Mee, 'Voluntary Conveyances of Land: The Presumption of Resulting Trust Redux?' [2018] *Conv* 184; *Lohia v Lohia* (2000) 3 ITELR 117; *Ali v Khan* [2002] EWCA Civ 974, but see *Prest v Petrodel* [2013] UKSC 34, [2013] 2 AC 415; *NCA v Dong* [2017] EWHC 3116.

[22] See, eg, *Vandervell v IRC* [1967] 2 AC 291 (HL) 312 (Lord Upjohn).

[23] Equality Act 2010, s 199; See J Glister, 'Section 199 of the Equality Act 2010: How not to Abolish the Presumption of Advancement' (2010) 73 *MLR* 807; after *Patel v Mirza* [2016] UKSC 42, [2017] AC 467 there is even less pressure to bring the section into force. See P Davies, 'Ramifications of Patel v Mirza in the Law of Trusts' in A Bogg and S Green (eds), *Illegality after Patel v Mirza* (Oxford, Hart Publishing, 2018) 241.

[24] *Re Vinogradoff* [1935] WN 68; *Re Muller* [1953] NZLR 879. See J Penner, *The Law of Trusts*, 12th edn (Oxford, OUP, 2022) para 10.12.

[25] J Mee, 'Presumed Resulting Trusts, Intention and Declaration' [2014] *CLJ* 86; E O'Dell, 'The Resulting Trust' in C Rickett and R Grantham (eds), *Structure and Justification in Private Law* (Oxford, Hart Publishing, 2008). For an assessment of the merits of the various alternative views concentrating on Swadling and Chambers, see J Penner, 'Resulting Trusts and Unjust Enrichment: Three Controversies' in C Mitchell (ed), *Constructive and Resulting Trusts* (Oxford, Hart Publishing, 2010).

Swadling argues that historically the fact presumed in the first type of case was a declaration of trust for the transferor,[26] or for the person who advances the purchase money. He argues that true legal presumptions are dispositive of the result, can be rebutted by contrary evidence, and are not invoked when there is no gap in the evidence. If there is good evidence of the party's intention, the presumption is not therefore in play,[27] which is why a presumption of a declaration of trust is rebutted by proof of an intention to do something else. All three conditions are met in resulting trust cases.[28] Once the presumption is made, a legal conclusion can be drawn. If the presumption is of a declaration of trust, a trust follows in the same way as if the declaration is proven by evidence. The contrary presumption of advancement is therefore simply a case where the presumption of resulting trust does not apply.[29] It is not a true presumption.

Chambers did not dispute the historical explanation offered by Swadling, but suggested, however, that the presumption later changed to a presumption that the claimant did not intend the recipient to benefit.[30] He has accepted Swadling's criticism that the presumption of resulting trust as a presumption 'that the provider did not intend to give the benefit of that property to the recipient'[31] is not a true presumption at all. Nonetheless, he still maintains that the lack of intention to give the benefit away is critical. There is no consideration for the transfer. The relevant legal ground at issue is therefore gift. Absent an intention to make a gift, there is no legal ground and restitution follows to prevent the unjustified enrichment of the defendant. Rebuttal of the presumption of advancement is therefore critical as removing a possible legal basis for the transfer. The presumption of advancement, unlike that of resulting trust, is therefore a true presumption, a presumption of an intention to make a gift.[32] The debate is as to what the presumptions are and what, if anything, is being presumed, although the presumptions have very little weight and very little evidence is required to rebut them.[33]

The substantive disagreement between the authors does, however, have implications not merely as to whether presumed resulting trusts are unjust enrichment trusts, but whether they are triggered by a civil law absence of basis structure. In chapter five, we saw that English law does not recognise a personal claim founded

[26] Swadling, 'A New Role for Resulting Trusts?' (n 19) 112; *Bosanac v Commissioner of Taxation* [2022] HCA 34, [104]–[110] (Gordon, Edelman JJ).

[27] As in, eg, *Aroso v Coutts & Co* [2002] 1 All ER (Comm) 241; *Goodman v Gallant* [1986] 1 All ER 311 (CA).

[28] Swadling, 'Explaining Resulting Trusts' (n 19) 77–79.

[29] ibid 93; *Bosanac v Commissioner of Taxation* [2022] HCA 34, [15] (Kiefel CJ, Gleeson J), [65] (Gageler J), [115] (Gordon, Edelman JJ).

[30] R Chambers, 'Resulting Trusts' in AS Burrows and A Rodger (eds), *Mapping the Law* (Oxford, OUP, 2006); PBH Birks, 'Restitution and Resulting Trusts' in S Goldstein (ed), *Equity and Contemporary Legal Developments* (Jerusalem, HUJ, 1992) 347.

[31] R Chambers, *Resulting Trusts* (Oxford, OUP, 1997) 19.

[32] R Chambers, 'Is there a Presumption of Resulting Trust?' in C Mitchell (ed), *Constructive and Resulting Trusts* (Oxford, Hart Publishing, 2010) 267–68.

[33] *Bosanac v Commissioner of Taxation* [2022] HCA 34, [31] (Kiefel CJ, Gleeson J).

purely on absence of basis. It is not enough as a matter of English law to say that performance rendered to the defendant was for no legal ground. A positive unjust factor must be shown. Unjust factors are simply never mentioned in presumed resulting trusts cases, so it is implausible to rest the trust on proven mistakes or duress. Can presumed resulting trusts be triggered purely by absence of basis? No. The first point must be that if personal and proprietary claims rest on different explanatory bases of the same area of the law, they are liable to undermine and undercut each other, risking incoherence in the law.

The second is that Chambers' conception of absence of basis is too broad and over-inclusive. As we have seen throughout this book, both the civil law system and English law (should) recognise a fundamental division between performance and non-performance claims. Absence of basis is best confined to the former as we saw in chapter two. The presumed resulting trust, as understood by Chambers, would cut across this distinction. This matters. If we attempt to explain English law by reference to a concept borrowed from another system, it seems a legitimate criticism that that concept works quite differently in its home jurisdiction from how it is being used to explain our own law. In *Chase Manhattan v Israel-British Bank*, the claimant bank paid the defendant twice believing it had not paid the first time.[34] It recovered. Goulding J called this a constructive trust;[35] Chambers has called it a resulting trust.[36] In either case, the bank paid under the erroneous belief that it had an obligation to do so. This would in a civil law system be a *condictio indebiti*. There is a transfer putatively to discharge an obligation which does not exist. Not all cases that Chambers explains on his absence of basis justification are *condictio*-claims, however. *Williams v Williams* cannot be explained in terms of performance.[37] The facts were that Williams Senior's solicitor transferred land owned by Williams Senior into his son's (Williams Junior's) name wrongly believing it Senior's intention that he do so. Senior, however, knew nothing of this, thus rebutting the presumption of advancement and leading to a resulting trust. That ignorance of Williams Senior rebuts any possibility of a putative performance by him. It is not a *condictio indebiti*, although Birks considered the ignorance cases a fortiori from the standard mistake claim.[38] In German law it would not be covered by § 812 at all, but by § 816(I) BGB, if property passes[39] and § 985 BGB if not. § 816(I) is a type of *actio de in rem verso* and provides:

> If an unauthorised person disposes of an object and the disposition is effective against the authorised person, then he is obliged to make restitution to the authorised person of

[34] *Chase Manhattan v Israel–British Bank* [1981] Ch 105.

[35] ibid 109.

[36] Chambers, *Resulting Trusts* (n 31) 128–29.

[37] *Williams v Williams* (1863) 32 Beav 370, 55 ER 145.

[38] PBH Birks, *An Introduction to the Law of Restitution*, rev edn (Oxford, Clarendon Press, 1989) 140–41.

[39] D Reuter and M Martinek, *Ungerechtfertigte Bereicherung* (Berlin, JCB Mohr, 1983) 328–29; B Dickson, 'The Law of Restitution in the Federal Republic of Germany: A Comparison with English Law' (1987) 36 *ICLQ* 751, 776–78.

> what he gains by the disposal. If the disposition is gratuitous, then the same duty applies to a person who as a result of the disposition directly gains a legal advantage.

The solicitor was an unauthorised person – he had no authority to transfer the land, although he thought he did. Williams Junior was a donee. As legal title passed from Senior to Junior, German law would put the latter under a duty of restitution to the former. Cases of claims by a trust beneficiary contingent on tracing (or by a principal consequent on unauthorised transfers by an agent) are said by Chambers and Penner, however, to be perfect examples of transfers *sine causa*.[40] This might be so on the very thin (even conclusory) conception of *sine causa* du Plessis raises that if all the prerequisites for a cause of action in unjust enrichment are met, the enrichment is *sine causa*.[41] That is not very useful. The important point is that a tracing claim is not a performance claim. The trustees or agents – not the claimant principals – transfer the assets. German law has no trust device, but the pattern is analogous. Trustee (A) transfers asset owned (in equity) by B to C. If C takes free under the bona fide purchase rules (in German law §§ 993–95 BGB) B has no claim. If C does not, B does have a claim against C. In Germany this is personal. In England it is proprietary, but in either case the comparative perspective tells us at the very least that absence of basis cannot explain them both. They cannot and should not be grouped together as Chambers does.

The second related difficulty of over-inclusion is that Chambers cannot distinguish between performance claims attracting a proprietary response and those not. How – on a pure absence of basis approach – is *Pitt v Holt*[42] (rescission) distinguished from *Chase Manhattan* (trust)?[43] If we try to do so on the basis that *Pitt* is a *causa donandi* case (a mistake made in making a gift) and *Chase Manhattan* a liability mistake, how do we account for *Westdeutsche Landesbank Girozentrale v Islington LBC*?[44] That too is, properly understood, a *condictio indebiti* claim in that the payments were made to discharge a (non-existent) debt,[45] but no proprietary claim lay at all.

This suggests that we are looking for a non-unjust enrichment explanation for presumed resulting trusts, and this is consistent with the recent High Court of Australia decision in *Bosanac v Commissioner of Taxation*,[46] which settles debate in Australia against the presumed resulting trust having anything to do with unjust enrichment.[47] One problem with Swadling's view, however, is that the presumed

[40] R Chambers and J Penner, 'Ignorance' in S Degeling and J Edelman (eds), *Unjust Enrichment in Commercial Law* (Sydney, Law Book Co, 2008).

[41] J du Plessis, *The South African Law of Unjustified Enrichment* (Durban, Juta, 2012) 53.

[42] *Pitt v Holt* [2006] UKHL 49, [2007] 1 AC 558.

[43] [1981] Ch 105.

[44] *Westdeutsche Landesbank Girozentrale v Islington LBC* [1996] AC 669 (HL); see J Mee, 'The Past, Present and Future of Resulting Trusts' [2017] *Current Legal Problems* 189, 209.

[45] D Sheehan, 'Resulting Trusts, Sine Causa and the Structure of Proprietary Restitution' (2011) 11 *Oxford University Commonwealth Law Journal* 1, 19–20.

[46] [2022] HCA 34.

[47] HJ Cooney, 'Presumed Resulting Trusts on the Move' [2023] *Lloyd's Maritime & Commercial Law Quarterly* 28, 29.

declaration exists in circumstances where we really do know there could not have been one. *Williams v Williams* is one such. We can, however, say that this is properly a tracing case. Williams Senior must trace his land into the hands of his son. Tracing cases can be thought of as giving rise to constructive trusts,[48] although Swadling would reject such a characterisation, as he believes constructive trusts are not true trusts.[49] *Hodgson v Marks* is another case where a valid declaration would seem impossible.[50] Hodgson transferred her house to her lodger (Evans), who ultimately sold it to Marks who granted a mortgage to the second defendant. The question in that case was whether Hodgson retained an equitable interest in the house which could bind the defendants via her actual occupation. The Court of Appeal held that there was a resulting trust. It did not matter that an express trust to the same effect would have been ineffective as not being evidenced in writing. This is a problem if the resulting trust is based on an implied declaration of trust. Why should an implied declaration of trust be valid if an express one is invalid? Russell LJ, however, rested the trust on the lack of intention to make a gift,[51] which in fact provides some support to Chambers. Swadling has argued that the express trust was enforced,[52] despite the informality and bases this result on *Rochefoucauld v Boustead*[53] and the argument that the transfer was intended to render Evans a trustee for her, and he committed fraud by going against that. Swadling though mistakes the substantive rule, the application of which is presumed. It is not that all trusts need to be declared expressly, but that on a voluntary transfer of property (or its purchase in the name of another) whether the transferee takes beneficially is dependent on the transferor's intention and it is significant in this context that virtually none of the cases talk about anything other than a presumption as to intention.[54]

B. Automatic Resulting Trusts

An example of an automatic resulting trust is of a transfer from B to A to hold on trust 'for my favourite student'.[55] We do not know who that is. It is difficult

[48] *Independent Trustees Ltd v GP Noble Trustee Ltd* [2012] EWCA Civ 195, [2013] 1 Ch 95.

[49] WJ Swadling, 'The Fiction of the Constructive Trust' [2011] *Current Legal Problems* 399; see Stevens, *The Laws of Restitution* (n 16) 262 for a valid response to Swadling's thesis.

[50] *Hodgson v Marks* [1971] Ch 892.

[51] ibid 933.

[52] ibid 907–08 (Ungoed-Thomas J) and in the CA 933 (Russell LJ); WJ Swadling, 'A Hard Look at Hodgson v Marks' in PBH Birks and FD Rose (eds), *Restitution and Equity: Volume 1 Resulting Trusts and Equitable Compensation* (Oxford, Mansfield Press, 2000); see also, *Re Vinogradoff* [1935] WN 68 where the resulting trustee had no capacity.

[53] *Rochefoucauld v Boustead* [1897] 1 Ch 196.

[54] Mee, 'Presumed Resulting Trusts, Intention and Declaration' (n 25) 90–94; an important exception decided after Mee's article was published is *Bosanac v Commissioner of Taxation* [2022] HCA 34, [104] (Edelman, Gordon JJ).

[55] Sheehan, *The Principles of Personal Property Law* (n 7) 164.

to say that the transfer is at the expense of the student because we cannot say who it is. One possibility as a cause of action is failure of consideration. Failure of consideration typically occurs where I do not obtain the quid pro quo or counter-performance I was expecting.[56] In these cases of automatic resulting trust, the term quid pro quo might be inappropriate but the basis on which the transfer takes place has failed. I transferred the assets on the basis that there would be a valid trust for my favourite student. There is no such trust.[57] We might say that the rules are simply part of our background property law.[58] Given that the resulting trustee will not be able to plead change of position against the settlor, it may seem to make little difference what view we take, although it may be important in questions of limitation periods, or choice of law.[59] We can, however, see that a performance analysis works through an examination of South African law.

In South African law neither the resulting trust nor the constructive trust exists. Since the trust in South Africa is a means of dividing enjoyment and administration of property, a constructive or resulting trust is said to be contradictory,[60] imposing unsought management duties. *Honoré's South African Law of Trusts* argues payments on trusts that fail are dealt with through the *condictio sine causa specialis*.[61] The *condictio sine causa specialis* is a bit of a ragbag. In this context there is an attempt to transfer assets to create an obligation to a third party. That aim cannot be met but does not fall within any of the other *condictiones* and is allocated to the *condictio sine causa*. It does not fall into the *condictio indebiti* for example as the settlor does not act under a non-existent obligation, purportedly applying to him. There is, however, a performance rendered – a transfer for the purpose of creating an obligation between trustee-recipient and a third party. The *condictio causa data causa non secuta* can apply where performance is rendered to obtain a non-contractual quid pro quo; the example often given is of a transfer in contemplation of marriage.[62] *Essery v Cowlard*[63] may therefore be a *condictio causa data causa non secuta* in South Africa. A settlement was made in 1877 in

[56] *Fibrosa Spolka Ackcjyna v Fairbairn Lawson* [1943] AC 32 (HL). Generally, failure of basis claims cannot be proprietary in nature: *Angove's Pty Ltd v Bailey* [2016] UKSC 47 [2016] 1 WLR 3179.

[57] D Sheehan, *The Principles of Personal Property Law*, 2nd edn (Hart Publishing Oxford 2017) 164–65.

[58] C Rickett and R Grantham, 'Resulting Trusts: The True Nature of the Failing Trust Cases' (2000) 116 *LQR* 15; Penner, *The Law of Trusts* (n 24) paras 10.69–10.72.

[59] See, eg, G Panagopoulos, *Restitution in Private International Law* (Oxford, Hart Publishing, 2000) 62–70 on characterisation of restitutionary claims in private international law.

[60] *Verseput v de Gruchy* 1977 (4) SA 440; *Ex Parte Estate Legrew* 1950 (2) SA 602; E Cameron, 'Constructive Trusts in South African Law: The Legacy Refused' [1999] *Edinburgh Law Review* 341, 352.

[61] E Cameron et al (eds), *Honoré's South African Law of Trusts*, 6th edn (Durban, Juta, 2018) 567–68.

[62] R Evans-Jones, 'The Claim to Recover what was Transferred for a Lawful Purpose Outwith Contract (the Condictio Causa Data Causa Non Secuta)' [1997] *Acta Juridica* 139, 142.

[63] *Essery v Cowlard* (1884) 26 Ch D 194; *Bond v Walford* (1886) 32 Ch D 238; F Maher, 'A New Conception of Failure of Basis' [2004] *Restitution Law Review* 96; see *Truter v Administrateur Kaapprovinsie* 1978 (4) SA 489 (CA), Cameron et al (eds) (n 61) 567 for the view that this too might be the *condictio sine causa*.

consideration of an intended marriage. Stock, the property of the intended wife, was declared to be in held trust for her, her husband and children's benefit. The marriage never took place. The trust, originally valid, therefore failed, and the fund resulted back to the intended wife who provided it. Absent this type of ring-fencing, subsequent failures of consideration never attract proprietary relief in English law. Although different *condictio* claims might be appropriate in the mixed jurisdictions, both scenarios can be included within a failure of basis analysis in English law. However, it is fundamental to the automatic resulting trust that it only operate where the defendant transferor was **not** to have free disposition of the asset in question, ie, he was not intended to have the full beneficial interest.[64] It is only in these cases that we conceptualise the putative performance of the claimant as the transfer of a right to the defendant.

III. Rescission

This section is divided into three. We first ask when a transaction is voidable. Second, we ask what type of right the voidability implies and last, whether rescission claims are unjust enrichment claims. A similar analysis is possible for rectification. Rectification is not primarily an unjust enrichment claim or remedy and we leave it largely to one side for that reason. It can, however, be available for common mistake in contract cases[65] and unilateral mistakes where there is a voluntary instrument. The same proprietary analysis applies to equities of rectification as to equities to rescind. It is a mere equity,[66] which can result in the specific restitution of property in cases where title is conveyed under the unrectified instrument and rectification implies the revesting of title.

A. Instances of Voidability

i. At Common Law

The doctrine of rescission at common law is a narrower one than its equitable counterpart. It operates for our purposes in the context of executory or executed contracts vitiated for fraud or duress. Where rescission takes place at common law the contract or other conveyance is extinguished *ab initio* and sums of money are

[64] One of two alternative necessary conditions in *Angove's Pty Ltd v Bailey* [2016] UKSC 47, [2016] 1 WLR 3179, [31].
[65] *Swainland Builders Ltd v Freehold Properties Ltd* [2002] EWCA Civ 560, [33]–[34] (Peter Gibson LJ); *Chartbrook Ltd v Persimmon Homes Ltd* [2009] UKHL 38, [2009] 1 AC 1101, [48] (Lord Hoffmann).
[66] C Mitchell, P Mitchell and S Watterson (eds), *Goff & Jones: The Law of Unjust Enrichment*, 10th edn (London, Sweet & Maxwell, 2022) paras 40.46–40.51; on how this works in registered land, see *Blacklocks v JB Developments (Godalming) Ltd* [1982] Ch 183.

recoverable from the defendant from the moment of disaffirmation as money had and received; the defendant has a claim to the counter-restitution of any benefits transferred to the claimant.

In cases of money, the orthodoxy is that rescission of the contract does not revert title to the money to the payer in the same way that legal title to goods reverts to the transferor. However, the same act will rescind the contract and require restitution of the payment.[67] Revesting may, however, take place in some limited circumstances where there is no mixing of the money with the defendant's own. This is what happened in *Banque Belge pour L'Etranger v Hambrouck*.[68] Hambrouck fraudulently obtained several cheques from the proceeds of which further cheques were paid to Spanoghe for no legally relevant consideration. The question was whether the money could be recovered from Spanoghe. Bankes LJ held that the bank had a power to revest title against Hambrouck, although he expressed it as Hambrouck's only having a voidable title.[69] Atkin LJ in the same vein talked of a 'voidable transaction' and title revesting in the plaintiff.[70] There was no problem of *restitutio in integrum*. No evidence had been led as to the manner of the fraud. The money in dispute had been paid into court, so there was no problem of mixing. It is uncontroversial, however, that rescission has proprietary effects in contracts for the sale of goods. Such contracts procured by fraudulent misrepresentation were described as voidable at common law after *Load v Green*.[71] To regain legal title to goods the defrauded seller must elect to disaffirm or rescind the contract. Title to goods passes under the voidable contract but does so defeasibly. Prior to any disposal of the goods by the fraudster to a bona fide purchaser for value,[72] the innocent party may reclaim it. This proprietary response is not available in the case of land or intangible property, because the common law does not know of any mechanism by which title to these assets can be reclaimed.

Duress also permits of rescission at common law, although there are no clear examples demonstrating its proprietary impact. Originally only duress to the person[73] and duress to goods, where goods were illegally detained,[74] would suffice. However, it is now clear that economic duress will also suffice.[75] The rules in duress cases should be the same and track those relating to fraud. It should therefore be possible to revest title in goods and money – at least to the extent that it is not mixed – and to allow personal claims to money where it is mixed and unidentifiable.

[67] D Fox, *Property Rights in Money* (Oxford, OUP, 2008) para 6.18.
[68] *Banque Belge pour L'Etranger v Hambrouck* [1921] 2 KB 321.
[69] ibid 325.
[70] ibid 332; see also, *FC Jones v Jones* [1996] Ch 159 (CA) which might be confined to its facts.
[71] *Load v Green* (1846) 15 M&W 216, 153 ER 828.
[72] *White v Garden* (1851) 10 CB 919, 138 ER 364.
[73] eg, *Barton v Armstrong* [1976] AC 104 (PC).
[74] *Skeate v Beale* (1841) 11 A&E 983, 113 ER 688.
[75] *The Evia Luck* [1992] 2 AC 152 (HL).

ii. In Equity

Rescission at common law for misrepresentation is only possible in fraud cases. In negligent and innocent misrepresentation, rescission is possible in equity only. *Re Glubb*[76] therefore the Court of Appeal held that testamentary gifts to charities induced by an innocent misrepresentation were voidable in equity. Importantly equitable rescission is possible in fraud cases as well. Clearly equity has no work to do if the election to rescind at common law is successful. However, if a bar to rescission – such as the impossibility of exact counter-restitution – applies to rescission at law, rescission in equity may still be possible,[77] because equity allows counter-restitution in money where the defendant can be put in substantially the same position as he was in before.[78]

Undue influence also allows rescission of gifts or contracts in equity, as we saw in chapter four. As an example of undue influence in *Allcard v Skinner*,[79] the claimant sought to recover gifts made to her religious order in pursuance of her vows after she decided to leave the order. The Court decided that the gifts were voidable, not void. She had been subject to undue influence in that she had not been in a position to make a fully independent decision as to the wisdom of the gifts to the order. They would therefore have been rescinded, except for the length of time that the claimant took to come to court.

Mistake is more complex and does not seem to support rescission of contracts. After *The Great Peace*,[80] it seems clear that common mistake (a mistake made by both parties) will not allow rescission of a contract in equity and unilateral mistake equally seems unable to support equitable intervention in England.[81] Intervention is therefore limited to non-contractual contexts. We have seen that *Chase Manhattan v Israel-British Bank* was likely mistakenly decided in chapter four, but to recap the mistake, as a liability mistake, should not attract proprietary consequences.[82] However, voluntary instruments – deeds of gift – can be rescinded in equity for mistake; after *Pitt v Holt* the law is that the mistake must be not merely causative but must be sufficiently serious.[83]

[76] *Re Glubb* [1900] 1 Ch 354; *Deutsche Morgan Grenfell v IRC* [2006] UKHL 49; [2007] 1 AC 558, 592 (Lord Scott).

[77] D O'Sullivan, S Elliott and R Zakrzewski (eds), *The Law of Rescission*, 3rd edn (Oxford, OUP, 2023) paras 10.44–10.45.

[78] *Erlanger v New Sombrero Phosphate Company* (1878) 3 App Cas 1218; conversely it is not available if he cannot. See, eg, *Campbell v Backoffice Investments Pty Ltd* [2008] NSWCA 95, (2008) 66 ACSR 359.

[79] *Allcard v Skinner* (1887) LR 36 Ch D 145; *Mitchell v Homfray* (1881) LR 8 QBD 587; *Wright v Vanderplank* (1856) 8 De GM&G 133, 44 ER 340; *Cheese v Thomas* [1994] 1 WLR 129.

[80] *Great Peace Shipping v Tsavliris International Shipping Ltd (The Great Peace)* [2003] QB 679.

[81] *Statoil ASA v Louis Dreyfus Energy Services LLP* [2009] 1 All ER (Comm) 1035, although rescission for unilateral mistake is possible in Singapore, for example. See *B2C2 Ltd v Quoine Pty Ltd* [2020] SGCA(I) 02.

[82] Fox, *Property Rights in Money* (n 67) paras 3.90–3.91 but see, defending the result in *Chase Manhattan*, D Salmons, 'The Availability of Proprietary Restitution in Cases of Mistaken Payments' [2015] *CLJ* 534, 563.

[83] See also, eg, *Re Magarey Farlam Lawyers Trust Account (No 3)* [2007] SASC 9, (2007) 96 SASR 337.

The final set of cases where equitable rescission is possible is when there is an unconscionable bargain and the principles are as set out in chapter four or for mental incapacity and intoxication which are governed by special rules apart from those on unconscionable bargains.[84] In these cases the party seeking rescission does not need to show exploitation or morally culpable conduct, although he does need to show that the counterparty was aware of the defect in his intention.[85]

B. What Kind of Right does the Claimant Have Prior to Rescission?

i. At Common Law

The first thing to say is that title to any asset is recovered whether it passed by way of delivery, contract or registration. It is recovered because the flaw that makes the contract voidable also renders title to any asset defeasible. The title is infected by the transferor's imperfect consent.[86] A personal claim to the recovery of money paid arises as does a claim for the payment for services rendered and these cannot be explained as proprietary claims. Rescission at common law therefore has two distinct effects – removal of a contract (say) *ab initio* but also revesting of title or the imposition of a personal claim. That claim also comes with a contingent – albeit fully independent – claim by the defendant, which accrues unconditionally on rescission.[87] In English common law it seems these can be seen as linked unjust enrichment claims, where the defendant has an action in failure of consideration because he performed on the basis of the counter-performance, which itself must now be returned to the claimant (eg, because of the defendant's fraud or duress).[88] The position in equity is more complex, but the substance is the same. The claimant's claim is conditional on repayment to the defendant, which is worked through in a court order; the claimant's award might be conditional and on terms, or it might occur through the making of allowances in an account.[89]

Rescission at common law is complete when the rescindor elects to disaffirm the contract and notifies the defendant. It has, however, been held that notice is not always needed. In *Car & Universal Finance Co v Caldwell*,[90] the fraudster could not be traced after he had purchased a car from the owner and sold it on. The

[84] O'Sullivan et al (n 77) para 7.41.
[85] ibid para 7.42.
[86] ibid paras 1.25–1.28.
[87] ibid para 15.62.
[88] E Bant, 'Rescission, Restitution and Compensation' in S Degeling and J Varuhas (eds), *Equitable Compensation and Disgorgement of Profit* (Oxford, Hart Publishing, 2017) 286–87; *Spence v Crawford* [1939] 3 All ER 271.
[89] O'Sullivan et al (n 77) para 15.62.
[90] *Car & Universal Finance Co v Caldwell* [1965] 1 QB 525; B Häcker, 'Proprietary Restitution after Impaired Consent Transfers' [2009] *CLJ* 324, 331–32.

owner, discovering the fraud, contacted the police and this was held to be sufficient to rescind the contract and vest title in the car. At that point the contract becomes void *ab initio* and the rescindor obtains legal title (at least to chattels) back. The exercise of the power does not retrospectively make the possessor a converter, although refusal to hand the asset over subsequent to rescission will be a conversion.[91] One question is what type of right or power the rescinding party has prior to the election. Although *Barclays Bank v Boulter* is authority that there is no vested common law property right,[92] analogies with equity suggest that a power to elect to rescind – and thereby revest legal title – is itself a proprietary right. The fact that the legal right to rescind and regain legal title is enforceable against donees of the asset sought to be recovered is further evidence of its proprietary nature.[93] It should be seen as a legal power to revest title.[94]

ii. In Equity

There is some controversy about the position in equity, but the preferable position is that rescission in equity is also effected by way of an election and that this entails the claimant has an equitable power *in rem* to vest equitable title back in himself, albeit one vulnerable to bona fide purchasers for value of an equitable interest.[95] Two lines of authority have grown up in equity. On the one hand there is a view that rescission for mistake, undue influence etc may be effected by the court order alone and not by any election by the claimant. In *Allcard v Skinner*[96] Lindley LJ referred to the claimant's having a right to have the gift set aside, which suggests a court order is needed.[97] The right to have a gift set aside for fraud or undue influence was said to devolve to the party's heirs,[98] however, which tends to suggest something of a proprietary flavour to the right. The point is perhaps clearer in *Gibbon v Mitchell*[99] where Gibbon was said to be applying to have the deed set aside (successfully) for mistake.

Under the second line of authority, rescission for misrepresentation may be effected by an election by the claimant. In *TSB v Camfield*,[100] there was an innocent misrepresentation by the husband as to his wife's liability and Roch LJ said:

[91] *Hunter BNZ Finance Ltd v CG Maloney Pty Ltd* (1988) 18 NSWLR 420.

[92] *Barclays Bank v Boulter* [1999] 1 WLR 1919.

[93] O'Sullivan et al (n 77) para 21.05.

[94] Häecker (n 90) 330.

[95] See, on bona fide purchase, *Phillips v Phillips* (1861) 4 De GF&J 208, 45 ER 1164; A Reilly, 'What Were Lord Westbury's Intentions in Phillips v Phillips? Bona Fide Purchase of an Equitable Interest' [2021] *CLJ* 156.

[96] (1887) LR 36 Ch D 145 (CA) 187.

[97] O'Sullivan et al (n 77) para 11.91.

[98] (1887) LR 36 Ch D 145 (CA) 187.

[99] *Gibbon v Mitchell* [1990] 1 WLR 1304; *SK Shipping Europe plc v Capital VLCC* 3 Corporation [2020] EWHC 2448, [2021] 2 Lloyds LR 109; *Harvard Nominees Pty Ltd v Tiller* [2020] FCAFC 229.

[100] *TSB v Camfield* [1995] 1 WLR 430.

> The right to set aside or rescind the transaction is that of the representee, not that of the court. The court's role in a disputed case will be to decide whether the representee has lawfully rescinded the transaction or is entitled to rescind it. Normally, if the representee is entitled to rescind the legal charge, that will have been effected by the representee's pleading that the transaction has been or should be set aside; that is to say, the transaction would have been set aside before the matter reaches the court. The court is not being asked to grant equitable relief; nor is it, in my view, granting equitable relief to which terms may be attached.[101]

Other authority suggests that rescission in equity is always effected by election. In *Brotherton v Asegudora Colseguros SA*,[102] the Court of Appeal was emphatic that rescission (making no distinction between common law and equity) was an act of the party.

The authorities are generally irreconcilable; a Supreme Court decision is needed to conclusively determine the law.[103] In principle, however, O'Sullivan et al argue, a transaction voidable in equity must be rescinded by court order unless it is voidable for fraud in which case equity assists the law by declaring that an election insufficient to avoid it at law does so in equity at least to the extent of revesting equitable title in the asset.[104] This, they suggest, is consistent with the Australian case of *Alati v Kruger*.[105] The respondent had bought a fruit business on the basis of a number of fraudulent misrepresentations regarding the business's average takings. He, within two weeks, brought proceedings to rescind the contract. The majority in the High Court decided that rescission would have been impossible at law as the respondent was not in a position to return the business *in specie* in the same state that he received it.[106] However,

> equity has always regarded as valid the disaffirmance of a contract induced by fraud even though precise *restitutio in integrum* is not possible, if the situation is such that, by the exercise of its powers, including the power to take accounts of profits and to direct inquiries as to allowances proper to be made for deterioration, it can do what is practically just between the parties, and by so doing restore them substantially to the *status quo* … rescission for misrepresentation is always the act of the party himself.[107]

In fraud cases, therefore, it is reasonable to talk of the claimant having an equitable power *in rem* to rescind the transaction and revest equitable title, creating a constructive or (maybe) resulting trust immediately on the election to rescind.

[101] ibid 438–39.

[102] *Brotherton v Asegudora Colseguros SA* [2003] 2 All ER (Comm) 298; *Drake Insurance plc v Provident Insurance plc* [2003] Lloyds Rep IR 78; *Reese River Silver Mining Co v Smith* (1869) LR 4 HL 64; *O'Sullivan v Management Agency and Music Ltd* [1985] QB 428; *Allied Irish Bank v Byrne* [1995] 1 FCR 430.

[103] *IGE USA Investments Ltd v HMRC* [2021] EWCA Civ 534, [2021] Ch 423, [91] (Henderson LJ).

[104] O'Sullivan et al (n 77) paras 11.107–11.112.

[105] *Alati v Kruger* (1955) 94 CLR 216.

[106] ibid 223.

[107] ibid 223–24.

Such an equitable election does not, however, affect legal title or extinguish the contract. This only occurs on the issuance of the court order.[108]

O'Sullivan, Elliott and Zakrzewski's argument seems flawed. First, if equitable rescission is possible by election to support the common law in fraud cases there seems little reason not to make it possible by election in duress where common law rescission is also possible. Second, the cases merely refer to misrepresentation – as above in *Alati v Kruger* – making no distinction between fraudulent and innocent. If equitable rescission is to be possible by election in innocent misrepresentation cases, which cannot be explained as equity assisting the law, why not rescission of mistaken voluntary instruments or rescission for undue influence which also fall within equity's exclusive jurisdiction? O'Sullivan et al argue not; while rescission is effected by election at common law, the fact that some discretionary reappraisal is possible in equity is inconsistent with rescission by election.[109] In principle this does not seem right either. The common law's very strict rules on restitution *in integrum* are not explicable by rescission's being effected by election. *Restitutio in integrum* should be seen as the claimant's recovery of his performance begetting a counter-claim for enrichments received by the claimant. The defendant has an independent free-standing claim to counter-restitution and restitution should be available in money. That this claim is not available seems an unjustifiable – although by now entrenched – restriction at law. The process is different in equity. Counter-restitution might be a condition of rescission, or an equitable accounting might be needed, but the substance is the same.[110]

Finally, the equity in the claimant seems to have proprietary qualities, being devisable to one's heirs. In *Stump v Gaby*[111] the deceased had executed a conveyance to his solicitor in what was described as 'embarrassed circumstances'. The right to rescind was devisable, an incident of a proprietary right, and the claimant's heir was therefore entitled to exercise the right to rescind. The case did not, however, preclude the characterisation of a right being a power *in rem* to vest title.[112] *Dickinson v Burrell*[113] was almost the same as *Stump v Gaby*; there was a voidable conveyance of land to the defendants by James Dickinson. He subsequently conveyed the same land on trust for himself for life and his children in remainder. The children sued to rescind the original conveyance. Lord Romilly MR held that the equitable right to rescind had passed to the new grantees.[114] The rights are also enforceable against third parties such as trustees in bankruptcy.[115]

[108] O'Sullivan et al (n 77) para 16.20.

[109] ibid para 11.95.

[110] Lodder (n 1) 124.

[111] *Stump v Gaby* (1852) 2 De GM&G 623; 42 ER 1015; *Cave v Cave* (1880) 15 Ch D 639; *Twinsectra Ltd v Yardley* [1999] Lloyds Rep Banking 438 (CA).

[112] *Gresley v Mousley* (1859) 4 de GM&G 78; 45 ER 31; *Melbourne Banking Corpn v Brougham* (1882) 7 App Cas 307; and *Latec Investments Ltd v Hotel Terrigal Pty Ltd* (1965) 113 CLR 265.

[113] *Dickinson v Burrell* (1866) LR 1 Eq 337.

[114] ibid 342; see also O'Sullivan et al (n 77) paras 22.05–22.08.

[115] *Re Eastgate* [1905] 1 KB 465; *Re Goldcorp* [1995] AC 74 (HL) 102 may suggest otherwise in corporate insolvency, but this inconsistency seems undesirable in policy terms.

C. A Claim in Unjust Enrichment?

There is some controversy over whether we can classify rescission claims as being unjustified enrichment claims. However, the better view is that we can do so and we can find comparative support for this too. First, let us look at the parallels in South African law. In that jurisdiction, rescission and the accompanying remedy of *restitutio in integrum* are seen as contractual.[116] *Restitutio in integrum* has provided important influence on the development of the *condictio indebiti*, however.[117] The instances where *restitutio in integrum* is possible following recission map closely onto cases where restitution for unjustified enrichment is possible, such as misrepresentation,[118] undue influence,[119] minority, and duress.[120] The remedy of *restitutio in integrum* was also made available outside that contractual context in the case of the payment of invalidly demanded taxes and other duties, which in South Africa can now be claimed in the *condictio indebiti*.[121] The fact the *restitutio in integrum* remedy was seen as restitutionary brings it very close to the *condictio indebiti*, and both were seen as founded in equity.[122] While *restitutio in integrum* has lost its old sweeping equitable character, there is little reason therefore why it cannot be seen as an unjustified enrichment remedy.[123]

Rescission in England (but not South Africa) can trigger proprietary claims. As such a claimant with the power to rescind a contract also has the power to avoid the conveyance of chattels transferred under it. The rule is that if the defendant is enriched by the receipt of rights, a proprietary claim is appropriate if the law allows for that claim.[124] That formulation seems unhelpful (even tautological), but Lodder suggests a proprietary claim is available when it is the right itself that is unjustly acquired by the defendant. What matters is that the law recognises the defective intention of the claimant with regard to a specific right.[125] This is a contingent decision. There is no necessary reason for it, but the law does, as seen, recognise such a right in different cases. Performance takes the form of the intentional transfer of (a thing of) value in personal claims, and the intentional transfer of rights in a rescission claim. Performance is conceptualised differently but remains performance and it is the defective performance which is reversed.[126]

[116] *Davidson v Bonafede* 1981 (2) SA 501.
[117] H Scott, *Unjust Enrichment in South African Law* (Oxford, Hart Publishing, 2013) 34–39.
[118] *Pretorius v Natal South Sea Investments Trust Ltd* 1965 (4) SA 410.
[119] *Preller v Jordaan* 1956 (1) SA 483.
[120] *Medscheme Holdings (Pty) Ltd v Bhamjee* 2005 (5) SA 339; D Visser, *Unjustified Enrichment* (Durban, Juta, 2008) 101; Scott (n 117) 37; *White Bros v Treasurer-General* (1883) 2 SC 322.
[121] *Willis Faber Enthoven v Receiver of Revenue* 1992 (4) SA 202 (A).
[122] *Rahim v Minister of Justice* 1964 (4) SA 630; *Port Elizabeth Divisional Council v Uitenhage Divisional Council* (1868) 1 Buch 221; Scott (n 117) 55.
[123] Visser (n 120) 111–13.
[124] Lodder (n 1) 218.
[125] ibid 218–19.
[126] Stevens, *The Laws of Restitution* (n 16) 229.

The opponent of treating rescission as unjust enrichment might reply that there was an inherent flaw in the contract that entitles the claimant to rescind. That act of rescission then triggers the revesting of title, because by the same token the passage of property was also inherently flawed from the beginning. It is revested at common law irrespective of whether it passed by contract or delivery or other event.[127] No other explanation is needed.[128] This is not quite right. There are essentially four reasons for scepticism.

The first reason for scepticism is that it would seem by a side wind to outlaw any proprietary claims in unjust enrichment (except the admittedly tenuous resulting trust), because they are all powers.[129] A second reason is that the view obscures the commonality of the normative reasons for restitution across rescission and non-rescission claims,[130] which we have also seen in South Africa, where *restitutio in integrum* is seen as unjust enrichment, as well as the commonality of their being performance claims. Rescission is available for duress and undue influence and (in some cases) for mistake. All of these are reasons for the reversal of payments by the claimant as well, although there is no exact correspondence in the conditions for relief. Rescission illustrates an important analytic similarity as well. In a personal claim for unjust enrichment the defendant is subject to a Hohfeldian liability to be made to repay, as we saw in chapter three. He is not under an immediate duty to repay the money. If the claim is to rescind a transaction the claimant also has a power, and so the defendant by the same token seems to be under no immediate duty to repay or re-transfer but is only liable to be made to do so.

The third reason is that not all claims consequential on rescission are proprietary. Imagine an executed contract rescinded at common law for fraud or duress. If services have been provided by the rescinding party, he should be able to argue that a quantum meruit is appropriate[131] for their value – a proprietary claim being inherently impossible. It seems very odd to say that the provision of services was inherently flawed in the same way Lionel Smith appears to regard the transfer of title (ie, rights) to a car as inherently flawed. The claim is, however, essentially the same as any other claim for performance rendered under duress or fraud. The claimant performed the services, intending to benefit the defendant-recipient, but that performance and the obligation to proffer it were vitiated by a recognised unjust factor – duress – and the claimant should receive the value of the performance back. O'Sullivan et al point out that the availability of equitable rescission means that the authority to the effect that this is not possible[132] will rarely matter, but in principle such relief should equally

[127] O'Sullivan et al (n 77) paras 14.03–14.09.
[128] LD Smith, 'Unjust Enrichment: Big or Small?' in S Degeling and J Edelman (eds), *Unjust Enrichment in Commercial Law* (Sydney, Law Book Co, 2008) 43–44.
[129] Lodder (n 1) 120.
[130] E Bant, *The Change of Position Defence* (Oxford, Hart Publishing, 2009) 90–92.
[131] O'Sullivan et al (n 77) para 14.41.
[132] *Selway v Fogg* (1839) 5 M&W 39, 151 ER 36.

be possible for those cases where equitable rescission may be barred.[133] Now imagine a contract rescinded in equity. If a contract is rescinded for (say) undue influence and services were provided, the party providing those services is entitled to their value.[134] A like argument applies here too. If therefore a claim for the value of services after rescission is an unjust enrichment claim so should a claim for the value of property. To claim otherwise sets up a distinction between services – and possibly money if no proprietary claim is available here either[135] – and chattels such that the chattels claim is a contractual (or property) claim and the services claim one in unjust enrichment. This seems inexplicable. All these claims follow the performance pattern, explained in chapter two, and involve the reversal of an intentional performance – be that payment, transfer or chattels or rendering of services – to the defendant. If so, while we might legitimately say that rescission followed by proprietary restitution is a different cause of action from one followed by personal restitution only, both cases of restitution must be sourced in unjust enrichment.

A final, fourth, point is that change of position might apply. In cases of fraud, duress and actual undue influence, the guilty party may not be able to avail themselves of the defence as we see in chapter eight. However, the mistaken payee in cases like *Pitt v Holt* should be able to rely on their change of position. An innocent third-party donee should be able to rely on change of position in principle whatever the initial cause of action.[136]

The kink this brings up is that rescissory powers, being proprietary, can be exercised against third parties. Rights of rescission cut across our neat division between performance and non-performance claims. This is true in both common law and equity. Donees of the transferred chattel are vulnerable to rescission.[137] One view is that this is simply because the original party can give no better title than he has. The title he received is flawed and defeasible, and so that is all he can give. From a comparative perspective there are two possibilities, each of which militates in favour of seeing rescission as restitutionary and based on unjust enrichment. The first is that it looks like an *actio de in rem verso*. The initial recipient (B), having no authority to do so from the claimant (A) who has equitable rights, transfers the asset to a third party (C). The transfer is effective at law, but the claimant has an equitable claim against the third party unless the bona fide purchase (of an equitable interest) defence applies. Tracing rules apply to identify the third party holding the asset over which the claimant can exercise the power to revest,[138] or to identify substitute

[133] O'Sullivan et al (n 77) para 14.44.
[134] ibid para 15.39; *O'Sullivan v Management Agency and Music Ltd* [1985] QB 428.
[135] O'Sullivan et al (n 77) para 16.05.
[136] But see, R Chambers, 'Proprietary Restitution and Change of Position' in A Dyson et al (eds), *Defences in Unjust Enrichment* (Oxford, Hart Publishing, 2016) 129.
[137] O'Sullivan et al (n 77) paras 21.04–21.05.
[138] *Bainbridge v Bainbridge* [2016] EWHC 898.

assets in the hands of the original recipient.[139] B, however, was never intended as an intermediary so the scenario more closely resemblances § 822 BGB than § 816(I) BGB although, in the absence of German law's recognition of proprietary claims, the analogy is far from perfect. A transfers assets to B by way of flawed performance. B, as a result of that flawed performance, now has legal title. He transfers to C. C is required to make restitution under § 822 BGB if B is no longer subject to an unjust enrichment claim. In England, B receives legal title subject to the equitable claim and may still be subject to a claim after the transfer of the asset or its traceable proceeds to C if both B and C now have traceable proceeds. There cannot, however, be a successful claim against both. It also seems odd, given that in each case we refer to the claim as one of rescission, to say that if against the initial recipient the action is in unjust enrichment, but if against a third party not.

IV. Trustee Misappropriation

Where a trustee misappropriates trust assets without authority and transfers them to a third party the beneficiary's claim against that third party is an unjust enrichment claim based on the trustee's lack of authority. In rare cases, an unauthorised substitution by a non-trustee might give the claimant a claim to the legal title,[140] although Goff and Jones suggest these cases should be re-analysed as giving the claimant merely equitable title.[141] For our purposes this difference does not matter. In either case the claim is dependent on unjust enrichment.

Some subrogation cases, based on the misappropriation of the claimant's funds, fit easily into this structure and depend on a tracing link. In *Boscawen v Bajwa*[142] the Abbey National's money was paid (without their consent and without their authority) by solicitors, holding it in their client account, to the Halifax Building Society, discharging their mortgage over Bajwa's house which was to be sold and the money to purchase it borrowed from the Abbey. But the sale fell through. The Abbey National was subrogated to the Halifax's mortgage, and this seems a typical example of an *actio de in rem verso* where an intermediary – the solicitors – transferred title to the money to the Halifax without authority and the remedy takes the form of a debt owed to one party being revived along with its accompanying security in favour of another, a remedial pattern also found in cases where equitable liens are used to secure unjust enrichment debts, for

[139] *Shalson v Russo* [2003] EWHC 1637, [2005] 1 Ch 281; *NCA v Robb* [2014] EWHC 4384; *Gladstone v Hadwen* (1813) 1 M&S 517, 105 ER 193; *Beverley v Pearce* [2013] EWHC 2627; A Nair, *Claims to Traceable Proceeds* (Oxford, OUP, 2017) paras 7.27–7.28.

[140] *Lipkin Gorman v Karpnale Ltd* [1991] 2 AC 548 (HL); *FC Jones v Jones* [1997] Ch 159.

[141] *Goff & Jones* (n 66) para 8.95.

[142] *Boscawen v Bajwa* [1996] 1 WLR 328; *Scotlife Home Loans (no 2) Ltd v Melinek* (1999) 78 P&CR 389; *Primlake Ltd v Matthews* [2006] EWHC 1227; C Mitchell and S Watterson (eds), *Subrogation: Law and Practice* (Oxford, OUP, 2007) paras 6.42–6.50; *Goff & Jones* (n 66) paras 8.145–8.147.

example, for improvements to land.[143] No claim was available against the Halifax who were bona fide purchasers, having validly discharged the mortgage debt. Bajwa, however, was enriched by the discharge of the liability.

To say that the trustee cases lie in unjust enrichment is controversial. Virgo has denied it,[144] as did Lord Millett in *Foskett v McKeown*, saying, 'The transmission of a claimant's property rights from one asset to its traceable proceeds is part of our law of property, not of the law of unjust enrichment'.[145] Birks maintained forcefully that in *Foskett* the life insurance beneficiaries, were unjustly enriched by the receipt of an asset, and rejected the contrary property characterisation of the action.[146] The reason for the claimants' interest in the express trust assets was the intention of the settlor. The life insurance policy was never an asset that the settlor had or would have ever considered. The reason for the interest in the policy monies could not, Birks argued, therefore be that the settlor of the original trust intended the claimants to have an interest in Murphy's (the trustee's) life insurance. Rather, the reason for their interest was that the trustee had without authorisation paid the premiums, the product of which was the eventual payout on the trustee's death. Birks' characteristically colourful way of putting this was that the original proprietary interest is not like a fishing line hooking onto assets like fish as they swim past.[147] The ability to choose in which asset to assert property rights after an unauthorised mis-transfer is instead a power *in rem* to vest an equitable interest in traceable assets.[148] There are two issues. The first is whether this is a newly created and different proprietary right from the original trust interest. The second is whether it is a right in unjust enrichment given the significant differences that it has from rights under a straightforward two-party performance claim.

To deny it is different from that original trust interest, we must deny, as Penner has, that the beneficiary's property rights are in individual assets. Penner argues that the beneficiary has property rights in a fund, reified separately from the assets contained within it. The third party to whom assets are mis-transferred, he argues, is liable proprietarily purely because the third party is bound by the beneficiary's interest in the trust property he or she received and, this being a fund interest, also in any property he or she acquires as traceable proceeds.[149] We only

[143] *Cooper v Phibbs* (1867) LR 2 HL 149.

[144] GJ Virgo, *The Principles of the Law of Restitution*, 3rd edn (Oxford, OUP, 2015) 11–17; but see, Burrows (n 12) 185–89.

[145] *Foskett v McKeown* [2001] 1 AC 102 (HL) 129. But see *Investment Trust Companies v HMRC* [2017] UKSC 29, [48] (Lord Reed); *CMOC Sales and Marketing v Persons Unknown* [2018] EWHC 2230 (Comm) [146].

[146] PBH Birks, *Unjust Enrichment*, 2nd edn (Oxford, OUP, 2005) 34–36.

[147] ibid 35.

[148] ibid 198–201; D Fox, 'Overreaching' in A Pretto and PBH Birks (eds), *Breach of Trust* (Oxford, Hart Publishing, 2002) 105–07.

[149] J Penner, 'Value, Property and Unjust Enrichment' in R Chambers, C Mitchell and J Penner (eds), *Philosophical Foundations of the Law of Unjust Enrichment* (Oxford, OUP, 2009); J Penner, 'Duty and Liability in Respect of Funds' in J Lowry and L Mistelis (eds), *Commercial Law: Perspectives and Practice* (London, Sweet & Maxwell, 2006) 207.

become concerned with the proprietary aspects when something goes wrong and the beneficiary is able to elect to enforce against any asset he or she chooses, or elects. There are significant difficulties with such a view. We can only identify a breach of trust obligations if we can identify an asset misused. Indeed, we cannot identify a fund without identifying the assets within it. The individual assets are consequently the critical feature, and it seems analytically more straightforward to accept that the beneficiaries always have proprietary interests in specifiable assets rather than positing a type of floating proprietary right, which does not attach to any particular asset until breach. Where dealings with the individual assets are authorised, the beneficiary obtains equitable title to any substitute and the third party obtains clean unencumbered legal title via overreaching.[150] Where unauthorised, the beneficiary obtains a power to revest equitable title in themselves.

The answer to the second question lies in five observations. The first is that the analytic debates tell us – not much. Claims to substitutes have some similarities with the standard unjust enrichment claims and some differences.[151] To be true to the methodology of the book, as outlined in chapter one, we must find significant normative and/or analytic family resemblances. The first point is the lack of authority of the trustee to deal with the asset in this particular way, which creates a defect in the transaction vis-a-vis the claimant beneficiary. This defect is created because in all these cases the defendant has a legal power to vary the claimant's rights over the asset, which is validly exercised vis-a-vis third parties even if in breach of obligations not to exercise the power in particular ways.[152] In the absence of bona fide purchase protecting the defendant recipient, he is affected by this defect vis-a-vis the claimant. Although this looks different from unjust factors like mistake or duress, in effect the claimant has outsourced the exercise of his autonomy and the trustee has overstepped the limits of this delegated autonomy.

The second point is that personal rights are available in the civil law of unjustified enrichment. Unless we take the implausible view, rejected in our discussion of Jaffey's writings in chapter three, that even personal claims to restitution are based in property law, the fact that some systems give personal claims (ie, not based on property) in these cases gives comparative support to the idea that a proprietary claim in the same cases can be unjust enrichment as well. German law for instance has no concept of the trust, although it does retain remnants of the *actio de in rem verso*.[153] The availability of the action is significantly narrower in Germany than in England.[154] Nonetheless, we can see parallels. A has transferred C's property to

[150] R Nolan, 'Property in a Fund' (2004) 120 *LQR* 132; D Sheehan, 'Property in a Fund, Tracing and Unjust Enrichment' (2010) 4 *Journal of Equity* 215, 227–31.

[151] C Webb, *Reasons and Restitution* (Oxford, OUP, 2016) 182.

[152] *Goff & Jones* (n 66) paras 8.02–8.03; Nair (n 139) para 6.84.

[153] § 816(I) BGB; § 822 BGB may apply in some cases.

[154] See G Dannemann, *The German Law of Unjustified Enrichment and Restitution: A Comparative Introduction* (Oxford, OUP, 2009) 130–32.

B without authority. A has an obligation vis-a-vis C to refund him under § 816(I) BGB, but if B receives gratuitously he also has an obligation to make restitution to C. Translated into the English trust context, B's restitutionary obligation, analogous to that of the donee, rests on the exercise of C's power, and A equally has a substitutive obligation to put back in the trust fund the missing value.[155] South African law accepts the concept of the trust, although claims against third parties in trust cases are not made using the *actio de in rem verso*, but the *condictio indebiti*.[156] It is a choice how far we go in protecting the trust beneficiary, the rescission claimant or mistaken payer. English law's choice is more protective of the claimant than others, but this need not deny that it is based on unjust enrichment.

The third point is that money, chattels and services have relational value in that they can be exchanged for other things and that value is realised by obtaining something I find more valuable in return for the thing I give up. Things and services have exchange potential, which I am entitled to realise. The law recognises this by, for example, rendering the defendant liable to pay the market value for services. Likewise, rights have exchange potential. Indeed, when I give my car to you, I am giving you rights to the car which is why the transaction can be analysed in one of two ways if it is reversible. Webb goes further, pointing out that giving me an interest in the substitute is a way of giving at least some effect to my original interest in the money used to buy it, since part of my interest in money is its exchangeability.[157] That makes property of relevance – indeed it is precisely Webb's point that we vindicate my property right here – but this does not, as we saw in chapter three, preclude unjust enrichment being of relevance given the parallel importance of exchangeability in both personal and proprietary claims; categorical overlaps are not *per se* problematic in law. Reflecting this,[158] both tracing and the attributive link between the parties in a personal performance claim bear some similarities in that each requires that there be a transactional link, governed by the parties' intention, between the claimant and defendant. A personal claim reflects the unrealised exchange value in the hands of the defendant and his consequent ability to exploit that (for free). A proprietary claim reflects the fact the defendant can exploit the exchange potential of the right transferred, which in turn entails that the defendant has or can realise the claimant's entitlement to the value of the asset. This is because, although value is not relevant to the order for specific restitution of the right, when I transfer rights to a chattel to you, I also give you the ability to realise its value. In a tracing case, the defendant has therefore received the

[155] On which, see D Sheehan, 'Equitable Remedies for Breach of Trust' in R Halson and D Campbell (eds), *Research Handbook on Remedies* (Cheltenham, Edward Elgar, 2019); *Target Holdings Ltd v Redferns* [1996] AC 421; *AIB v Mark Redler & Co* [2014] UKSC 58, [2015] AC 1503.

[156] See generally on this, du Plessis (n 41) 149–50; *Bowman de Wet and du Plessis NNO v Fidelity Bank Ltd* 1997 (2) SA 35.

[157] Webb (n 151) 183–85.

[158] D Sheehan, '"At the Expense of": Linking Claimant and Defendant in the Law of Unjust Enrichment' (2020) 20 *Oxford University Commonwealth Law Journal* 235, 240; T Cutts 'Tracing, Value and Transactions' (2016) 79 *MLR* 381, 395–403.

rights (and the attendant ability to realise) without authorisation, which generates a defect in the transaction vis-a-vis the claimant.

In *Relfo v Varsani*, both analyses – the tracing analysis and the personal unjust enrichment claim analysis – can be seen side by side.[159] Money was transferred inappropriately by Gorecia from the company's accounts ultimately to Intertrade. Those payments went first to accounts held by Mirren Ltd and then onto Intertrade. The Court of Appeal accepted that the payments by Gorecia were the source of the payments to Varsani. At first instance, Sales J had thought these were sham transactions.[160] In the Court of Appeal, Floyd LJ refers to the 'economic reality' of the situation and suggested that the 'meaningless' intermediate steps did not render the payments insufficiently 'proximate'.[161] This entails that intermediate steps never intended to have any particular purpose can be skipped. Goff and Jones have noted the sham explanation for the case,[162] but they prefer an argument that successive payments were recharacterised as one composite coordinated transaction.[163] In line with this as well, both Gloster and Floyd LJJ refer to the payment as equivalent to a direct payment.[164] The real position therefore was that the intention of the parties that the series of transactions be used as a means to pay Intertrade is respected and the series is construed as one transaction. The same analysis is adopted for tracing. Sales J may have denied that a tracing link was strictly necessary for an unjust enrichment claim,[165] but he did accept that there was a tracing link and both he and the Court of Appeal brought the parties' intention that the transactions be connected into account in making that tracing link.[166]

The fourth point relates to the availability of change of position, explored in greater detail in chapter eight. Lord Millett said in *Foskett v McKeown* that change of position was available in unjust enrichment actions, and bona fide purchase was available in proprietary actions.[167] Change of position was not therefore available in *Foskett v McKeown* itself, as an action in property not unjust enrichment law. As a matter of legal policy, making change of position available in such cases prior to the claimant's exercise of his right to vest title seems right, however.[168] The third-party defendant must be able to take advantage of the protection that change of position provides to prevent the need to impose unnecessary safeguards 'just

[159] *Relfo v Varsani* [2014] EWCA Civ 360.

[160] [2012] EWHC 2168, [59]; *Investment Trust Companies v HMRC* [2017] UKSC 29, [48].

[161] [2014] EWCA Civ 360 [110].

[162] *Goff & Jones* (n 66) para 6.58.

[163] ibid para 6.59.

[164] [2014] EWCA Civ 360, [103] (Gloster LJ), [115] (Floyd LJ); See, *CMOC Sales and Marketing v Persons Unknown* [2018] EWHC 2230 (Comm) [147]–[151].

[165] [2012] EWHC 2168, [88].

[166] ibid [77]; [2014] EWCA Civ 360, [56]–[63] (Arden LJ).

[167] *Foskett v McKeown* [2001] 1 AC 102 (HL) 129; Lord Millett, 'Proprietary Restitution' in S Degeling and J Edelman (eds), *Equity in Commercial Law* (Sydney, Law Book Co, 2006) 315.

[168] D Sheehan, 'The Scope and Rationale(s) of the Defence of Change of Position' (2023) 74 *Northern Ireland Legal Quarterly* 269.

in case' he must repay,[169] and to preclude his being made irreversibly worse off as a result of the claim. The defence precludes the result's being different depending on the essentially random nature of which bank account an innocent party uses to spend money in reliance on a belief that he is entitled to the money received. Once the claimant has exercised his right to vest title and the defendant knows of his obligation to refund, the defence is unavailable. The susceptibility of the claim to the defence prior to this is not conclusive in that some non-unjust enrichment actions attract change of position, but it suggests that these actions can be included in unjust enrichment. Indeed, one of the reasons why the defence should be available is that the defendant has done nothing, and this is our final observation. The third-party donee is liable to the beneficiary immediately. The beneficiary has a power to recover the asset and the donee is liable to be ordered to do so. This is a Hohfeldian power-liability relation; the personal claim between a mistaken payer and payee is also analytically a power-liability relation, as we saw in chapter three. The defendant cannot be seen as being under a duty because he has no reason necessarily to know he has received assets subject to a claim or that the trustee had no authority to transfer them. In both the personal and proprietary claims, the defendant would seem subject to a liability not a duty.[170] Not every strand of Wittgenstein's rope[171] is present, but enough are for this to be considered as an unjust enrichment claim.

V. Conclusion

There are good reasons therefore to suspect that many proprietary claims can be coherently grouped with unjust enrichment. Rescission claims, for example, are in essence performance claims. In some cases, restitution is personal and in others proprietary, but this merely reflects that the law sometimes sees the performance rendered as the transfer or provision of services or (a thing of) value and in other cases as the transfer of rights. From a comparative perspective, each is a performance claim. Likewise, the comparative perspective suggests that trustee misapplication of property can be seen as unjust enrichment. In both German and South African law there is an unjustified enrichment claim in the troublesome case of a party (A) transferring an asset of B to C. The next chapter is the final substantive chapter of the book and deals with the question of defences, including that most typical of unjust enrichment defences – change of position.

[169] PBH Birks, 'Change of Position and Surviving Enrichment' in WJ Swadling (ed), *The Limits of Restitutionary Claims: A Comparative Analysis* (London, UKNCCL, 1997) 50–51; Bant (n 130) 211–14.

[170] See S Smith, *Rights, Wrongs and Injustices* (Oxford, OUP, 2019) 243–45; see also P Jaffey, 'The Hohfeldian Power-Liability/Right-Duty Distinction in the Law of Restitution' (2004) 17 *Canadian Journal of Law & Jurisprudence* 295.

[171] See ch 1 for the analogy.

8

Defences to Unjust Enrichment Claims

Introduction

This chapter concludes the substantive argument of the book. The first three chapters explored how we should go about classifying areas of law and set out a roughly civilian structure for the English law of unjust enrichment, although one that still makes heavy use of unjust factors. We explored the operation of different causes of action in unjust enrichment and how they fit that scheme in chapters four to seven. This chapter explores the impact of defences on our understanding of unjust enrichment. A preliminary point is therefore needed. We can distinguish between defences and denials.[1] A denial is a statement to the effect that one (or more) element of the cause of action has not been made out. The 'defence' of good consideration – as discussed in chapter two – is therefore not a true defence as it serves to deny the necessary element of all unjust enrichment claims that the defendant does not have an otherwise valid reason for keeping the enrichment. A defence accepts that the action is made out but seeks nonetheless to exculpate the defendant. For the same reason natural obligations do not represent a defence as such. Because the effect of a natural obligation is a claim that the performance was in fact owing, although it could not be enforced, performance of a natural obligation allows the defendant to raise good consideration. The primary, true, defence examined is change of position. We also look at its relationship with estoppel. We then examine the defences of passing on, illegality and bona fide purchase. Other defences exist, but these are the most important in practice and theory.

I. Change of Position

The defence of change of position was introduced into English law by *Lipkin Gorman v Karpnale*.[2] Lord Goff suggested that it would apply in cases where the defendant had so changed his position that it would be unconscionable to make

[1] C Mitchell and J Goudkamp, 'Defences and Denials in the Law of Unjust Enrichment' in WJ Swadling (ed), *Restatement the Third of Restitution and Unjust Enrichment: Critical Essays* (Oxford, Hart Publishing, 2013).

[2] *Lipkin Gorman v Karpnale* [1991] 2 AC 548 (HL).

the defendant repay or repay in full.[3] The typical case is where the defendant has detrimentally relied on the receipt in making extra-ordinary expenditure that is now irreversible and has done so in good faith. In *Lipkin* itself Cass, a partner at the claimant firm, stole money and gambled it away at the defendant's casino. Change of position succeeded because the club had changed their position in paying out Cass' winnings in reliance on the receipt of the initial stakes.[4] In early analyses the defence was seen through the lens of a mistake claim; the suggestion was that when relief for mistake was relatively restricted, succeeding only in cases of liability mistakes, the defence was not needed, but if all causal mistakes allow relief, the defence was required to cut back restitution.[5] The first subsection examines the scope of change of position as a defence to personal unjust enrichment claims; the second looks at the rationale for the defence before the third examines its operation as a possible defence to proprietary claims and restitution for wrongs. The defence does not extend to all unjust enrichment claims and should extend outside unjust enrichment. It should apply to innocent wrongdoing[6] where the defendant is unaware of the wrong, often a trespass or conversion. The defence should apply to proprietary claims and the argument that it should does not depend on the claim being an unjust enrichment claim. Last, we look at the relation with estoppel.

A. Scope of the Defence within Personal Unjust Enrichment Claims

The defendant must reasonably rely on receipt by making an irreversible change in his position. There are several different issues which need to be separated. We can start with reliance. Reliance is primarily a causal issue.[7] If the defendant relies on the receipt in deciding to spend the money, the receipt causes the expenditure in the sense that it causes the defendant to make a particular assumption about the facts or law relating to his being able to use the money or chattels and then this assumption causes the change in his position. This points up a difference between the narrow view limiting the defence to defendant-instigated changes of position (ie, the view that reliance is necessary) and the broader view where independently caused changes of position count. This is one line of fracture in the case law and commentary. There was formerly some dispute as to what sorts of reliance counted

[3] ibid 577–83; other cases have also rested relief on inequitability. See, *Garland v Consumer Gas* 2004 SCC 25, [2004] 1 SCR 629, [64]; *Dextra Bank v Bank of Jamaica* [2001] UKPC 45; [2001] 1 All ER (Comm) 195, 204.

[4] [1991] 2 AC 548, 582–83.

[5] *Barclays Bank v WJ Simms, Son & Cooke (Southern) Ltd* [1980] QB 677, 695–96 (Goff J); PBH Birks, 'Change of Position and Surviving Enrichment' in WJ Swadling (ed), *The Limits of Restitutionary Claims: A Comparative Analysis* (London, UKNCCL, 1997) 40–41.

[6] *Cavenagh Investment Pte Ltd v Kaushik Rajiv* [2013] SGHC 45 (trespass to land); *Kuwait Airways v Iraqi Airways* [2002] 2 AC 883, [79] (Lord Nicholls) (conversion).

[7] E Bant, *The Change of Position Defence* (Oxford, Hart Publishing, 2009) 147.

in cases of a defendant-instigated change of position and whether reliance could take place in anticipation of receipt. It can.[8] Detrimental reliance does not require a link to be proven between specific receipts and specific items of expenditure;[9] general reliance on increased assets will suffice.[10] Reliance, however, has no role where the change in the defendant's position is independently caused by a third party (eg, theft) or act of God (eg, destruction by lightning strike). The wide view of the defence, accepted in England,[11] accommodates this; the narrow view of the defence does not. The wide view is in principle more attractive. It should not matter for the purposes of deciding whether a party has suffered an irreversible detriment – which we take to be the preferred justification of the defence – if the defendant made a conscious choice to divest himself of the assets or if they were stolen or destroyed. The two types of change of position differ merely in how causation is proven.

Another line of fracture is between disenriching cases and non-disenriching cases where the defendant is not financially worse off but is still deemed to have changed his position, although it seems extremely difficult to identify clear case law examples of the latter.[12] In principle, however, disenrichment is not co-extensive with irreversible detriment and so, taking that as the preferred justification, non-disenriching changes of position should be possible.

Separate questions emerge around the reasonableness of the reliance, bad faith and the knowledge of the defendant. It is said, therefore, that the defendant is disqualified from relying on the defence if he had no legitimate expectation of being able to rely on the receipt of the asset. This might be because he knew or was wilfully blind[13] to the fact that the claimant made a mistake or was in bad faith.[14] It may be sufficient that the defendant should have made further enquiries as to their entitlement.[15] These issues need to be carefully separated out. The true requirement is one of objective reasonableness. If the defendant acts, knowing

[8] *Lipkin Gorman v Karpnale* [1991] 2 AC 548 (HL); *Dextra Bank v Bank of Jamaica* [2001] UKPC 45; [2001] 1 All ER (Comm) 195.

[9] Paying off debts will not suffice; *Scottish Equitable BS v Derby* [2001] 3 All ER 818; *Credit Suisse v Attar* [2004] EWHC 374 (Comm), [98]; C Mitchell, P Mitchell and S Watterson (eds), *Goff & Jones: The Law of Unjust Enrichment*, 10th edn (London, Sweet & Maxwell, 2022) para 27.15.

[10] *Philip Collins v Davis* [2000] 3 All ER 818; *Skyring v Greenwood* (1825) 4 B&C 281, 107 ER 1064; *Holt v Markham* [1923] 1 KB 504.

[11] A Burrows, 'Change of Position: The View from England' (2003) 36 *Loyola of Los Angeles Law Review* 803; *Scottish Equitable BS v Derby* [2001] 3 All ER 818.

[12] PBH Birks, *Unjust Enrichment*, 2nd edn (Oxford, OUP, 2005) 258–61.

[13] *Harrison v Madejski* [2014] EWCA Civ 361, [61]; *Port of Brisbane Authority v ANZ Securities* [2003] 2 Qd R 661, 674–75.

[14] *Lipkin Gorman v Karpnale* [1991] 2 AC 548 (HL) 577.

[15] *Jones v Churcher* [2009] EWHC 722, [46]; *Niru Battery Manufacturing v Milestone Trading* [2004] QB 985; *State Bank of NSW v SBC* (1995) 39 NSWLR 350; *Heperu Pty Ltd v Belle* [2009] NSWCA 84, (2009) 76 NSWLR 195; *Citigroup v National Australia Bank* [2012] NSWCA 381, (2012) 82 NSWLR 391; *Cavenagh Investments Pte Ltd v Kaushik Rajiv* [2013] SGHC 45, [2013] 2 SLR 543, [71] (Chan Seng Onn J). For comment, see eg, R Chambers, 'Change of Position on the Faith of Receipt' [1996] *Restitution Law Review* 103, 107–08; and *Goff & Jones* (n 9) paras 27.47–27.55.

facts which objectively contradict the basis on which he purports to act, he does not act reasonably and cannot rely on the defence.[16] This is not the same as a good faith requirement, but good faith is assumed within reasonableness; one cannot act dishonestly and reasonably at the same time and although we can act honestly but unreasonably, the defence will not apply in these cases.[17]

This brings the debate round to questions of which claims are vulnerable to the defence. Mistake claims clearly are and we saw earlier in chapter four that this might extend to some non-performance claims as well. It is, however, hard to see many cases where a duressor would not know he was not entitled to the money; a duress claim is therefore not normally susceptible to the defence because the duressor does not act in reasonable reliance on the receipt. One exception may be where the duress was applied by A to make B pay C and C is innocent of all fault.[18] Change of position in actual undue influence and unconscionable dealings should be unavailable on the same basis. We require proof here of an abuse of a position of influence. Lindley LJ in *Allcard v Skinner* talked of coercion, cheating and unfair conduct.[19] It is hard again to see how a claimant could prove this and the defendant still to be able to claim that he was reasonably relying on the receipt.[20] Presumed undue influence claims do exist, however, where the defendant was able to rely on the defence[21] because it was reasonable to rely on the receipt.

Possibly change of position does not apply to failure of consideration claims, or at least not all such. In *Haugusund Kommune v Depfa ACS Bank*,[22] for example, the Court of Appeal had to decide whether the local authorities having entered a void swaps agreement with the banks were able to rely on change of position in answer to a claim for restitution. They were not able to do so. Aikens LJ drew a distinction between two cases. The first is where the defendant receives money believing it is his to keep, and the second is where he receives money, knowing that he will have to repay it at some point.[23] In such a case he cannot rely on a change of position defence to justify a refusal to repay because the enrichment was accepted on the basis that it would have to be repaid/paid for. The defendant will have acted as if his interest in the asset were absolute even though he knows it is still conditional. On the facts, Aikens LJ held that the authorities did take the money on the basis that it was repayable. The agreements were always void, but that 'cannot change the basis on which the kommunes received the money'.[24]

[16] Bant, *The Change of Position Defence* (n 7) 154.
[17] ibid 45.
[18] Bant discusses, ibid 175, a scenario in which even here C might be unable to rely on the defence.
[19] *Allcard v Skinner* (1887) 36 Ch D 154, 181.
[20] *Waikato Regional Airport v A-G of New Zealand* [2001] 2 NZLR 670.
[21] eg, *Cheese v Thomas* [1994] 1 WLR 129; M Chen-Wishart, 'Loss-Sharing, Undue Influence and Manifest Disadvantage' (1994) 111 *LQR* 173.
[22] *Haugusund Kommune v Depfa ACS Bank* [2010] EWCA Civ 579, [2012] QB 549; *Goss v Chilcott* [1996] AC 788 (HL).
[23] [2010] EWCA Civ 579, [2012] QB 549, [123].
[24] ibid [124].

Burrows (now Lord Burrows) makes a convincing argument that while this holds in loan cases, it does not always hold. His example is a builder who receives money in advance, pays for material and a holiday. The builder does not take on any obligation to repay money, but to do the work. If there is a failure of consideration, he ought to be able to rely on the holiday expenditure to found the defence.[25] This is incomplete, however. The builder may be the guilty party, refusing to work or working so shoddily that the client is entitled to terminate the contract for breach. At this point there may be a question as to whether the fact the builder is in breach justifies the refusal of the defence. We may, as we saw in chapter five, legitimately say that it should, and this draws support from the proposition that he cannot found a defence on his own failure to render his interest in the claimant's performance unconditional. However, he should be able to rely on change of position if the contract is terminated because of the other party's failures (ie, in rendering it impossible for him to perform).

There are, therefore, as we discussed in chapter five, important questions regarding the allocation of risks between the claimant and the defendant to work out. If change of position is available to the party in breach, he is in effect acting as an insurer for the innocent party in cases where the asset is destroyed or lost; this is justified because he is the wrongdoer, had possession of the asset and is best placed to bear the loss. Where both parties are innocent, the defendant may have a better claim to avail himself of the defence. All other things being equal, if we allow the defence, the person who makes the performance (in either direction) takes the risk as the defence is available to both parties. The fact you cannot give back what you have received is irrelevant as the two claims are independent of each other. This is not German law, which in the context of unjustified enrichment claims accepts not the *Zweikondiktionentheorie* of the two independent claims but the *Saldotheorie*, whereby the claimant's claim is reduced by or netted off against the amount of the enrichment he has lost.[26] In English law, Popplewell LJ in *SFM v Christ the King College* held, consistently with the two claims theory, that where benefits acquired by the claimant were sufficiently closely connected to the gain for which restitution was sought, the claimant had to make counter-restitution of them.[27] This would generally be true where the benefits were in exchange for each other – ie, where performance was reciprocal.[28] The counter-restitution obligation is engaged where the defendant's compliance with an order to make restitution entails the failure of the basis upon which the defendant's own performance to the

[25] AS Burrows, *The Law of Restitution*, 3rd edn (Oxford, OUP, 2011) 544–45; AS Burrows, *A Restatement of the English Law of Unjust Enrichment* (Oxford, OUP, 2012) §23(2)(iii); Stevens claims this is still incompatible with the basis of the claim. R Stevens, 'The Unjust Enrichment Disaster' (2018) 134 *LQR* 574, 587. See also, *Goff & Jones* (n 9) paras 27.68–27.70.

[26] M Jewell, 'The Boundaries of Change of Position: A Comparative Study' [2000] *Restitution Law Review* 1, 31–32.

[27] *SFM v Christ the King College* [2021] EWCA Civ 1053, [78]–[79].

[28] ibid [80]; this is an example of equitable transaction set-off as discussed in ch 5.

claimant was subject.[29] The decision also raised (but did not answer) the question of the impact of the claimant's change of position on the defendant's claim for counter-restitution.[30] This must be carefully worked through to ensure that the risk is on the correct party, but as we saw in chapter five the same policy questions must be addressed in these cases whether they are void, voidable or terminated contracts and to deal with them in different places of the law can cause problems.[31]

In the context of rescission, which needs to be treated in parallel to non-rescissory cases, Bant also proposes a two-claims approach for English law whereby the linked requirement of *restitutio in integrum* is viewed as a bilateral process of claim and set-off.[32] In other words, the defendant may be liable for mistake, duress or undue influence and having successfully made a case for rescission and restitution of benefits transferred, the basis for the transfer of any benefits by the defendant fails. This is seen in terms of the claimant's unjust enrichment.[33] Considerations underpinning the defence of change of position have a part to play and should help determine both the claimant's liability in counter-restitution, but also the defendant's liability under the primary claim.[34] It is difficult to see therefore why the two areas of rescission and personal restitution (in *SFM* the contract was claimed to be void) should not inform each other. Bant rejects the *Saldotheorie* approach in part because the German (and South African) approach to change of position is to regard it largely as a disenrichment defence, which in turn leads it to quantify relief to the claimant in terms of the net enrichment of the defendant. The *Saldotheorie* therefore sits very easily within the general approach of German law, and although South African law has adopted the two-claims theory,[35] it remains open to South African courts, if the defendant raises loss of enrichment, to adopt the *Saldotheorie*. Since disenrichment and net enrichment do not represent the English approach to justifying change of position, there is a much less good fit. This is supported by the case law which suggests that a prime requirement of *restitutio in integrum*, and therefore change of position, is reciprocity. If the claimant wants to be restored to the status quo ante so must the defendant.[36] This in turn

[29] T Pilkington and D Winterton, 'Void Contracts, Counter-Restitution and Change of Position' (2022) 138 *LQR* 21, 24; A Lodder, *Enrichment in the Law of Unjust Enrichment and Restitution* (Oxford, Hart Publishing, 2012) 123–24; *Spence v Crawford* [1939] 3 All ER 271; *David Securities Pty Ltd v Commonwealth Bank of Australia* (1992) 127 CLR 353, 382; *Ovidio Carrideo Nominees (Pty) Ltd v The Dog Depot (Pty) Ltd* [2006] VSCA 6.

[30] Pilkington and Winterton (n 29) 22.

[31] S Meier, 'Unwinding Failed Contracts: New European Developments' [2017] *Edinburgh Law Review* 1.

[32] Bant, *The Change of Position Defence* (n 7) 94–103.

[33] E Bant, 'Rescission, Restitution and Compensation' in S Degeling and J Varuhas (eds), *Equitable Compensation and Disgorgement of Profit* (Oxford, Hart Publishing, 2017) 286–87; *Spence v Crawford* [1939] 3 All ER 271.

[34] Bant, *The Change of Position Defence* (n 7) 94–95.

[35] *Yarona Healthcare Network (Pty) Ltd v Medshield* 2018 (1) SA 513, 530–31.

[36] Bant, *The Change of Position Defence* (n 7) 118; *Brown v Smitt* (1924) 34 CLR 160; *Spence v Crawford* [1939] 3 All ER 271; *Erlanger v New Sombrero Phosphate Company* (1878) 3 App Cas 1218; *Alati v Kruger* (1955) 94 CLR 216.

implies that the worst outcome for either party is that the counter-claim is reduced to zero. The defendant cannot therefore be expected to shoulder losses suffered by the claimant above and beyond the claimant's counter-restitutionary liability.[37] Bant accepts the defence has different application in different contexts, but argues that counter-restitution, seen as the defendant's failure of consideration claim, is vulnerable to change of position.

Two points must be made. First, the discussion above demonstrates the need for unjust factors to apply in some way in our law of restitution. It is much more difficult to justify the lack of the defence if the law's focus is on the payment which, as we saw in chapter five, is fictionally deemed to be to discharge the non-existent debt. This provides no way to discriminate between the mistaken payment case and the payment by duress. This explains why German law resorts to a non-codal requirement of claimant voluntariness to exclude the duressor from being able to rely on the defence. Second, it is an example of the essentialist error we have been arguing against to say that because change of position applies to some unjust enrichment performance claims, it must apply to all.

B. Rationale of the Defence: Disenrichment and Irreversible Detriment

The defence of change of position has been linked to disenrichment.[38] The rationale is that where the defendant is no longer enriched, he should no longer be liable for the enrichment he no longer has. If we take this seriously, we should measure enrichment at the time of trial as opposed to the time of transfer[39] and ignore everything else. We do not; bad faith defendants are disentitled from the defence and the disenrichment view is over-inclusive. German[40] and South African law come much closer to a simple net enrichment approach. In South Africa, the relevant authority is *Kudu Granite Operations (Pty) Ltd v Caterna Ltd*[41] which is seen to have committed the law to such a net enrichment approach. Both jurisdictions, however, qualify the defence's availability. South African law, for instance, bars the defence in cases of a bad faith defendant who parts with the enrichment knowing that it was received *indebite*.[42] The 'disenrichment' approach in both jurisdictions

[37] Bant, 'Rescission, Restitution and Compensation' (n 33) 300–02.

[38] *Test Claimants in the FII Litigation v HMRC* [2014] EWHC 4302 (Ch), [2015] STC 1471, [354] (Henderson J).

[39] Stevens, 'The Unjust Enrichment Disaster' (n 25) 577.

[40] § 818 BGB; Jewell (n 26) 11–12.

[41] *Kudu Granite Operations (Pty) Ltd v Caterna Ltd* 2003 (5) SA 193 (SCA); see also *King v Cohen, Benjamin & Co* 1953 (4) SA 641; see also, J du Plessis, 'Determining the Moment when Enrichment Liability is Quantified: The Curious Case of *Paschke v Frans*' [2016] *Journal of South African Law* 281.

[42] *African Diamond Exporters (Pty) Ltd v Barclays Bank International Ltd* 1978 (3) SA 699; *Glenrand MIB Financial Services (Pty) Ltd v Willem van den Heever NO* [2012] ZASCA 195; §818-819 BGB; Jewell (n 26) 20.

is in tension with the competing idea that unjust enrichment law is concerned with the reversal of failed performances and the idea, much more apparent in Germany than South Africa, that the actual thing transferred should be returned to the claimant. Such an approach is rather less generous to the defendant because it allows for greater differentiation between enrichment claims. For Krebs, the tension is prosaic in nature – a question about the relative generosity of the law to the defendant.[43] However, there may be important conceptual consequences. One we have already seen. Seeing bilateral cases in terms of two potentially reversible performances (the *Zweikondiktionentheorie*) implies that each requires independent valuation. A second is that seeing the law as being based on failed performances allows us to explain why we do not (in England) measure enrichment at trial.[44] The reason on this view is that we reverse not the enrichment but the performance.

This latter explanation does not, however, apply to non-performance claims and so leaves a gap. The irreversible detriment view by decoupling the defence from the enrichment enquiry fills the gap. The reason we do not measure enrichment at trial is not therefore because we reverse performances, but because to do so would not allow us to consider other loss-generating but non-disenriching changes of position. The example normally given is *Commerzbank v Price-Jones*[45] where the claimant had foregone an increase in salary by not applying for jobs elsewhere. The fact the claimant might not have succeeded in his applications made the claimed change rather too speculative, however. It does not make a good test case, but the suggestion was also raised of seeking a divorce as a suitable change;[46] Bant also suggests getting married or having a child.[47] Closely related to this, irreversible detriment will apply when the defendant ostensibly remains enriched as by the purchase of new furniture.[48] Change of position, therefore, prevents the defendant from being placed in a worse or entirely different position by the reversal of the transfer.[49] Second, an advantage of the approach over disenrichment is that it emphasises that detriment as assessed at the time of the claim rather than the time the change of position occurred. This is because the irreversibility criterion tells us that the defendant is not now able to recover the money he paid away.[50] Finally, by decoupling the defence from the enrichment enquiry, the detriment view allows us to entertain the possibility of the defence's application to non-unjust enrichment claims.[51]

[43] T Krebs, 'Disenrichment in German Law' in E Bant et al (eds), *Research Handbook on Unjust Enrichment and Restitution* (Cheltenham, Edward Elgar, 2020) 438–39.

[44] Stevens, 'The Unjust Enrichment Disaster' (n 25) 586–87.

[45] *Commerzbank v Price-Jones* [2003] EWCA Civ 1664.

[46] ibid [68].

[47] Bant, *The Change of Position Defence* (n 7) 134.

[48] As in *RBC v Dominion Securities* (1994) 111 DLR (4th) 240.

[49] Bant, *The Change of Position Defence* (n 7) 171.

[50] ibid 135.

[51] ibid 171, 206; see E Bant, 'Change of Position: Outstanding Issues' in A Dyson et al (eds), *Defences in Unjust Enrichment* (Oxford, Hart Publishing, 2016) 146–49.

The rationale was enunciated judicially in the High Court of Australia decision of *Australian Financial Services Pty Ltd v Hills Industries*,[52] relying explicitly on the work done by Elise Bant.[53] AFSL was induced by a fraudster to make payments to Hills for non-existent equipment and to enter leaseback arrangements regarding the equipment with companies owned by the fraudster. Hills treated the payment, as requested by the fraudster, as discharging certain debts owing to them from other companies, themselves owned by the fraudster, and refrained from taking action against them. AFSL performed vis-à-vis the fraudsters and to allow a claim against Hills is to allow AFSL to leapfrog the correct defendant.[54] The case has parallels with *Aiken v Short*,[55] but the High Court instead considered change of position. They emphatically rejected disenrichment as the defence's rationale in large measure because some relevant changes of position will be difficult or impossible to value.[56] The plurality also criticised 'disenrichment' as being overly mathematical when the law should ask who should bear the loss and why.[57] French CJ argued that disenrichment was at best a circumstance defining a class of case in which recovery could be held inequitable, and founded the defence very firmly on 'a general rubric of inequitable recovery'[58] as set out in *Lipkin Gorman v Karpnale* and subsequently in *Dextra Bank v Bank of Jamaica*.[59] More broadly, the Court did not therefore adopt an unjust enrichment analysis of restitution and so the apparent symmetry of enrichment versus disenrichment did not arise. Instead, the Court[60] founded recovery on the equitable roots of the action in *Moses v Macferlan*,[61] something to which both French CJ and the plurality referred in discussing the foundations of the defence. Gageler J described change of position as being the second stage of an analysis based on 'notions of conscience'.[62] In the end it is reasonably clear that whether we talk of conscience, as preferred in Australia, or unjust enrichment, makes little real difference to the overall shape of the area of law.[63] Little is of course utterly irreversible, but it appears purchases of, or improvements to land, may be taken as irreversible.[64] If litigation is needed

[52] *Australian Financial Services Pty Ltd v Hills Industries* [2014] HCA 14, (2014) 253 CLR 560; again, relying on Bant, the court in Singapore adopted 'irreversible detriment' in *Cavenagh Investments Pte Ltd v Kaushik Rajiv* [2013] SGHC 45, [2013] 2 SLR 543.

[53] Irreversibility first appears in her writing in E Bant and P Creighton, 'The Australian Change of Position Defence' (2002) 30 *University of Western Australia Law Review* 208.

[54] R Stevens, *The Laws of Restitution* (Oxford, OUP, 2023) 365.

[55] *Aiken v Short* (1856) 1 H&N 210, 156 ER 1180.

[56] [2014] HCA 14, (2014) 253 CLR 560, [23] (French CJ).

[57] ibid [78], [84].

[58] ibid [23] (French CJ); [79]–[80] (Hayne J et al); [144]–[145] (Gageler J).

[59] *Dextra Bank v Bank of Jamaica* [2002] 1 All ER (Comm) 193 (PC).

[60] [2014] HCA 14, (2014) 234 CLR 560, [65]–[76] (Hayne J et al); [105]–[126] (Gageler J).

[61] *Moses v Macferlan* (1760) 2 Burr 1005, 97 ER 676.

[62] [2014] HCA 14, (2014) 234 CLR 580, [143].

[63] K Barker, 'Unjust Enrichment in Australia: What Is(n't) It? Implications for Legal Reasoning and Practice' (2020) 43 *Melbourne University Law Review* 903.

[64] *Saunders & Co v Hague* [2004] 2 NZLR 475; see, for discussion, eg, C Mitchell, 'Change of Position: The Developing Law' [2005] *Lloyd's Maritime & Commercial Law Quarterly* 168.

for the defendant to recover money paid away we might deem it irreversible.[65] In *AFSL* itself, the debts owed to Hills by the fraudster's companies were effectively unenforceable and the change of Hill's position in discharging those debts was irreversible 'as a practical matter of business'.[66]

C. Proprietary Claims and Restitution for Wrongs

The leading case in favour of allowing the defence in cases of innocent trespass is *Cavenagh Investments Pte Ltd v Kaushik Rajiv*.[67] The decision involved a condominium development at Pebble Bay in Singapore. An employee of the management company forged signatures on the lease agreement, allowing him to lease the apartment to the defendant without the defendant realising that the lease was unauthorised, and he was paying rent to the employee personally. When this came to light the plaintiff sued for trespass. Kaushik claimed change of position and succeeded. Chan Seng Onn J said:

> I do not take the view that there should be a blanket ban on the defence of change of position applying to all cases of restitution for wrongs … Where there is no moral turpitude but the wrong involved is one where the law has prescribed the remedy for a particular policy reason, the defence should also not apply … In the present case I do not see why the defence should not apply.[68]

The judge said that the policy behind rendering the conduct wrongful would not be defeated by providing a change of position defence. This must be right. Kaushik was just the wrong defendant in that the real wrongdoer was the fraudster, but as importantly he had irreversibly changed his position through his payments to the fraudster, which were practically irrecoverable in the absence of litigation.[69] The fact that Kaushik was innocent meant that the trade-off between the strictness of the liability and the availability of the defence was resolved in favour of the latter. The importance of the property right needs to be balanced against the defendant's freedom of action. Importantly the innocent defendant, if he has changed his position, would not be free to determine his own spending priorities if liability were imposed.[70]

[65] *K&S Corporation v Sportingbet (Australia) Pty Ltd* [2003] SASC 98, (2003) 86 SASR 313.
[66] [2014] HCA 14, (2014) 253 CLR 580, [95].
[67] [2013] SGHC 45, [2013] 2 SLR 543.
[68] ibid [64]–[65].
[69] D Sheehan, 'The Scope and Rationale(s) of the Change of Position Defence' (2023) 74 *Northern Ireland Legal Quarterly* 269.
[70] C Rotherham, 'Morally Blameless Wrongdoers and the Change of Position Defence' (2018) 30 *Singapore Academy of Law Journal* 149, 167; see also on the possibility of change of position being available to innocent converters & trespassers *Kuwait Airways v Iraqi Airways (Nos 4 & 5)* [2002] UKHL 19, [2002] 2 AC 883 (HL).

Proprietary claims are likewise susceptible to the defence.[71] A quick comment is needed. We saw in chapter seven that claims for specific restitution of a right are proprietary; change of position allows the defendant to set off a detriment against the claim for specific restitution. Let us imagine a trustee who misappropriates trust funds and gives them to a third party. *Foskett v McKeown*[72] is authority that these claims are not claims in unjust enrichment, but, even if right, this does not affect the argument. The strictness of the liability of the innocent third-party donee to return assets and the effect of the claim on his creditors in insolvency can be set against the need for the donee's freedom of action to be respected. That the defendant (and by extension his creditors) knows nothing of, and cannot guard against, the claimant or his claim militates in favour of the defence irrespective of whether we think the claim is an unjust enrichment claim. Had the defendant withdrawn money from the very bank account in which the unauthorised transfer was paid, the claimant's tracing claim could be reduced. The defendant's moral position should not depend on which bank account he decides (arbitrarily) to withdraw from; if he takes money from a separate unconnected account and is forced to repay the defendant, he will be made irreversibly 'worse off'.[73] The same justification for the defence therefore applies to both wrongs and proprietary claims contingent on tracing.

In addition, as we saw in chapter seven, the defendant is not subject to a duty to return the mistaken payment or to return the misapplied trust asset. Rather, as we saw in chapter three, reflecting the fact that he cannot on receipt know there is a cause of action against him, he is subject to a liability to be made to repay in Hohfeldian terms. Other proprietary claims, reflecting the same Hohfeldian structure, include rescission claims where the reason behind the voidability of the contract or other instrument is one of the standard unjust factors, be that duress or undue influence, or (outside contract) mistake. Such claims should be seen as unjust enrichment claims as they are performance claims, as understood in chapter two. If the defendant can take advantage of the defence in answer to a personal claim in unjust enrichment, he should by analogy be able to do so in the rescission cases or misapplied trust asset cases. In all these cases the absence of any duty on the defendant to return immediately on receipt provides conceptual space for a defence of change of position designed to prevent the defendant from being made 'worse off'.

D. Relation with Estoppel

Common law estoppels are rules of evidence.[74] In an estoppel by representation, therefore, A must reasonably rely on the representation – ie, it was reasonable for

[71] *Goff & Jones* (n 9) paras 27.84–27.88; but see, R Chambers, 'Proprietary Restitution and Change of Position' in A Dyson et al (eds), *Defences in Unjust Enrichment* (Oxford, Hart Publishing, 2016).

[72] *Foskett v McKeown* [2001] 1 AC 102 (HL).

[73] Sheehan, 'The Scope and Rationale(s) of the Change of Position Defence' (n 69) 300.

[74] *RE Jones Ltd v Waring & Gillow Ltd* [1926] AC 670 (HL) 683–84.

him to take the view induced by the representation and it must be reasonable to act on it. In an estoppel by convention, the matter of fact or law adopted must be mutually assumed (and communicated between) by the parties. To allow one party to depart from the adopted state of affairs infringes the other's autonomy.[75] Not all estoppels are evidentiary. Equitable estoppels by contrast have a substantive effect and can – at least in Australia – act as a cause of action as well as a defence.[76] Common law estoppels, however, ensure the representee's expectations are met. As such, unlike change of position, they are all-or-nothing. They do not operate *pro tanto*.[77]

Fung and Ho by contrast argue that estoppel by representation should not operate in an all-or-nothing fashion,[78] and this plainly affects the relation with change of position if both operate *pro tanto*. *Scottish Equitable BS v Derby* illustrates that a *pro tanto* response might be justifiable if the detriment suffered and the size of the mistaken payment (say) are out of proportion to each other;[79] in the same vein, *National Westminster Bank v Somer* suggests that *pro tanto* operation will avoid unconscionability.[80] A mistaken payment was made of $77,000, and in reliance on a representation that the money was owing, made a series of deliveries of goods worth $13,000. The Court of Appeal held that on such facts it was unconscionable for the company to rely on the representation to avoid repaying the full $77,000. On this basis, the all-or-nothing defence should be excised completely as it is always unconscionable to retain a balance.[81] Fung and Ho also comment that equitable estoppel is not always all-or-nothing and, while acknowledging the differences, argue that fusion demands the two be merged so that the level of detriment can be assessed in each case.[82] Fusion between law and equity, however, only requires this if the two types of estoppel have the same function. It is simply not clear that they do, despite comments to that effect in *NatWest v Somer International (UK) Ltd*.[83] Detriment is a requirement of common law estoppel, but it need not be financially

[75] J Hudson, 'The Price of Coherence in Estoppel' (2017) 39 *Sydney Law Review* 1, 11–12; *Goff & Jones* (n 9) paras 30.01, 30.18.

[76] *Giumelli v Giumelli* (1999) 196 CLR 101; for an argument that both common law and equitable estoppels should be unified, see E Bant and M Bryan, 'Fact, Fiction and Future: Risk and Reasonable Reliance in Estoppel' (2015) 35 *OJLS* 427.

[77] *Avon County Council v Howlett* [1983] 1 WLR 605; J Taylor, 'The Role of Estoppel as a Defence to Claims in Unjust Enrichment' (2003) 9 *Auckland University Law Review* 1208, 1233; E Cooke, *The Modern Law of Estoppel* (Oxford, OUP, 2000) 151.

[78] E Fung and L Ho, 'Establishing Estoppel after the Recognition of Change of Position' [2001] *Restitution Law Review* 52, 62–63.

[79] *Scottish Equitable BS v Derby* [2001] EWCA Civ 369, [2001] 3 All ER 818.

[80] *National Westminster Bank v Somer* [2001] EWCA Civ 970, [2002] 1 All ER 198.

[81] Burrows, *The Law of Restitution* (n 25) 557; see also, K Dore, 'Change of Position and Estoppel as Defences to an Action for Money Paid by Mistake' (1992) 15 *Dalhousie Law Review* 615, 627, but see Hudson, 'The Price of Coherence in Estoppel' (n 75) 18–19.

[82] Fung and Ho, 'Establishing Estoppel' (n 78) 60; equitable estoppel concentrating on resiling from a promise is different from repudiation of a statement of fact in common law. See B McFarlane 'The Limits of Estoppel' (2013) 7 *Journal of Equity* 250.

[83] [2001] EWCA Civ 970, [2002] 1 All ER 198, 213.

quantifiable;[84] it merely triggers the concern for defendant autonomy, which is the primary concern. Equitable estoppels are not primarily concerned with detriment either, but with the unconscionable behaviour that triggers it.[85]

Nevertheless, pressure remains to recognise estoppel as a *pro tanto* defence. One way to argue for this is to say that change of position is just estoppel minus a representation. Gageler J in *AFSL v Hills Industries*[86] took this view, which led to the rather strange suggestion by his Honour, not that estoppel operate *pro tanto*, but that change of position as a species of estoppel operate absolutely, unless that would be disproportionate.[87] This is an entirely novel idea and without any further supporting authority should be rejected. A related strategy is to sideline estoppel,[88] barring it if change of position is available. Key argued in this vein that in all cases where there is an estoppel there is also a change of position; the detriment required for change of position is present in the reliance on the representation.[89] Estoppel should not make the defendant better off than he would have been relying on a *pro tanto* change of position. At a minimum, this means the defences overlap and can operate concurrently. It might also mean that one defence displaces the other. Robert Walker LJ in *Scottish Equitable BS v Derby* raised an interesting fact scenario in support of this argument. He posits a case where A pays B £1,000 and represents that to be owed to B. B throws a party for £250 and puts the rest in a bank account. A claims that since he cannot recover the £250 (change of position) B has suffered no detriment and cannot rely on estoppel.[90] Likewise, the defendant, Key suggests, cannot have a legitimate complaint if his detriment is reversed and no more and in the usual case the representation by the claimant will be innocent so there is little justification for an arguably punitive response requiring that the claimant lose the claim altogether.[91] In *TRA Global Pty Ltd v Kebakoska*,[92] Osborn J disputed this line of argument, suggesting that given that estoppel is evidentiary in character it should, if anything, operate before the substantive defence of change of position,[93] and held that the extent of the detriment required to establish estoppel and change of position were not in any event co-extensive.[94]

[84] *Kelly v Fraser* [2013] 1 AC 450, 460.

[85] Hudson, 'The Price of Coherence in Estoppel' (n 75) 18–19.

[86] [2014] HCA 14, (2014) 253 CLR 560.

[87] ibid [158].

[88] *Philip Collins Ltd v Davis* [2000] 3 All ER 808; *RBC v Dominion Securities* (1994) 111 DLR (4th) 240; *Citigroup Pty Ltd v National Australia Bank* [2012] NSWCA 381, (2012) 82 NSWLR 391, [64]; but see, E Fung and L Ho, 'Change of Position and Estoppel' (2001) 117 *LQR* 14, 17.

[89] P Key, 'Excising Estoppel by Representation as a Defence to Restitution' [1995] *CLJ* 525, 531–32.

[90] [2001] 3 All ER 818, [46].

[91] Key, 'Excising Estoppel by Representation' (n 89) 534–35; P Key, 'Estoppel by Representation as a Defence to Restitution: The Exception Proves the Rule?' [2001] *CLJ* 465.

[92] *TRA Global Pty Ltd v Kebakoska* [2011] VSC 480.

[93] ibid [73]; J Hudson, 'Estoppel by Representation as a Defence to Unjust Enrichment: The Vine has not Withered Yet' [2014] *Restitution Law Review* 19, 29.

[94] [2011] VSC 480, [73]–[74].

Osborn J is correct in this. The detriment with which estoppel is concerned is not the same as that with which change of position is concerned. It is concerned with the detriment that would be incurred if the other party departed from the representation.[95] That could well, in part, be because of differences of timing of determining the detriment – at trial in change of position and at the point the party attempted to resile in estoppel – mean that the detriment is different in the two defences.[96] There would also be an undesirable division in the operation of estoppel between the unjust enrichment context and elsewhere were the defences to be merged;[97] put differently, concentrating on alleged similarities between estoppel and change of position and ignoring the resemblances with the significant features we pick out to ground estoppels by representation and their operation as rules of evidence elsewhere in the law, flies in the face of the proper application of the methodology used here.

II. Passing On

Passing on does not exist as a general defence to an unjust enrichment claim in English law.[98] In England, the decision in *Kleinwort Benson v Birmingham CC* is key.[99] The bank and local authority had entered into void interest rate swap agreements; the bank also entered into protective hedging transactions. When the bank therefore claimed its money back because of the nullity of the contract and the consequent failure of consideration, the local authority countered that it had lost nothing because of the hedge transactions. Saville LJ argued that mitigation was irrelevant, and that 'at the expense of' referred to immediate expense,[100] uncorrected by subsequent actions by the claimant, and so ruled passing on inadmissible as a defence, although Evans LJ in obiter dicta left it open in the mistaken tax context,[101] saying only that there was a public law element to those cases. This

[95] Hudson, 'Estoppel by Representation' (n 93) 20; *Grundt v Great Boulder Proprietary Gold Mines Ltd* (1937) 59 CLR 641.

[96] Bant, *The Change of Position Defence* (n 7) 226–27, although they are sometimes described in identical terms. *Barons Finance Ltd v Kensington Mortgage Co Ltd* [2011] EWCA Civ 1592.

[97] Hudson, 'Estoppel by Representation' (n 93) 27–28.

[98] Birks, *Unjust Enrichment* (n 12) 219–21; Stevens, *The Laws of Restitution* (n 54) 374–76; *Croxen v Gas and Electricity Markets Authority* [2022] EWHC 2826 (Ch), [190]–[196] (Zacaroli J).

[99] *Kleinwort Benson v Birmingham CC* [1997] QB 380; *Kleinwort Benson Ltd v South Tyneside Metropolitan BC* [1994] 4 All ER 972. For Australia, see *Commissioner of State Revenue v Royal Insurance Australia Ltd* (1994) 182 CLR 51; *Roxborough v Rothman's Pall Mall of Australia* (2001) 208 CLR 516 (HCA); *Mason v New South Wales* (1959) 102 CLR 108; *Hilliard v Westpac Banking Corporation* [2009] VSCA 211, [83]–[84]. For Canada, see *Air Canada v British Columbia* [1989] 1 SCR 1161; see M Rush, *The Defence of Passing On* (Oxford, Hart Publishing, 2006) 35–52.

[100] [1997] QB 380, 394–95; *Roxborough v Rothman's Pall Mall of Australia* (2002) 208 CLR 516, 528–30 (Gleeson CJ); 541 (Gummow J); *Commissioner of State Revenue v Royal Insurance Australia* (1994) 126 ALR 1.

[101] [1997] QB 380, 385.

seems insufficient to explain the distinction; indeed, if the policy behind recovery of overpaid tax is to ensure state legality, it might be thought contradictory. There have, however, been legislative interventions, for example in the context of VAT, where a defence that the claimant would be unjustly enriched exists.[102]

In principle, the lack of a passing on defence seems right. This book adopts a structure for unjust enrichment law reminiscent of that in South Africa. It is worth noting therefore that Visser advocates no defence of passing on for South Africa,[103] although the reason he does this is pragmatic rather than the principled rejection of the defence argued for in this book. In South Africa, the second of the general requirements for unjust enrichment is one of impoverishment and a double cap rule applies so that relief is no greater than either the claimant's loss or the defendant's enrichment.[104] In other words, the 'at the expense of' requirement in South Africa demands a corresponding loss on the part of the claimant. The logic of impoverishment demands a passing on defence;[105] quantum is calculated at the date of the commencement of the action and if at that point the claimant is no longer impoverished, it should reduce the quantum of relief. As a matter of positive law, however, this seems not to be followed through in South Africa.[106] Visser suggests that the logistics are just too difficult in terms of calculating any pass-through from a claimant to his customers. If, therefore, a customer purchasing from a cartelist pays inflated prices for his raw materials (the defendant's gain) how do we work out whether and how much that is recouped by increased prices for the finished product?

English law does not have a double-cap rule; in principle it should be sufficient to prove that the gain comes 'from' the claimant.[107] This is consistent with the logic of a performance claim. There is only one rather weak authority, which contains no detailed discussion of the authority or principle,[108] that there needs to be an equivalent loss to the claimant corresponding to the defendant's gain. In performance claims, the purpose of the attributive transactional link is not to demonstrate some arithmetical equivalence between the defendant's enrichment and the claimant's loss. It is to demonstrate the intentionality of the transfer or rendering of the services. Claims for restitution are concerned with reversing defective performances and the fact that the claimant may have passed on his loss

[102] VAT Act 1994, s 80(3); arguing that the common law might follow suit in recognising a defence in the *Woolwich BS v IRC* case, see *Goff & Jones* (n 9) para 32.20.

[103] D Visser, *Unjustified Enrichment* (Durban, Juta, 2008) 752.

[104] ibid 161.

[105] ibid 748; J du Plessis, 'The Relevance of the Plaintiff's Impoverishment in Awarding Claims Based on Unjustified Enrichment' (2009) 20 *Stellenbosch Law Review* 494, 502–04.

[106] *Govender v Standard Bank of South Africa Ltd* 1984 (4) SA 392 (*condictio sine causa specialis*); *St Helena Primary School v Department of Education* 2007 (4) SA 16 (imposed enrichment).

[107] Rush (n 99) 154–63; Stevens, *The Laws of Restitution* (n 54) 30–31.

[108] *Re BHT (UK) Ltd* [2004] EWHC 201; Rush (n 99) 117–18; see also *Investment Trust Companies v HMRC* [2017] UKSC 29, [2018] AC 275, [44]–[45] (Lord Reed) making it clear that loss is not understood in the same way as damages for loss.

does not, vis-a-vis the defendant, affect the defectiveness of the performance. Like reasoning applies in improvement cases where the purpose of the attributive link is to show that the immediate enrichment of the defendant was causally from the claimant.

III. Illegality

Illegality operates a defence to a claim in unjust enrichment, but it is a different sort of defence in that it responds to substantive policy concerns. It is also not just concerned with unjust enrichment. It operates as a defence to tort and contract claims as well as to resulting trust claims. A contract, for example, might be rendered illegal for any one of several reasons concerned to deter the substantive transaction in progress. It ensures that a claim in unjust enrichment fails, or alternatively that a defence fails if the illegality bites upon the defendant's change of position, for example.[109] The claimant might, for example, have paid under the contract, not received the illegal counter-performance and now seeks to recover. Whether he can do so ought to depend entirely on whether the policy behind the illegality is stultified or advanced,[110] and this can be decided as a matter of statutory construction or by examining the policy behind the common law decision. The substance of the matter should not depend on whether the illegality derives from common law or statute.

Prior to the decision in *Patel v Mirza*,[111] a claimant who withdrew from the transaction prior to the fulfilment of the illegal purpose may have been able to rely on a principle of *locus poenitentiae* as a cause of action. Essentially, the action allowed for recovery of the assets transferred purely in order to encourage withdrawal from the transaction. It was not necessary to prove a failure of basis or mistake.

It is interesting to compare this with civil law systems which begin with illegality as grounding a cause of action. In South Africa, the *condictio ob turpem vel iniustam causam* has a restricted ambit of operation,[112] and now has some constitutional implications.[113] The central requirement for the *condictio* is that it is used where the basis for the payment – the contract – was an illegal one.[114] The illegality

[109] *Barros Mattos Junior v McDaniels Ltd* [2004] EWHC 1188, [2005] 1 WLR 247.

[110] PBH Birks, 'Recovering Value Transferred under an Illegal Contract' (2000) 1 *Theoretical Inquiries in Law* 155; *Equuscorp Pty Ltd v Haxton* [2012] HCA 7, (2012) 246 CLR 446; *Nelson v Nelson* (1995) 184 CLR 584; *Ochroid Trading Ltd v Chua Siok Liu* [2018] SGCA 5; *Kim v Choi* 2020 BCCA 98; D Sheehan, 'Reconsidering the Defence of Illegality in Unjust Enrichment' [2009] *Lloyd's Maritime & Commercial Law Quarterly* 319.

[111] *Patel v Mirza* [2016] UKSC 42, [2017] AC 467.

[112] R Zimmermann, *The Law of Obligations* (Durban, Juta, 1996) 860.

[113] H Scott, 'Transforming the South African Law of Unjustified Enrichment' [2017] *Restitution Law Review* 29, 37–42.

[114] *Afrisure v Watson* 2009 (2) SA 127, 131–32.

of the transaction explains why the payment was *sine causa*.[115] The *condictio ob turpem vel iniustam causam* lies both if the transaction is uncompleted and if it has been completed.[116] The claimant must, it is said, tender back what he received and be free of 'turpitude'.[117] The defendant must know of the unlawfulness of the contract either at the time of the transfer, or after the transfer but before the institution of the action; he must still have the asset in his hands when he discovered the illegality.[118] The *condictio ob turpem vel iniustam causam* is a cause of action in illegality; it is an assertion that the transaction was a nullity because of illegality, of which the defendant knew or became aware, justifying restitution. The defendant may then assert a defence of *in pari delicto* – that the claimant was just as guilty or knowledgeable of the illegality and therefore restitution should be barred.[119]

The foundational case on the *par delictum* rule in modern South African unjust enrichment law is *Jajbhay v Cassim*[120] which suggested that, although the general rule was that the claim would only succeed if the parties were *non in pari delicto*, the rule was subject to public policy and whether policy was best served by the grant or refusal of the action. No definite criteria have ever been laid down, however, as to when the general rule against relief should be relaxed. This makes South African law vulnerable to the criticism that public policy when 'at large' can justify almost any answer, although in practice the discretion has caused few problems. In South Africa, therefore, the claimant claims restitution on the basis that the transfer was not due because of the illegality; the defendant raises the plaintiff's turpitude as a defence, and in the third step this defence may be discretionarily disapplied.[121] It seems preferable, however, for South African law to recognise a cause of action based on the illegality of the transfer, but that whether the prerequisites for that action are satisfied depends on the policy behind the illegality and its stultification,[122] and so in *Afrisure v Watson*[123] the *in pari delicto* rule was disallowed because the infringed statutory scheme was aimed at protecting scheme members and this purpose would be stultified by non-recovery.[124]

[115] This is the narrow view of illegality under which all illegal contracts are void. Some illegal contracts, on the wide view, are valid but unenforceable. J du Plessis, 'Some Thoughts on the Consequences of Illegal Contracts' [2021] *Acta Juridica* 177.

[116] Zimmermann (n 112) 845.

[117] *National Credit Regulator v Oppermann* 2013 (2) SA 1, 9–10; *First National Bank of Southern Africa v Perry* 2001 (3) SA 960.

[118] *First National Bank of Southern Africa Ltd v Perry* 2001 (3) SA 960.

[119] *Afrisure v Watson* 2009 (2) SA 127; the burden of proof is on the defendant. See LTC Harms (ed), *Amler's Precedents of Pleading*, 9th edn (Durban, Lexis, 2018) 120, but South African courts are not 'hung up' on exact pleading in this context: *Klokow v Sullivan* 2006 (1) SA 259.

[120] *Jajbhay v Cassim* 1939 AD 537.

[121] Visser (n 103) 417–18; J du Plessis, *The South African Law of Unjustified Enrichment* (Durban, Juta, 2012) 204–06.

[122] H Scott, *Unjust Enrichment in South African Law* (Oxford, Hart Publishing, 2013) 13–14; *First National Bank of Southern Africa v Perry* 2001 (3) SA 960, [20]–[23]; see also, J du Plessis 'Comparative Observations on the Consequences of Illegality' [2022] *Edinburgh Law Review* 408.

[123] 2009 (2) SA 127.

[124] ibid 142–45; for further examples of relaxing the par delictum rule, see Visser (n 103) 448–53.

There is also a *condictio ob turpem vel iniustam causam* in German law. Section 817 BGB provides:

> If the purpose of performance was determined in such a way that that the recipient, in accepting it, was violating a statutory prohibition or public policy, then the recipient is obliged to make restitution. A claim for return is excluded if the person who rendered performance was likewise guilty of such a breach, unless the performance consisted in entering into an obligation; restitution may not be demanded of any performance rendered in fulfilment of such an obligation.

The provision has little ambit of operation. As we have seen, one of the features of the German law of unjustified enrichment is its automatic nature, so if the illegality renders a contract or obligation '*nichtig*', it is covered by the general provision of § 812[125] so that a payment under a void illegal contract is recoverable as being made without any basis.

The classic English case on the use of illegality as a defence to an unjust enrichment claim is now *Patel v Mirza*; in principle the test laid down applies across private law, not just in unjust enrichment although we concentrate on its effects in unjust enrichment in this chapter. The decision involved the respondent's transfer of £620,000 to the appellant for use in an illegal insider trading operation. The inside information was never forthcoming, and the investment never made. The respondent claimed in unjust enrichment for failure of basis and succeeded in the Supreme Court. The justices adopted a flexible test as to how illegality should be judged. Lord Toulson identified two underlying policies in the law of illegality. The first was that a person should not be allowed to profit from his own wrongdoing, and the second that the law be coherent and not self-defeating.[126] From there, observing that there can be no mechanistic process, he identified three factors. First, what was the underlying purpose of the prohibition? Second, what other public policies would be rendered ineffective by denying the claim? Third, the role of proportionality.[127] It is not clear, however, even how those factors were applied in *Patel* itself. For example, no scale was ever proffered to explain how one should judge proportionality,[128] although a further range of factors was proffered including the seriousness and intentionality of the illegality and the parties' relative culpability.[129] The minority criticised the judgment therefore on the ground that Lord Toulson's proposals were too vague and too wide,[130] although Lord Toulson did approve of Gloster LJ's approach of asking if the policy behind the insider trading provisions were stultified.[131] On the facts, the basis for the payment

[125] T Krebs, *Restitution at the Crossroads* (London, Cavendish, 2001) 186–87.
[126] [2016] UKSC 42, [2017] AC 467, [99].
[127] ibid [101].
[128] GJ Virgo, 'Illegality after Patel v Mirza: One Step Forward, Two Steps Back' (2016) 22 *Trusts and Trustees* 1090, 1093–94.
[129] [2016] UKSC 42, [2017] AC 467, [107].
[130] ibid [204] (Lord Mance), [217] (Lord Clarke), [265] (Lord Sumption).
[131] ibid [115].

had simply failed, the securities transaction never took place and that it did so was the condition of the payment. No question of giving effect to the illegal insider dealings was at issue and Lord Toulson never found it necessary to consider how he might apply the various factors he identified. He simply agreed with Gloster LJ that denying restitution was 'not a just and proportionate response'.

The *locus poenitentiae* principle is unlikely to stand.[132] The minority, for instance, disapproved of the doctrine's moral overtones in requiring 'genuine' repentance of the illegality,[133] and Lord Neuberger's characterisation of the governing principle was broad enough to take in cases where there was genuine and voluntary withdrawal from the purpose and any other case where the purpose was not fulfilled. Despite its still not being explicitly recognised, *Patel v Mirza* is therefore consistent with recognition of partial failure of consideration,[134] and Lord Toulson concluded by commenting that,

> [a] claimant, such as Mr Patel, who satisfies the ordinary requirements of a claim for unjust enrichment, should not be debarred from enforcing his claim by reason only of the fact that the money which he seeks to recover was paid for an unlawful purpose.[135]

The defence should therefore bite in rare cases.

Although Lord Toulson suggests that the claimant will plead one of the standard unjust enrichment actions and wait for the defendant to pose illegality as a defence, the tenor of the decision is mixed. There are suggestions that all illegal executed contracts can be unwound, simply because of the illegality.[136] Lord Sumption buttressed this by remarking that failure of consideration will not work in *locus poenitentiae* cases where recovery is sought prior to the time for the other party's performance,[137] or in cases of full execution of the contract. Mistake as to the illegality would still work, however. The question seems open for now, not least because the claimant had suffered a failure of consideration in *Patel*; he had not received the counter-performance bargained for. If contracts are unwound merely because of the illegality, however, English law tracks South African where the *condictio ob turpem vel iniustam causam* is invariably used in preference to others such as the *condictio indebiti* or *condictio causa data causa non secuta*.

Returning to the operation of the multi-factorial test, we can see that its application in practice is, however, still unclear. There remains a good deal of vagueness,

[132] ibid [82] (Lord Toulson), [162] (Lord Neuberger).

[133] ibid [202] (Lord Mance), [248]–[249] (Lord Sumption).

[134] G Virgo, 'Illegality and Unjust Enrichment' in A Bogg and S Green (eds), *Illegality after Patel v Mirza* (Oxford, Hart Publishing, 2018) 226.

[135] [2016] UKSC 42, [2017] AC 467, [121].

[136] Virgo, 'Illegality and Unjust Enrichment' (n 134) 226–28; *Patel v Mirza* [2016] UKSC 42, [2017] AC 467, [145]–[146], [167] (Lord Neuberger), [197] (Lord Mance), [245]–[250] (Lord Sumption); B Häecker, 'The Impact of Illegality and Immorality on Contract and Restitution from a Civilian Angle' in A Bogg and S Green (eds), *Illegality after Patel v Mirza* (Oxford, Hart Publishing, 2018) 353–57.

[137] *Patel v Mirza* [2016] UKSC 42, [2017] AC 467, [249] (Lord Sumption).

leeway and discretion in how courts might approach it.[138] Despite Lord Toulson's endorsement of Gloster LJ's approach in the Court of Appeal, it may not always be quite as simple as asking whether the policy behind the prohibiting rule is furthered or stultified by allowing the claim. One issue is whether a quantum meruit will be permitted given that this is sometimes seen as part enforcement.[139] Lord Toulson approved the decision in *Mohamed & Co v Alaga*[140] where the solicitor's firm had agreed an illegal fee-sharing contract with the claimant for introducing clients. Enforcement of this was prohibited and a quantum meruit calculated by reference to the contract equally impossible. The plaintiff was in good faith, with no knowledge of any illegality and was able to recover a quantum meruit for translation services, which were not illegal, but not the introduction services which were illegal. On this basis, Lord Toulson suggested that cases where illegality would bar a claim in unjust enrichment will be rare,[141] although one where the claim was barred is *Awwad v Geraghty & Co* where the policy behind the prohibition was to preclude solicitors from acting under conditional fee arrangements. Geraghty did so act and knew it was illegal.[142]

Patel was subject to considerable discussion in the Singapore Court of Appeal in *Ochroid Trading Ltd v Chua Siok Liu*.[143] The Court distinguished between cases where the contract itself was prohibited in which case it was void and unenforceable in all cases and where the conduct was prohibited – but not the contract per se. In the latter cases, it had to be considered whether the contract's nullity was a proportionate response to the illegality.[144] The second stage of the enquiry was whether there could be restitutionary relief and the Court of Appeal agreed with *Patel* that where the ordinary requirements of unjust enrichment were met that was normally possible. In most circumstances the cause of action will be failure of consideration,[145] although the Singaporean court argued, albeit tentatively, for a narrow view of the *locus poenitentiae* decisions as requiring genuine repentance[146]

[138] J Goudkamp, 'The End of an Era: Illegality in Private Law in the Supreme Court' (2017) 133 *LQR* 14, 17–19; J Fisher, 'The Latest Word on Illegality' [2016] *Lloyd's Maritime & Commercial Law Quarterly* 483, Stevens, *The Laws of Restitution* (n 54) 404–08; but see, E Lim, '*Ex Turpi Causa*: Reformation not Revolution' (2017) 80 *MLR* 927, 935–37.

[139] G Dannemann, 'Illegality as a Defence against Unjust Enrichment Claims' [2000] *Oxford University Comparative Law Forum* 4, text at fns 218–19; or repayment of an illegal loan. See *Goff & Jones* (n 9) para 35.43.

[140] *Mohamed & Co v Alaga* [2000] 1 WLR 1815; See Virgo, 'Illegality and Unjust Enrichment' (n 134) 231–32.

[141] [2016] UKSC 42, [2017] AC 467, [116]–[121]; G Virgo, 'The Defence of Illegality in Unjust Enrichment' in A Dyson et al (eds), *Defences in Unjust Enrichment* (Oxford, Hart Publishing, 2016) 192–93.

[142] *Awwad v Geraghty & Co* [2001] QB 570.

[143] *Ochroid Trading Ltd v Chua Siok Liu* [2018] SGCA 5.

[144] ibid [36]–[39], [113] (Andrew Phang JA).

[145] ibid [139]–[141].

[146] ibid [174]–[175]; but see, WJ Swadling, 'The Role of Illegality in the English Law of Unjust Enrichment' [2000] *Oxford University Comparative Law Forum* 5; Stevens *The Laws of Restitution* (n 54) 409–11.

as a separate cause of action in Singapore. Such a claim in failure of consideration would be subject to the defence of illegality and the question to be asked is whether the fundamental policy underlying the prohibition (whether common law or statutory) would be stultified by allowing the claim.[147] *Ochroid* therefore posits a basis for the application of the illegality defence which threatens much less uncertainty and posits a clear link between the effect of the illegality and its justification, lacking in *Patel*. The Singaporean approach is to be preferred,[148] with the caveat that no special *locus poenitentiae* doctrine is necessary. The standard unjust factors will suffice. On the facts of the case, which were that the transactions in question were extortionate loans banned under the Moneylenders Act, the Court of Appeal decided that to permit even the recovery of the principal under failure of basis would defeat the point of the prohibition to remove and deter illegal moneylending as a serious social menace.[149]

IV. Bona Fide Purchase

Bona fide purchase protects a party who gives valuable consideration and does not know, nor has any reason to think that there has been (say) a breach of trust by the seller. It is not primarily a defence to unjust enrichment,[150] but a way of protecting the marketability of property subject to equitable interests and of money. It creates a good title where one would otherwise not be available. It is therefore a narrowly construed defence.

To take advantage of bona fide purchase in equity the claimant must not have constructive notice of any defects in the title and the consideration must be executed, although no enquiry is made into the adequacy of the consideration.[151] All equitable interests are vulnerable to the bona fide purchase of a legal estate and equitable rescissory powers are vulnerable to bona fide purchase of an equitable estate.[152] No legal title is vulnerable to bona fide purchase except title in money or bills of exchange.[153] The reason for these exceptions is essentially that money would not fulfil its purpose of being freely exchangeable if we had to stop and wonder if the person handing it over had good title. Bills of exchange are designed

[147] [2018] SGCA 5, [145], [159].

[148] GJ Virgo, 'The State of Illegality' (2019) 31 *Singapore Academy of Law Journal* 747; see also, J Goudkamp, 'The Law of Illegality: Identifying the Issues' in A Bogg and S Green (eds), *Illegality after Patel v Mirza* (Oxford, Hart Publishing, 2018) 45–47.

[149] [2018] SGCA 5, [219].

[150] E Bant and J Edelman, *Unjust Enrichment*, 2nd edn (Oxford, Hart Publishing, 2016) 371–74; K Barker, 'Bona Fide Purchase as a Defence to Unjust Enrichment Claims: A Concise Restatement' [1999] *Restitution Law Review* 75.

[151] *Goff & Jones* (n 9) paras 29.09–29.10.

[152] *Phillips v Phillips* (1861) 4 De GF&J 208, 45 ER 1164; A Reilly, 'What Were Lord Westbury's Intentions in Phillips v Phillips? Bona Fide Purchase of an Equitable Interest' [2021] *CLJ* 156.

[153] *Miller v Race* (1738) 1 Burr 452, 97 ER 398.

to be as good as money. They are documents of title to money and so the holder in due course takes free of all defects in prior title when the bill is negotiated to him for value and without notice of any prior defects.[154] The requirements of bona fide purchase in law of money are different from those in equity. Actual notice is required to defeat the defence as constructive notice is not known to the common law.[155] The better view is that, again unlike in equity, the consideration given may be either executed or executory.[156]

V. Conclusion

We have examined four defences: change of position, passing on, illegality and briefly bona fide purchase. The first three defences in English law parallel South African law. There is, properly understood, no defence of passing on in either jurisdiction. Change of position exists in both jurisdictions, and rules on illegality also exist. However, there may be significant differences in their operation. Change of position reflects a greater emphasis on net enrichment in South Africa than in England. We should not see change of position in terms of disenrichment in English law, but in terms of irreversible detriment. This difference, however, seems to have another implication and one which highlights historical contingencies in the development of the different systems, just as we saw in chapter four with the mistaken improvement of property cases. The implication of the disenrichment approach in South Africa and in Germany is that the defence does not apply outside unjustified enrichment. In England, however, the wider scope of detriment as a basis for the defence allows for the defence to be applied outside the unjust enrichment context, in cases of innocent wrongdoing.

South African law has a special *condictio* for illegality cases which is then tempered by the operation of public policy. English law – for historical reasons – has not had such a special action, allowing for general recovery of performances purely on the grounds of the illegality of the transaction. There are suggestions of such a development in *Patel v Mirza*, but the better view of the positive law is that one of the standard unjust enrichment claims must be made out and the defendant can then make use of illegality as a defence. Recovery will therefore be possible in, for example, cases of failure of basis and where a mistake as to the illegality has been made.

[154] Bills of Exchange Act 1882, ss 29–30; D Sheehan, *The Principles of Personal Property Law*, 2nd edn (Oxford, Hart Publishing, 2017) 136–39.

[155] *Goff & Jones* (n 9) para 29.05; on notice generally see *Armstrong v Winnington Networks Ltd* [2012] EWHC 10, [2012] 3 WLR 835, [111–123] (Morris QC); *Great Investments Ltd v Warner* [2016] FCAFC 85, [103]–[122].

[156] Sheehan, *The Principles of Personal Property Law* (n 154) 79–80.

9

Conclusion

Unjust enrichment scholarship has got into a mess, but it is not a disaster. We can and should retain a category of unjust enrichment as part of our law. The distinctive contribution to the debate that this book makes is twofold. First, it has defended the inclusion of disparate strands into the law of unjust enrichment (or indeed any area of the law) on the basis that they have illuminating family resemblances, understood in a Wittgensteinian sense. While this type of categorisation might be criticised on the basis that anything might be a family resemblance – after all there is always a claimant – this critique misses its mark. What gives unjust enrichment its unity is its **function**. Unjust enrichment law reverses defective enrichments, whether they are by way of performance or through some other way. However, this does not tell us precisely what counts as a defect. Its function is **under-determinative** and unjust enrichment is free to draw on principles found across the law. It is therefore **normatively pluralistic**, and this reflects the Dworkinian approach taken by this book to the way principles interact across the law. Those principles that it draws on are **historically contingent**, shaped to some degree by conventional morality and past political practices. My description of the function of unjust enrichment has deliberate echoes of civilian systems and the second distinctive contribution the book makes is that it has defended a view of the English law of unjust enrichment as following a pattern similar (but not identical) to South African law. English law therefore recognises a distinction between performance and non-performance claims, but one which (unlike German law, say) makes explicit additional use of unjust factors. The book then takes this insight and develops it by mapping the English causes of action against this structure in a way never before done. The result is highly illuminating. Not only are unjust factors not causes of action in that 'mistake' for instance forms the core of several causes of action, but we can draw on the civilian experience to show why some of the actions drawn into unjust enrichment's ambit in Birks' original thinking must be left out of our subject.

Just like English law, civilian and mixed jurisdictions include a mixed bag of actions in their law of unjustified enrichment. It is important we recognise the nature of this mixed bag, because only by accepting the differences between the actions can we avoid the difficulties of over-generalisation that are increasingly recognised in some current unjust enrichment scholarship. Scott has commented, however, that there is little that connects the civil law actions together; *sine causa* is a very thin idea indeed.[1] The critique of incoherence has therefore been levelled, not just at English law, but at civil law jurisdictions too.[2] If true, this would undermine the book's thesis and the usefulness of the comparisons drawn. It is not true. The different claims can be brought together in English law and are justifiably collected in civilian and mixed jurisdictions as well. How do we answer this critique of incoherence?

This is what we discussed in chapter one. We started with the question of what a cause of action is. It is a set of idealised normative requirements that are collectively necessary and sufficient for relief to be justified. Because it is an abstract idealised set of conditions, our cause of action cannot exactly describe any set of facts at all. This implies that our cause of action is a Weberian ideal type. The action's connection with any given set of facts that satisfies it is one of Wittgensteinian family resemblance where the significant normative elements of cause of action reflect significant features of the facts to hand. What then counts as a significant normative element? To answer this, we must recognise that the way we classify in law depends crucially on why we do so. For what purpose are we classifying? In our case we are classifying in order to understand the normative rationale for reversing an enrichment. This might be because the defendant committed a wrong and we hive these cases off because the rationale in a breach of duty case is rather different from that where there is no breach of duty. The method is therefore to abstract a set of normatively significant features, illuminating the function of the action. We then turn to an 'amorphous mass' of empirical material and sort through it, using the ideal type's suggestions, identifying where and how the ideal type's governing principles, function or ideas manifest themselves empirically and also crucially where they do not. A Weberian ideal-type is a work-in-progress, endlessly being reformulated as a result of its contact with real-world facts and by reference to other ideal types. The idea of a work-in-progress is consistent with Dworkinian jurisprudence; Dworkin suggests that the law works its way pure as we continue to search for the right answer to any given question of law. Causes of action, as ideal types, have an argumentative function. Larger category-concepts equally have such an argumentative function. There is an iterative process where we can identify some normative features which are shared by different causes of action, bearing in mind that, in line with Wittgenstein's analogy of the rope, not all such features crop up in all actions. This justifies the recognition of an area of law and allows us to derive a doctrinal and normative theme to it. That theme in turn lends our higher-level category extra legitimacy and can be used to better delineate the area's precise scope and boundary by identifying changes that can justifiably be made to our lower-level concepts. With these foundational elements in place, we asked what the significant features of unjust enrichment liability are. Not every feature is present in every case, but this is to be expected and implies that different

[1] H Scott, 'Rationalising the South African Law of Enrichment' [2014] *Edinburgh Law Review* 433, 449.
[2] N Jansen, 'Farewell to Unjustified Enrichment?' [2016] *Edinburgh Law Review* 123.

normative considerations from different areas can be at play in the same cause of action, and by extension by the same area of law.

The English law of unjust enrichment does not follow the exact same pattern as any civil law or mixed jurisdiction, but there are important parallels discussed in chapter two. English law includes a set of performance claims. Performance claims involve an intentional transfer of money or goods or an intentional rendering of services by the claimant to the defendant. It is the performance or its value which is returned. It is that which was requested, accepted or which was legally or factually necessary. In that latter case there need not be acceptance, but the defendant is disentitled from saying that he would not have accepted. In rescission cases it is the exact right transferred that is returned. As in South Africa, performance claims revolve around unjust factors; the claimant must prove a positive reason to grant restitution alongside the need to prove that there was no obligation to make the payment. English law also includes a set of non-performance claims – basically any unjust enrichment claim that is not a performance claim. In English law, non-performance claims can be divided into primarily intermediary claims and imposed enrichment claims, encroachment claims where the claimant relies on unjust enrichment rather than the wrong of (say) conversion being largely of no advantage. Intermediary claims I analogised to the civil law *actio de in rem verso*. Imposed enrichment claims typically involve no intentional transaction between the parties at all; the claimant may have been mistaken as to the ownership of the asset improved, believing it his own. These actions are significantly different in some respects from each other and from performance claims; the rules on attribution and 'at the expense of' in performance and imposed enrichment cases are quite different, for example. The approach to attribution in performance claims, which relies on the intentionality of the transfer or the rendering of services to another clearly cannot take in non-performance claims, precisely because there is no such intentional performance. In imposed enrichment cases attribution is purely causal in character.

In chapter three, we saw how principles from different areas overlapped in unjust enrichment and looked for the required family resemblances between the causes of action that make up unjust enrichment. Unjust factors, understood as broad reasons for restitution, can take up part of this unifying role and mistake, in particular, provides an important element of normative 'glue' sticking the two parts of unjust enrichment together. Defending this proposition required us to face an important objection to the effect that concentrating on mistake is immoral as it involves using the defendant as a means to the claimant's ends. The view is based on the Kantian/Hegelian idea that we must be formally independent of each other to be autonomous. Chapter three challenged this view, and indeed the book's general approach to law, of looking for substantive significant normative similarities, can be contrasted with the formalist view of private law as largely apolitical or pre-political in character. Some attempts to square this Kantian/Hegelian view with the presence of liability for mistaken payments are tortured, to say the least, and end effectively accepting the importance of a much thicker substantive view of personal autonomy rather like that defended in chapter three itself. This is that the law disrespects me as an autonomous entity if it forces me to go against norms governing my actions by refusing to allow restitution for mistake at all. The second part of the chapter gave a brief response to two important critics of unjust enrichment, Jaffey and Hedley.

The next few chapters mapped out the detailed description of the causes of action that make up unjust enrichment. We looked at mistake, duress and undue influence in chapter four and failure of basis in chapter five. We saw, as well, in chapter five that a pure absence of basis approach to English law performance claims fails. The civilian law cannot be imported wholesale. While absence of basis and unjust factors may purport to be incompatible explanations, the two systems do meet in the middle. An 'unjust factors' approach to performance claims needs absence of basis to prevent inappropriate restitution where there is a basis for the payment made and the pure absence of basis approach needs some nuanced use of unjust factors with regard, for instance, to the availability (or non-availability) of the defence of change of position.

In chapter six, we examined two actions – the *Woolwich v IRC*[3] claim, and necessity. We suggested that the former can be included in unjust enrichment. It has many of the features of a performance claim, but also imports vital normative considerations from public law. Depending on which normative features we pick out as significant, it can be seen as either (or both) unjust enrichment or public law. The latter cannot be included, and this demonstrates the power of the performance idea. Moral necessity, included in South African law as *negotiorum gestio*, provides a defence to intentional torts as well as the ground for recognising a duty of care. In other words, what would otherwise be a trespass to goods is lawful because of the necessity and provides a claim to reimbursement of expenses. Just as in South African law, English law ought to recognise that such cases justify relief because they are **valid** transactions – not because they are invalid. Legal necessity claims, often contribution, subrogation or reimbursement claims, are not unjust enrichment claims either. They are simply based on the defendant being primarily liable and they 'order' the liabilities so that those who should pay, do pay. Unjust enrichment adds nothing to the analysis.

English law in effect recognises a proprietary *actio de in rem verso*, discussed in chapter seven. The proprietary claim contingent on tracing depends on a trustee or agent breaching their obligations and mis-transferring assets to a third party. Those claims based on the trustee or agent's lack of authority to make the transaction can also be seen, loosely, as based on defective transactions and this forms a significant resemblance with other unjust enrichment claims. Vis-a-vis the principal, the transfer to the defendant is defective. The *actio de in rem verso* has withered in civil law jurisdictions but forms an important part of the historical pedigree of unjustified enrichment in such jurisdictions. From a comparative perspective, it is

[3] *Woolwich BS v IRC* [1993] AC 70 (HL).

therefore worth bringing these claims into the English law of unjust enrichment, but there are good reasons to bring proprietary claims in beside this. Many of the unjust factors also allow for the rescission of contracts or deeds of gift. The unity of the reasons for relief and provision of restitution suggests that such rescission claims be included within unjust enrichment. English law recognises rescission claims as performance claims; the claimant is attempting to reverse the effects of a performance made to the defendant on the basis of, for example, mistake or undue influence.

We finally discussed some important defences – change of position, passing on, illegality and bona fide purchase – in chapter eight. As in previous chapters we took a comparative approach and noted some possible developing similarities with the South African *condictio ob turpem vel iniustam causam* in that illegality may in time *per se* be enough to justify restitution.

Reasonable people can, of course, disagree with the arguments of the book. Others might pick out different normative features as being significant; they might argue to include actions I have excluded or exclude from unjust enrichment those I have included. Indeed, it will still be open to opponents of unjust enrichment to say that there are no significant normative resemblances here at all and, even on my less theoretically demanding view of taxonomy, these cases are too disparate. Two closing points might therefore be made. The first is that the methodology of looking for important significant analogies and family resemblances is a wider methodology of taxonomising the law that can be used to justify and describe other areas as well. Hercules will create an analysis of the entire legal system by roughly this method. Secondly, we started this book and this concluding chapter by observing that unjust enrichment scholarship has got into a mess. One aspect of this mess is the way in which proponents and opponents tend to adopt different views of concepts and then talk past each other. Chapter one provides a methodology around which both opponents and proponents could gather so that we can talk to each other and not past each other. If the book only achieves this, it will be job well done, whatever the reader thinks about my own normative preferences, civilian law structure for the area, and argued-for family resemblances.

INDEX

www.ingramcontent.com/pod-product-compliance
Ingram Content Group UK Ltd.
Pitfield, Milton Keynes, MK11 3LW, UK
UKHW020139290926
15471UKWH00003B/593

9 781509 942435